The A-Z of
Health and Safety

eremy Stranks

THORO*g*OOD

Published by
Thorogood Publishing Ltd
10-12 Rivington Street
London EC2A 3DU

Telephone: 020 7749 4748
Fax: 020 7729 6110
Email: info@thorogood.ws
Web: www.thorogood.ws

A CIP catalogue record for this book is
available from the British Library.

RB: ISBN 1 85418 382 6
PB: ISBN 1 85418 387 7

Cover and book designed and typeset in
the UK by Driftdesign

Printed in India by Replika Press

Special discounts for bulk
quantities of Thorogood
books are available to
corporations, institutions,
associations and other
organizations. For more
information contact
Thorogood by telephone on
020 7749 4748, by fax on
020 7729 6110, or e-mail
us: info@thorogood.ws

The author

Jeremy Stranks MSc FCIEH FIOSH RSP

Jeremy Stranks was a public health inspector (environmental health officer) with two local authorities in the Midlands before going into industry as a regional health inspector with a large food manufacturing organization. After completing the MSc in Occupational Safety and Hygiene course at Aston University in 1975, he was appointed chief health and safety adviser to the Milk Marketing Board and its commercial subsidiary, Dairy Crest Limited, a position he held for 15 years.

In 1990 he established Safety & Hygiene Consultants, a small business specializing in health and safety training, expert witness work and consultancy.

He is a regular seminar speaker with several training organizations and is the author of over 20 books, including *The Handbook of Health and Safety Practice* (Pearson Prentice Hall), which is now in its seventh edition, *Health and Safety Law* (Prentice Hall), *A Manager's Guide to Health and Safety at Work* (Kogan Page) and *Stress at Work: Management and Prevention* (Elsevier Butterworth Heinemann).

He was a founder member of the National Examination Board in Occupational Safety and Health (NEBOSH) and a chief examiner for that Board many years. He is currently an examiner for the Chartered Institute of Environmental Health and the Royal Institute of Public Health.

Jeremy Stranks recently received the Award for Distinguished Service of the Royal Society for the Prevention of Accidents.

Contents

List of abbreviations

ACAS	Advisory, Conciliation and Arbitration Service
ACOP	Approved Code of Practice
AER	All England Reports
BS	British Standard
CDMR	Construction (Design and Management) Regulations
CHIPR	Chemicals (Hazard Information and Packaging for Supply) Regulations
CORGI	Council for the Registration of Gas Installers
COSHHR	Control of Substances Hazardous to Health Regulations
dB(A)	Decibels measured on the A-network of a sound pressure level meter
DSE	Display screen equipment
EA	Enforcing authority
EHSRs	Essential health and safety requirements
HAVS	Hand-arm vibration syndrome
HSWA	Health and Safety at Work etc Act
HSC	Health and Safety Commission
HSE	Health and Safety Executive

Hz	Hertz
ISO	International Standards Organization
LEV	Local exhaust ventilation
LOLER	Lifting Operations and Lifting Equipment Regulations
LTEL	Long term exposure limit
MEL	Maximum exposure limit
MHSWR	Management of Health and Safety at Work Regulations
OES	Occupational exposure standard
OLA	Occupiers' Liability Act
PAT	Portable appliance test
PPE	Personal protective equipment
PUWER	Provision and Use of Work Equipment Regulations
PWP	Powered working platform
RCD	Residual current device
RIDDOR	Reporting of Injuries, Diseases and Dangerous Occurrences Regulations
RoSPA	Royal Society for the Prevention of Accidents
RPE	Respiratory protective equipment
RSI	Repetitive strain injury
SFARP	So far as is reasonably practicable
STEL	Short term exposure limit
SWL	Safe working load
TLV	Threshold Limit Value

VCM	Vinyl chloride monomer
VWF	Vibration-induced white finger
WHSWR	Workplace (Health, Safety and Welfare) Regulations
WVB	Whole body vibration

List of figures

List of tables

A

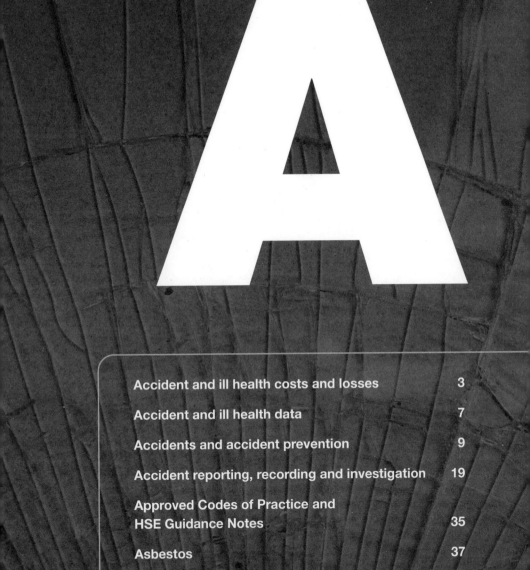

Accident and ill health costs and losses

Organizations are generally good at measuring the costs of accident and ill health prevention. Making health and safety improvements, however, may be restricted due to the need to stay within a defined safety budget (see *Safety budgets*).

All accidents and ill health, however, represent considerable losses to an organization. They include losses:

a) of a direct nature, such as fines levied in a court, following prosecution; or

b) indirect costs, such as those associated with time lost by a variety of people, such as managers, employees, first aid staff and the injured person, following an accident at work.

Accident and ill health costing

One way of assessing the losses associated with accidents and ill health is through the operation of an accident costing exercise carried out over a specific period of time, such as six months. This will enable the organization to identify both the direct and indirect costs of accidents, such as fines imposed by a court, repairing damage to structural items, replacement of work equipment and the cost of replacement labour.

Form

A specimen accident costing form is shown below in Figure 1.

Figure 1: Accident costing form

ACCIDENT AND ILL HEALTH COSTS

Costing no_____Date_____

Accident/case of ill health

Name _____Age _____

Job title_____Department_____

Accident/ill health details_____

_____

£   p

Direct costs

1. % Employer's liability premium
2. % Increased premiums payable   } These figures to be inserted by the insurance company
3. Civil claim award
4. Fines
5. Court and legal representation costs

Indirect costs

6. Treatment costs
   a) First aid
   b) Transport
   c) Hospital
   d) Others

7. Lost time costs
   a) Injured/ill person
   b) Management
   c) Supervisor
   d) First aiders
   e) Others

8. Operational costs
   a) Lost production/service
   b) Overtime payments
   c) Damage to plant, structure, vehicles, etc
   d) Training/supervision of replacement labour

9. Investigation costs
   a) Management
   b) Safety adviser
   c) Safety representative
   d) Liaison with enforcement officers

10. Other costs
    a) Replacement of personal items
    b) Other miscellaneous costs

TOTAL COSTS

See:

- *Accident and ill health data*
- *Accidents and accident prevention*
- *Accident reporting, recording and investigation*
- *Safety budgets*

Accident and ill health data

Many organizations collect and analyse accident and ill health data. In some cases, the information derived from this exercise is used to measure and compare safety performance across different parts of the organization.

Standard indices

A number of standard indices are used

Frequency rate	$\dfrac{\text{Total number of accidents}}{\text{Total number of man-hours worked}}$	x 100,000
Incident rate	$\dfrac{\text{Total number of accidents}}{\text{Number of persons employed}}$	x 1,000
Severity rate	$\dfrac{\text{Total number of days lost}}{\text{Total number of man-hours worked}}$	x 1,000
Mean duration rate	$\dfrac{\text{Total number of days lost}}{\text{Total number of accidents}}$	
Duration rate	$\dfrac{\text{Number of man-hours worked}}{\text{Total number of accidents}}$	

Trends

These indices are useful in identifying trends in accident and ill-health experience and much useful feedback for future health and safety strategies can be obtained from their analysis and study. They can, however, be subject to abuse and misuse and are not a true measure of safety performance.

See:

- *Accident and ill health costs*
- *Accidents and accident prevention*
- *Accident reporting, recording and investigation*

Accidents and accident prevention

What is an accident?

1. **Oxford Dictionary**

   An unforeseeable event often resulting in injury.

2. **British Safety Council**

   A management error; the result of errors or omissions on the part of management.

3. **Royal Society for the Prevention of Accidents (RoSPA)**

   Any deviation from the normal, the expected or the planned usually resulting in injury.

4. **Frank Bird, American Exponent of 'Total Loss Control'**

   An unintended or unplanned happening that may or may not result in personal injury, property damage, work process stoppage or interference, or any combination of these conditions under such circumstances that personal injury might have resulted.

5. **Health and Safety Unit, University of Aston**

   An unexpected, unplanned event in a sequence of events that occurs through a combination of causes. It results in physical harm (injury or disease) to an individual, damage to property, business interruption or any combination of these effects.

The pre-accident situation

In any situation prior to an accident taking place, two important factors must be considered, namely:

a) **The objective danger**

This is the objective danger associated with a particular machine, system of work, hazardous substance, etc. at a particular point in time.

b) **The subjective perception of risk on the part of the individual**

People perceive risks differently according to a number of behavioural factors, such as attitude, motivation, training, visual perception, personality, level of arousal and memory. People also make mistakes. Ergonomic design is significant in preventing human error.

The principal objectives of any accident prevention programme should be, firstly, that of reducing the objective danger present through, for instance, effective standards of machinery safety and, secondly, bringing about an increase in people's perception of risk, through training, supervision and operation of safe systems of work.

Pre-accident strategies

These can be classified as 'Safe Place' and 'Safe Person' strategies.

'Safe place' strategies

The principal objective of a 'safe place' strategy is that of bringing about a reduction in the objective danger to people at work. These strategies feature in much of the occupational health and safety legislation that has been enacted over the last century, in particular, the HSWA.

'Safe place' strategies may be classified under the following headings:

- Safe premises

- Safe plant, equipment and machinery

- Safe processes

- Safe materials

- Safe systems of work

- Safe access to and egress from the workplace

- Adequate supervision and control

- Competent and trained employees.

'Safe person' strategies

Generally, 'safe place' strategies provide better protection than 'safe person' strategies. However, where it may not be possible to operate a "safe place" strategy, then a 'safe person' strategy must be used. In certain cases, a combination of 'safe place' and 'safe person' strategies may be appropriate.

The main aim of a 'safe person' strategy is to increase people's perception of risk. One of the principal problems of such strategies is that they depend upon the individual conforming to certain prescribed standards and practices, such as the use of certain items of personal protective equipment. Control of the risk is, therefore, placed in the hands of the person whose appreciation of the risk may be lacking or even non-existent.

'Safe person' strategies may be classified as follows:

- care of the vulnerable, such as pregnant employees and young persons;

- personal hygiene;

- personal protective equipment;

- safe behaviour;

- caution in the face of danger.

Post accident (reactive) strategies

Whilst principal efforts must go into the implementation of proactive strategies, it is generally accepted that there will always be a need for reactive or 'post-accident' strategies, particularly as a result of failure of the various 'safe person' strategies. The problem with people is that they forget, they take short cuts to save time and effort, they sometimes do not pay attention or they may consider themselves too experienced and skilled to bother about taking basic precautions.

Post-accident strategies can be classified as follows:

- disaster/contingency/emergency planning;
- feedback strategies, such as those arising from accident investigation;
- improvement strategies.

The cause of accidents

The actual causes of accidents are many and varied. In endeavouring to identify the causes of accidents, the following more common contributory factors to the causes of accidents should be considered:

- the design and layout of the workplace or working area;
- structural features, such as floors, staircases and elevated working platforms;
- environmental factors, such as temperature, lighting and ventilation;
- operational methods;
- mechanical or materials failure;
- maintenance arrangements;
- machinery safety elements;
- personal protective equipment;
- cleaning and housekeeping arrangements;

- the level of supervision;

- health and safety training provided;

- rules and instructions to employees and others;

- unsafe attitudes to work;

- ergonomic factors in the work;

- physical and mental disability or incapacity;

- safety monitoring systems in operation; and

- stress arising from work activities.

The prevention or control of risks

One of the significant outcomes of the risk assessment process is the identification and specification of preventive and protective measures.

The risk assessment process incorporates the following procedures:

Recognition/identification of hazards

Recognition of the hazards implies some form of safety monitoring, such as a safety inspection or audit, together with feedback from accident investigation in certain cases.

Assessment and evaluation of the risks

Risk assessment requires a measurement of the magnitude of the risk based on factors such as probability or likelihood of the risk arising, the severity of outcome, in terms of injury, damage or loss, the frequency of the risk arising and the number of people exposed to the risk. Following assessment, evaluation of risk must take into account the current legislation applying to that particular risk situation.

Implementation of a control strategy

Once the risk has been assessed, it must either be eliminated or controlled. Elimination or avoidance of the risk may not be possible for a variety of reasons and, inevitably, some form of control must be implemented.

Monitoring of control strategy

It is essential that any control strategy applied is subject to regular monitoring to ensure continuing effectiveness and use of the control.

Prevention and control strategies in accident prevention

Prohibition

This is the most extreme control strategy that can be applied, in particular where there is no known form of operator protection available e.g. in the case of potential exposure to carcinogenic substances, or where there is an unacceptable level of risk in certain activities.

Substitution

This implies the substitution, for instance, of a less dangerous substance for a more dangerous one, or of a less dangerous system of work for a more dangerous one.

Change of process

Design or process engineering can usually change a process to afford better operator protection.

Controlled operation

This can be achieved through isolation of a particularly hazardous operation, the use of Permit to Work systems, method statements, mechanical or remote control handling systems, machinery guarding, restriction of certain operations to highly trained operators, i.e. competent and/or authorized persons, and in the case of hazardous airborne contaminants, the use of various forms of arrestment equipment.

Limitation

The limitation of exposure of personnel to specific environmental and chemical risks, e.g. noise, gases, fumes, on a time-related basis, may be appropriate in certain cases.

Ventilation

The operation of mechanical ventilation systems e.g. receptor systems and captor systems, which remove airborne contaminants at the point of generation, or which dilute the concentration of potentially hazardous atmospheres with ample supplies of fresh air (dilution ventilation) is generally required where substances are known to be hazardous to health.

Housekeeping, personal hygiene and welfare amenity provisions

Poor levels of housekeeping are a contributory factor in many accidents. The maintenance of high standards of housekeeping is vital, particularly where flammable wastes may be produced and stored.

Staff must be trained in maintaining good standards of personal hygiene, particularly where they may be handling hazardous substances.

The provision of suitable and sufficient sanitary accommodation, washing and showering arrangements, facilities for clothing storage and the taking of meals must be considered.

Personal protective equipment (PPE)

The provision and use of various items of PPE, e.g. safety boots, eye protectors, gloves, etc.

is a commonly used strategy. It has severe limitations in that an operator must wear the PPE correctly all the time that he is exposed to the risk. However, the provision and use of any item of PPE must be viewed as the last resort, when all other strategies have failed, or an interim measure until some other form of control strategy can be applied. The limitations of PPE should be clearly established and systems for maintenance and cleaning of same established and implemented.

Employers should ensure that PPE is 'suitable' in that it is appropriate for the risks and conditions where exposure may occur, takes account of ergonomic requirements and the state of health of the wearer, is capable of fitting the wearer correctly and, is effective in preventing or adequately controlling the risks without increasing the overall risk.

Health surveillance

Health surveillance implies monitoring the health of identified persons on a regular basis. It may include the exclusion of certain people from specific processes or practices e.g. women and young persons, medical surveillance of certain personnel, medical examinations, health checks, health supervision, biological monitoring e.g. blood tests, urine tests, and other forms of testing, such as audiometry.

Information, instruction and training

The provision of information to staff and the instruction and training of specific management, safety personnel and operators in the recognition of risk and the assessment of same is crucial to the success of any accident prevention programme. Staff must know why certain management action is taken and orders given, and must be fully aware that their co-operation is needed to make the workplace a safe and healthy one for themselves and others.

See:

- *Accident and ill health costs*
- *Accident and ill health data*
- *Accident reporting, recording and investigation*
- *Emergency procedures*
- *Health surveillance and health protection*
- *Information for employees*
- *Information, instruction and training*
- *Method statements*
- *Permit to work systems*
- *Personal protective equipment*
- *Risk assessment*
- *Ventilation in the workplace*

Accident reporting, recording and investigation

Reporting of injuries, diseases and dangerous occurrences regulations (RIDDOR) 1995

These regulations lay down the requirements for the reporting of certain types of injury and disease to the enforcing authority, together with specific events listed in the Schedule to the regulations known as 'dangerous occurrences'.

Definitions

The following definitions are significant:

Major injuries

These are:

1. Any fracture, other than to the fingers, thumbs or toes

2. Any amputation

3. Dislocation of the shoulder, hip, knee or spine

4. Loss of sight (whether temporary or permanent)

5. A chemical or hot metal burn to the eye or a penetrating injury to the eye

6. Any injury resulting from electric shock or electrical burn (including any electrical burn caused by arcing or arcing products) leading to unconsciousness or requiring resuscitation or admittance to hospital for more than 24 hours

7. Any other injury:

   a) leading to hypothermia, heat-induced illness or to unconsciousness;

   b) requiring resuscitation; or

   c) requiring admittance to hospital for more than 24 hours

8. Loss of consciousness caused by asphyxia or by exposure to a harmful substance or biological agent

9. Either of the following conditions which result from the absorption of any substance by inhalation, ingestion or through the skin:

   a) acute illness requiring medical treatment; or

   b) loss of consciousness

10. Acute illness which requires medical treatment where there is reason to believe that this resulted from exposure to a biological agent or its toxins or infected material

Reportable diseases

Examples include:

Column 1	Column 2
Disease	**Work activity**
18. Hepatitis	Work involving exposure to human blood products or body secretions or excretions
19. Legionellosis	Work on or near cooling systems which are located in the workplace and use water; or work on hot water service systems located in the workplace which are likely to be a source of contamination
25. Tetanus	Work involving contact with soil likely to be contaminated by animals

Duties of the responsible person

The responsible person (see definition) must forthwith send a report to the enforcing authority on the approved form (Form 2508A) wherever a person suffers from one of these diseases.

Dangerous occurrence

This is an occurrence which arises out of or in connection with work and is of a class specified in Part 1 of Schedule 1 of the Regulations.

Example:

3. Explosion, collapse or bursting of any pressure vessel, including a boiler or boiler tube, in which the internal pressure was above or below atmospheric pressure, which might have been liable to cause the death of, or any of the injuries or conditions covered by Regulation 3(2) to, any person, or which resulted in stoppage of the plant involved for more than 24 hours.

Responsible person

In the case of a reportable injury or disease:

a) involving an employee at work – the employer; and

b) involving a person undergoing training for employment – the person whose undertaking makes the immediate provision of that training.

In any other case, the person for the time being having control of the premises in connection with the carrying on by him of any trade, business or other undertaking (whether for profit or not) at which, or in connection with, the work at which the accident, disease or dangerous occurrence happened.

Work

This means work as an employee, as a self-employed person or as a person undergoing training for employment (whether or not under any scheme administered by the Manpower Services Commission).

Principal requirements of the regulations

- Where any person, as a result of an accident arising out of or in connection with work, dies or suffers any of the specific major injuries or conditions, or where there is a dangerous occurrence, the responsible person shall:

    a) forthwith notify the enforcing authority by quickest practicable means; and

    b) within ten days send a report thereof to the enforcing authority on a form approved for this purpose (Form 2508).

- Where a person at work is incapacitated for work of a kind which he might reasonably be expected to do, either under his contract of employment, or, if there is no such contract, in the normal course of his work, for more than three consecutive days (excluding the day of the accident but including any days which would not have been working days) because of an injury (other than a specified major injury) resulting from an accident at work, the responsible person shall within ten days of the accident send a report thereof to the enforcing authority on the form approved for this purpose (Form 2508). (See Fig 2: **Report of an injury is dangerous occurrence.**)

- Where an employee, as a result of an accident at work, has suffered a specified major injury or condition which is the cause of his death within one year of the date of the accident, the employer shall inform the enforcing authority in writing of the death as soon as it comes to his knowledge, whether or not the accident had been reported previously.

- Where a person at work suffers from a reportable disease, the responsible person shall forthwith send a report thereof to the enforcing authority on the form approved for this purpose (Form 2508A). (See Fig 3: **Report of a case of disease.**)

This requirement applies only if:

a) in the case of an employee or a person undergoing training, the responsible person has received a written statement prepared by a registered medical practitioner diagnosing the disease as one of the reportable diseases, or

b) in the case of a self-employed person, that person has been informed by a registered medical practitioner that he is suffering from the disease so specified.

• Whenever a conveyor of flammable gas through a fixed pipe distribution system, or a filler, importer or supplier (other than by means of retail trade) of a refillable container containing liquefied petroleum gas receives notification of any death or any major injury which has arisen out of or in connection with the gas, distributed, filled, imported or supplied, as the case may be, by that person, he must forthwith notify the HSE of the incident and within 14 days send a report on the approved form (Form 2508G).

• Whenever an employer or self-employed person who is a member of the class of person approved by the HSE for the purposes of paragraph (3) of the Gas Safety (Installation and Use) Regulations 1994 (i.e. a CORGI registered gas installation business) has in his possession sufficient information for it to be reasonable for him to decide that a gas fitting or any flue or ventilation used in connection with that fitting, by reason of its design, construction, manner of installation, modification or servicing, is or has been likely to cause death, or any major injury by reason of:

a) accidental leakage of gas;

b) inadequate combustion of gas;

c) inadequate removal of the products of combustion of gas,

he must within 14 days send a report of it to the HSE on the approved form, (Form 2508G) unless he has previously reported such information.

Health and Safety at Work etc Act 1974
The Reporting of Injuries, Diseases and Dangerous Occurrences Regulations 1995

HSE
Health & Safety
Executive

Report of an injury or dangerous occurrence

Filling in this form
This form must be filled in by an employer or other responsible person.

Part A

About you

What is your full name?

! What is your job title?

| What is your telephone number?

About your organisation

What is the name of your organisation?

What is its address and postcode?

What type of work does the organisation do?

Part B

About the incident

On what date did the incident happen?

/ /

At what time did the incident happen?
(Please use the 24-hour clock eg 0600)

Did the incident happen at the above address?

Yes ☐ Go to question 4

No ☐ Where did the incident happen?

☐ elsewhere in your organisation – give the
name, address and postcode

☐ at someone else's premises – give the name,
address and postcode

☐ in a public place – give details of where it
happened

If you do not know the postcode, what is
the name of the local authority?

In which department, or where on the premises,
did the incident happen?

Part C

About the injured person

If you are reporting a dangerous occurrence, go
to Part F.
If more than one person was injured in the same incident,
please attach the details asked for in Part C and Part D for
each injured person.

1 What is their full name?

2 What is their home address and postcode?

3 What is their home phone number?

4 How old are they?

5 Are they

☐ male?

☐ female?

6 What is their job title?

	☐☐☐

7 Was the injured person (tick only one box)

☐ one of your employees?

☐ on a training scheme? Give details:

☐ on work experience?

☐ employed by someone else? Give details of the
employer:

☐ self-employed and at work?

☐ a member of the public?

Part D

About the injury

1 What was the injury? (eg fracture, laceration)

	☐☐

2 What part of the body was injured?

	☐☐

3 Was the injury (tick the one box that applies)

- [ ] a fatality?
- [ ] a major injury or condition? (see accompanying notes)
- [ ] an injury to an employee or self-employed person which prevented them doing their normal work for more than 3 days?
- [ ] an injury to a member of the public which meant they had to be taken from the scene of the accident to a hospital for treatment?

4 Did the injured person (tick all the boxes that apply)

- [ ] become unconscious?
- [ ] need resuscitation?
- [ ] remain in hospital for more than 24 hours?
- [ ] none of the above.

Part E

About the kind of accident

Please tick the one box that best describes what happened, then go to Part G.

- [ ] Contact with moving machinery or material being machined
- [ ] Hit by a moving, flying or falling object
- [ ] Hit by a moving vehicle
- [ ] Hit something fixed or stationary

- [ ] Injured while handling, lifting or carrying
- [ ] Slipped, tripped or fell on the same level
- [ ] Fell from a height

    How high was the fall?

    [_____] metres

- [ ] Trapped by something collapsing

- [ ] Drowned or asphyxiated
- [ ] Exposed to, or in contact with, a harmful substance
- [ ] Exposed to fire
- [ ] Exposed to an explosion

- [ ] Contact with electricity or an electrical discharge
- [ ] Injured by an animal
- [ ] Physically assaulted by a person

- [ ] Another kind of accident (describe it in Part G)

Part F

Dangerous occurrences

Enter the number of the dangerous occurrence you are reporting. (The numbers are given in the Regulations and in the notes which accompany this form.)

[_____]

Part G

Describing what happened

Give as much detail as you can. For instance
- the name of any substance involved
- the name and type of any machine involved
- the events that led to the incident
- the part played by any people.

If it was a personal injury, give details of what the person was doing. Describe any action that has since been taken to prevent a similar incident. Use a separate piece of paper if you need to.

[ ]

Part H

Your signature

Signature

[_____]

Date

[/ /]

Where to send the form

Please send it to the Enforcing Authority for the place where it happened. If you do not know the Enforcing Authority, send it to the nearest HSE office.

Health and Safety at Work etc Act 1974
The Reporting of Injuries, Diseases and Dangerous Occurrences Regulations 1995

Report of a case of disease

Filling in this form

This form must be filled in by an employer or other responsible person.

Part A

About you

1 What is your full name?

2 What is your job title?

3 What is your telephone number?

About your organisation

4 What is the name of your organisation?

5 What is its address and postcode?

6 Does the affected person usually work at this address?

Yes ☐ Go to question 7

No ☐ Where do they normally work?

7 What type of work does the organisation do?

Part B

About the affected person

1 What is their full name?

2 What is their date of birth?

/ /

3 What is their job title?

4 Are they
☐ male?
☐ female?

5 Is the affected person (tick one box)
☐ one of your employees?
☐ on a training scheme? Give details:

☐ on work experience?
☐ employed by someone else? Give details:

☐ other? Give details:

F2508A (01/96)

Continued overleaf

Part C

The disease you are reporting

1 Please give:

- the name of the disease, and the type of work it is associated with; or
- the name and number of the disease (from Schedule 3 of the Regulations – see the accompanying notes).

2 What is the date of the statement of the doctor who first diagnosed or confirmed the disease?

/ /

3 What is the name and address of the doctor?

Part D

Describing the work that led to the disease

Please describe any work done by the affected person which might have led to them getting the disease.

If the disease is thought to have been caused by exposure to an agent at work (eg a specific chemical) please say what that agent is.

Give any other information which is relevant.

Give your description here

Continue your description here

Part E

Your signature

Signature

Date

/ /

Where to send the form

Please send it to the Enforcing Authority for the place where the affected person works. If you do not know the Enforcing Authority, send it to the nearest HSE office.

For official use	
Client number	Location number
Event number	☐ INV REP ☐ Y ☐ N

- The responsible person shall keep a record of:

  a) any event which is required to be reported under Regulation 3 i.e. specified major injury or condition or dangerous occurrence; and

  b) any case of disease required to be reported under Regulation 3.

- The records shall be kept at the place where the work to which they relate is carried on or, if that is not reasonably practicable, at the usual place of business of the responsible person and an entry in either of such records shall be kept for at least three years from the date on which it is made.

- The responsible person shall send to the enforcing authority such extracts from the records required to be kept as the enforcing authority may from time to time require.

In the case of (a) above, the following particulars shall be kept in records of any event which is reportable under Regulation 3:

1. Date and time of the accident or dangerous occurrence.

2. The following particulars of the person affected:

   a) full name;

   b) occupation;

   c) nature of the injury or condition.

3. Place where the accident or dangerous occurrence occurred.

4. A brief description of the circumstances.

In the case of (b) above, the following records shall be kept of instances of the diseases specified in Schedule 2 and reportable under Regulation 5:

1. date of diagnosis of the disease;

2. occupation of the person affected;

3. name and nature of the disease.

- It shall be defence in proceedings against any person for an offence under these Regulations for that person to prove that he was not aware of the event requiring him to notify or send a report to the enforcing authority and that he had taken all reasonable steps to have all such events brought to his notice.

- As part of the recording requirements, copies of Forms 2508 and 2508A should be maintained by employers for at least 12 months.

Social Security Act 1975

Under this legislation:

- Employees must notify their employer of any accident resulting in personal injury in respect of which benefit may be payable.
  - Notification may be given by a third party if the employee is incapacitated.

- Employees must enter the appropriate particulars of all accidents in an Accident Book (Form BI 510)
  - This may be done by another person if the employee is incapacitated. Such an entry is deemed to satisfy the requirements in 1 above.

- Employers must investigate all accidents of which notice is given by employees. Variations in the findings of this investigation and the particulars given in the notification must be recorded.

- Employers must, on request, furnish the Department of Social Security with such information as may be required relating to accidents in respect of which benefit may be payable e.g. Forms 2508 and 2508A.

- Employers must provide and keep readily available an Accident Book in an approved form in which the appropriate details of all accidents can be recorded (Form BI 510). Such books, when completed, should be retained for three years after the date of the last entry.

- For the purposes of the above, the appropriate particulars should include:
  - name and address of injured person
  - date and time of accident
  - place where accident happened
  - cause and nature of injury
  - name and address of any third party giving notice.

- Under the Social Security Act employers must provide an Accident Book in which employees may enter details of accidents they have sustained at work. The Accident Book must be made freely available to employees. Managers should monitor entries in the Accident Book regularly.

- Accident Books must comply with the requirements of the Data Protection Act 1998 and employers must use the latest version of the Accident Book. This requires all personal details to be removed from the book and stored in a secure location whilst retaining a reference number.

Accident investigation

Investigation should identify:
- the type of accident, e.g. fall on the same level;
- the form and severity of injury e.g. an amputated hand;
- evidence of trends in current accident experience;
- the evidence of involvement with machinery, hand tools or hazardous substances;
- breaches of statute or regulations by the organization, the accident victim, the manufacturers and/or suppliers of articles and substances used at work, or other persons;
- whether the injury is be reportable to the enforcing authority (HSE, local authority) under RIDDOR;

- evidence of lost production;

- damage to plant and equipment; and

- the need for immediate remedial action to prevent a recurrence of this accident; and

- the potential for a civil claim by the injured party based on negligence.

'Near misses'

A 'near miss' is defined as 'an unplanned and unforeseeable event that could have resulted, but did not result in human injury, property damage or other form of loss'. The identification of the causes of 'near misses' and the taking of remedial action is important on the basis that "Yesterday's 'near miss' could be tomorrow's fatal accident". 'Near misses' commonly follow other accident trends.

Practical accident investigation

In any serious incident situation, such as a fatal accident, an accident resulting in major injury e.g. fractures, amputations, or where there has been a scheduled dangerous occurrence, such as the collapse of a crane, speed of action is essential. This is particularly the case when it comes to interviewing injured persons and witnesses.

The following procedure is recommended:

- Establish the facts as quickly and completely as possible with regard to:

  a) the general environment;

  b) the particular plant, machinery, practice or system of work involved; and

  c) the sequence of events leading to the accident.

- Take photographs of the accident scene prior to any clearing up that may follow the accident.

- Produce sketches and take measurements; produce a scale drawing of the events leading up to the accident.

- Identify all witnesses i.e. those who saw, heard, felt or smelt anything; interview them thoroughly, in the presence of a third party if necessary, and take full statements. Increasingly, there is a need to formally caution witnesses prior to their making a statement. Do not prompt or lead witnesses.

- Evaluate the facts, and individual witnesses' versions of same, as to accuracy, reliability and relevance.

- Identify the direct and indirect causes of the accident on the basis of the relevant facts.

- Examine closely any contradictory evidence. Never dismiss a fact that does not fit in with the rest. Find out more.

- Examine fully about the system of work involved.

- Where appropriate, arrange for plant and equipment, such as lifting appliances, machinery and vehicles to be examined by a specialist e.g. a consultant engineer.

- Produce a report for the responsible manager emphasizing the causes and remedies to prevent a recurrence, including any changes necessary.

- In complex and serious cases, consider the establishment of an investigating committee comprising managers, supervisors, technical specialists and trade union safety representatives.

Any accident report produced must be accurate, comprehensible and identifies the causes of the accident, both direct and indirect. It must be recognized that the purpose of accident investigation is that of identifying the causes and not of apportioning blame.

The provision of feedback on the causes of accidents is crucial in large organizations, especially those who operate more than one site or premise. Above all, a system of monitoring should be implemented to ensure that the lessons which have been learned from the accident are put into practice or incorporated in future systems of work, and that procedures and operating systems have been produced for all grades of staff.

See:

- *Accident and ill health costs*
- *Accident and ill health data*
- *Accidents and accident prevention*
- *Hazard reporting*
- *Reportable and prescribed diseases*

Approved Codes of Practice and HSE Guidance Notes

Approved codes of practice

The need to provide elaboration on the implementation of regulations is recognized in Section 16 of the HSWA, which gives the HSC power to prepare and approve codes of practice on matters contained not only in regulations but in sections 2 to 7 of the Act. Before approving a code, the HSE, acting for the HSC, must consult with any interested body.

An Approved Code of Practice (ACOP) has a special legal status similar to the Highway Code. Although failure to comply with any provision of an ACOP is not in itself an offence, the failure may be taken by a court in criminal proceedings as proof that a person has contravened the regulation to which the provision relates. In such a case, however, it will be open to that person to satisfy a court that he has complied with the regulation in some other way, e.g. undertaking works of an equivalent nature.

An ACOP is a quasi-legal document and, although non-compliance does not constitute a breach, if the contravention of the Act or regulations is alleged, the fact that the ACOP was not followed could be accepted as evidence of failure to comply, or do all that was practicable or reasonably practicable.

Examples of ACOPs are:

- Management of health and safety at work (Management of Health and Safety at Work Regulations 1999)

- Control of substances hazardous to health (Control of Substances Hazardous to Health Regulations 2002)

HSE guidance notes

The HSE issues Guidance Notes in some cases to supplement the information in both regulations and ACOPs. These Guidance Notes have no legal status and are purely of an advisory nature.

Categories

HSE Guidance Notes fall into six categories:

1. General Safety
2. Chemical Safety
3. Environmental Hygiene
4. Medical series
5. Plant and Machinery
6. Health and Safety

Examples of Guidance Notes are:

EH40	Occupational exposure limits
MS20	Pre-employment health screening
HS(G)37	Introduction to local exhaust ventilation

Other Guidance Notes are issued specifically with Regulations as with, for example, the Manual Handling (Manual Handling Operations Regulations 1992).

Asbestos

Asbestos is a broad term applied to a number of substances falling into two chief varieties, chrysotile and amphiboles. These substances are naturally occurring iron, sodium, calcium and magnesium hydrated silicates. They have a fibrous structure and are incombustible.

Chrysotile asbestos (white asbestos) is a hydrated magnesium silicate found in serpentine rock. It is widely distributed in nature and accounts for some 93% of the world's asbestos production. Amphibole asbestos varieties include amosite, crocidolite, anthophyllite, tremolite and actinolyte. The last two substances have few industrial applications but are sometimes found as impurities in talc.

Pathological effects of exposure to asbestos

The risks to health result from the inhalation of the fibrous dust and its subsequent dispersion within the lung and other parts of the body. This may occur in those extracting the fibre and processing same, and subsequent manufacture and application of products. In practice, exposure to asbestos alone is uncommon. Other mineral dusts are frequently inhaled along with the asbestos and may influence its effects. The effect of these and other pollutants, especially cigarette smoke, may adversely influence the type and severity of disease produced by asbestos.

Several types of diseases may result from the inhalation of asbestos:

- asbestosis, a fibrous (thickening and scarring) of the lung itself and of its outer surface, and the pleura, which may become calcified;
- cancer of the bronchial tubes; and

- cancer of the pleural surface (diffuse mesothelioma), which may also occur in the abdominal cavity (peritoneal mesothelioma).

There is also some evidence that cancers in other sites of the body may occasionally become asbestos-linked.

These types of disease have a long latent period in that they first become evident as long as 20 years after the first exposure to the fibres.

Control of exposure

Exposure to all forms of asbestos should be reduced to the minimum level reasonably practicable. In addition, the personal exposure of workers should not exceed the current action levels and control limits. Action levels refer to cumulative exposures over a continuous 12 week period. Control limits refer to concentrations of asbestos in the atmosphere. They do not represent safe levels which, once attained, make further improvements in dust control unnecessary. They represent the upper level of permitted exposure, for each form of asbestos, above which the risk to health is unacceptable.

Control of Asbestos At Work Regulations 2002

The Regulations impose extensive duties on employers, occupiers and controllers of premises, other than of non-domestic premises, (duty holders) to manage asbestos.

Asbestos is defined as meaning the following minerals, namely crocidolite, amosite, chrysotile, fibrous actinolite, fibrous anthophyllite or fibrous tremolite or any admixture containing any of those minerals.

Important definitions

Action level means one of the following cumulative exposures to asbestos over a continuous 12 week period when measured or calculated by a method approved by the HSC, namely:

- where the exposure is solely to chrysotile 72 fibre-hours per millilitre of air;

- where the exposure is to any other form of asbestos either alone or in mixtures including mixtures of chrysotile with any other form of asbestos, 48 fibre-hours per millilitre of air; or

- where both types of exposure occur separately during the 12 week period concerned, a proportionate number of fibre-hours per millilitre of air.

Control limit means any of the following concentrations of asbestos in the atmosphere when calculated or measured by a reference method described in Annex 1 to Council Directive 83/477/EEC or by a method giving equivalent results to that reference method approved by the HSC, namely:

- for chrysotile
  - i)   0.3 fibres per millilitre of air averaged over a continuous period of four hours,
  - ii)   0.9 fibres per millilitre of air averaged over a continuous period of ten minutes;

- for any other form of asbestos either alone or in mixtures including mixtures of chrysotile with any other form of asbestos:
  - i)   0.2 fibres per millilitre of air averaged over a continuous period of four hours;
  - ii)   0.6 fibres per millilitre of air averaged over a continuous period of ten minutes.

Principal requirements of the regulations

- Occupiers and controllers of non-domestic premises must ensure that a suitable and sufficient assessment is carried out as to whether asbestos is, or is liable to be present in, the premises.

- Where the assessment shows that asbestos is or is liable to be present in any part of the premises, the duty holder shall ensure that:

  - a determination of the risk from that asbestos is made;

  - a written plan identifying those parts of the premises concerned is prepared; and

  - the measures which are to be taken for managing the risk are specified in the written plan.

- An employer shall not carry out work which exposes or is liable to expose his employees to asbestos unless:

  - before commencing that work, he has identified by analysis or otherwise, the type of asbestos involved in the work; or

  - he has assumed that the asbestos is not chrysotile alone and for the purposes of these regulations has treated it accordingly.

- An employer shall not carry out work which exposes or is liable to expose his employees to asbestos unless he has made a suitable and sufficient assessment of the risks, the steps that need to be taken and has implemented these steps.

- An employer shall not undertake any work with asbestos unless he has prepared a suitable written plan of work detailing how that work is to be carried out.

- The employer shall ensure, so far as is reasonably practicable, that the work is carried out in accordance with the plan.

- An employer shall not carry out work with asbestos unless he has notified the HSE in writing of the particulars specified in Schedule 1 at least 14 days before commencing that work. Where there is a material change in that work, the HSE shall be notified of the change in that work.

- Every employer shall ensure that adequate information, instruction and training is given to those of his employees who are, or are liable to be, exposed to asbestos, or who supervise such employees.

- Every employer shall:
  - prevent the exposure of his employees to asbestos so far as is reasonably practicable;
  - where it is not reasonably practicable to prevent such exposure:
    i) reduce that exposure to the lowest level reasonably practicable by measures other than the use of RPE; and
    ii) ensure the number of employees who are exposed to asbestos is as low as is reasonably practicable.

- Every employer shall take immediate steps to remedy the situation where the concentration of asbestos in air inhaled by an employee exceeds the relevant control limit.

- Every employer who provides any control measure, other thing or facility pursuant to these regulations shall ensure so far as is reasonably practicable that it is properly used or applied.

- Every employee shall make full and proper use of any control measure or other thing or facility provided and, where relevant, shall take all reasonable steps to ensure it is returned after use to any accommodation provided for it and, if he discovers a defect therein, report it forthwith to his employer.

- The employer shall ensure that any control measure is maintained in an efficient state, in efficient working order, in good repair and in a clean condition.

- Every employer shall provide adequate and suitable protective clothing, ensuring it is either disposed of as asbestos waste or adequately cleaned at suitable intervals.

- Employers must make arrangements to deal with accidents, incidents and emergencies, including the provision of safety drills and the provision of information to employees on such arrangements.

- There is a general duty on employers to prevent or, where this not reasonably practicable, reduce to the lowest level reasonably practicable, the spread of asbestos from any place where work under his control is carried out.

- Premises and plant must be kept in a clean state and where work involving asbestos has been completed, the premises or appropriate parts of same must be thoroughly cleaned.

- Employers must ensure that any area in which work under his control is carried out is designated as:
  - an asbestos area, where exposure would or could exceed the action level; and
  - a respirator zone, where the concentration of asbestos in that area would or could exceed a relevant control limit.

- Asbestos areas and respirator zones must be clearly marked and access to these areas restricted.

- Employers must monitor exposure of their employees to asbestos by measurement of asbestos fibres present in the air. Records of monitoring must be maintained.

- Employers who carry out air monitoring shall ensure that they meet criteria equivalent to those set out in the paragraphs of ISO 17025.

- Where an employer undertakes air monitoring of asbestos fibres he must ensure he meets the criteria equivalent to those set out in ISO 17025. Any person carrying out measurement of the concentration of asbestos fibres present in the air shall be accredited by an approved body as complying with ISO 17025.

- Employers must maintain health records of all employees exposed to asbestos, keeping same for at least 40 years from the date of the last entry. Such employees must be under adequate medical surveillance by a relevant doctor unless exposure to asbestos does not exceed the action level.

- Employees must be provided with adequate washing facilities, together with facilities for the storage of protective clothing, personal clothing not worn during working hours and RPE which must be separate from each other.

- Asbestos or asbestos waste must not be stored, received into or dispatched from any place of work, or distributed within any place of work, except in a totally enclosed distribution system, unless it is in a sealed container clearly marked as showing that it contains asbestos.

- Where asbestos is supplied for use as a product at work it must be labelled in accordance with the provisions of Schedule 2.

Schedules

1. Particulars to be included in a notification.

2. The labelling of raw asbestos, asbestos waste and products containing asbestos.

ACOPS

The regulations are accompanied by several ACOPs including:

- *Work with asbestos insulation, asbestos coating and asbestos insulation board*

- *The management of asbestos in non-domestic premises*

- *Control of asbestos at work*

- *Work with asbestos that does not normally require a licence*

B

Benchmarking

A benchmark is a reference point which is commonly used in surveying practice. More recently the term has been used to imply some form of standard against which an organisation can measure performance and, as such, is an important business improvement tool in areas such as quality management. Health and safety benchmarking follows the same principles whereby an organization's health and safety performance can be compared with a similar organization or 'benchmarking partner'.

The HSE publication *Health and Safety Benchmarking – Improving Together* (IND G301/1999) defines health and safety benchmarking as a planned process by which an organization compares its health and safety processes and performance with others to learn how to:

- reduce accidents and ill-health;
- improve compliance with health and safety law; and/or
- cut compliance costs.

The benchmarking process

Health and safety benchmarking is a five-step cycle aimed at ensuring continuous improvement.

At the commencement of the process, it would be appropriate to form a small benchmarking team or group, perhaps comprising a senior manager, health and safety specialist, line managers, employee representatives and representatives from the benchmarking partner or trade association.

Step 1 – Deciding what to benchmark

Benchmarking can be applied to any aspect of health and safety, but it is good practice to prioritize in terms of high hazard and risk areas, such as with the use of hazardous substances, with certain types of workplace or working practice. Feedback from the risk assessment process and accident data should identify these priorities. Consultation with the workforce should take place at this stage, together with trade associations who may have experience of the process.

Step 2 – Deciding where you are

This stage of the exercise is concerned with identifying the current level of performance in the selected area for consideration and the desired improvement in performance. Reference should be made at this stage to legal requirements, such as regulations, to ACOPs and HSE Guidance on the subject and to any in-house statistical information. It may also be appropriate to use an audit and/or questionnaire approach to measure the current level of performance.

Step 3 – Selecting partners

In large organizations it may be appropriate to select partners both from within the organization, perhaps at a different geographical location (internal benchmarking) and from outside the organization (external benchmarking). With smaller organizations, trade associations or the local Chamber of Commerce may be able to assist in the selection of partners. Local benchmarking clubs operate in a number of areas. Reference should be made to the *Benchmarking Code of Conduct* to ensure compliance with same at this stage.

Step 4 – Working with your partner

With the right planning and preparation, this stage should be straightforward. Any information that is exchanged should be comparable, confidentiality should be respected and all partners should have a good understanding of the other partners' process, activities and business objectives.

Step 5 – Acting on the lessons learned

Fundamentally, the outcome of any benchmarking exercise is to learn from other organizations, to learn more about the individual organization's performance compared with working partners and to take action to improve performance.

According to the HSE, any action plan should be 'SMARTT', that is:

- **S**pecific
- **M**easurable
- **A**greed
- **R**ealistic
- **T**rackable and
- **T**imebound.

As with any Action Plan, it should identify a series of recommendations, the member(s) of the organization responsible for implementing these recommendations and a timescale for their implementation. Progress in implementation should be monitored on a regular basis. In some cases, it may be necessary to re-define objectives in the light of, for example, recent new legislation. There should be continuing liaison with benchmarking partners during the various stages of the Action Plan.

Pointers to success

To succeed in health and safety benchmarking, there should be:

- senior management resources and commitment;
- employee involvement;
- a commitment to an open and participative approach to health and safety, including a willingness to share information with others within and outside the organization;
- comparison with data on a meaningful 'apples with apples' basis; and
- adequate research, planning and preparation.

See:

- *Safety management systems*

Biological agents

Schedule 9 to the COSHH Regulations covers the special provisions relating to biological agents. These provisions are, in the majority of cases, additional to the other provisions of the Regulations and are directed at protecting employees against risks to their health, whether immediate or delayed, arising from biological agents.

Classification of biological agents

The Schedule enables the HSC to approve and publish a document *Categorization of Biological Agents According to Hazard and Categories of Containment* containing a list of biological agents together with the classification of each agent which it has approved.

Where a biological agent does not have an approved classification, the employer shall provisionally classify that agent in accordance with the classification below, having regard to the nature of the agent and of the properties to which he may reasonably be expected to be aware. The employer shall assign that agent to one of the following Groups according to its level of risk of infection and, if in doubt as to which of the two alternative Groups is the most appropriate, he shall assign it to the higher of the two:

- **Group 1** – unlikely to cause human diseases;

- **Group 2** – can cause human disease and may be a hazard to employees; it is unlikely to spread to the community and there is usually effective prophylaxis or treatment available;

- **Group 3** – can cause severe human disease and may be a serious hazard to employees; it may spread to the community, but there is usually effective prophylaxis or treatment available;

- **Group 4** – can cause severe human disease and is a serious hazard to employees; it is likely to spread to the community and there is usually no effective prophylaxis or treatment available.

Assessment of health risks

Every employer who intends to carry on any work which is liable to expose his employees to any biological agent shall take account of the Group into which that agent is classified when making an assessment of the risks created by that work.

Prevention of exposure to a biological agent

If the nature of the activity so permits, every employer shall ensure that the exposure of his employees to a particular biological agent is prevented by substituting a biological agent which is less hazardous.

Control of exposure to biological agents

Where there is a risk of exposure to a biological agent and it is not otherwise reasonably practicable to prevent that exposure then it shall be adequately controlled, in particular by the following measures which are to be applied in the light of the results of the assessment:

a) keeping as low as practicable the number of employees exposed, or likely to be exposed, to the biological agent;

b) designing work processes and engineering control measures so as to prevent or minimize the release of biological agents into the place of work;

c) displaying the biohazard sign and other relevant warning signs;

d) drawing up plans to deal with accidents involving biological agents;

e) specifying appropriate decontamination and disinfection procedures;

f) instituting means for the safe collection, storage and disposal of contaminated waste, including the use of secure and identifiable containers, after suitable treatment where appropriate;

g) making arrangements for the safe handling and transport of biological agents, or materials that may contain such agents, within the workplace;

h) specifying procedures for taking, handling and processing samples that may contain biological agents;

i) providing collective prevention measures and, where exposure cannot be adequately controlled by other means, individual protection measures including, in particular, the supply of appropriate protective clothing or other special clothing;

j) where appropriate, making available effective vaccines for those employees who are not already immune to the biological agent to which they are exposed or are liable to be exposed;

k) instituting hygiene measures compatible with the aim of preventing or reducing the accidental transfer or release of a biological agent from the workplace, including, in particular:

   i) the provision of appropriate and adequate washing and toilet facilities; and

   ii) the prohibition of eating, drinking, smoking and application of cosmetics in working areas where there is a risk of contamination by biological agents.

In this paragraph, 'appropriate' in relation to clothing and hygiene measures means appropriate for the risks involved and the conditions at the place where exposure to the risk may occur.

Special control measures are laid down in the Schedule with respect to:

a) health and veterinary care facilities; and

b) laboratories, animal rooms and industrial processes.

Examination and maintenance of PPE

Every employer who provides PPE, including protective clothing, to meet the requirements of these Regulations as they apply to biological agents shall ensure that it is:

a) properly stored in a well-defined place;

b) checked and cleaned at suitable intervals; and

c) when discovered to be defective, repaired or replaced before further use.

PPE which may be contaminated by biological agents shall be:

a) removed on leaving the working area; and

b) kept apart from uncontaminated clothing and equipment.

In the above case, the employer shall ensure that the equipment is subsequently decontaminated and cleaned or, if necessary, destroyed.

Other provisions of the Schedule

These include:

a) a duty on employers to provide written emergency instructions, together with displaying notices, in the event of an accidental release of a biological agent;

b) a duty on employees to report accidents or incidents which have or may have resulted in an accidental release which could cause severe human disease to the employer;

c) a duty on employers to inform his employees forthwith of an accidental release, and subsequently, of the causes of the accident and the measures taken, or to be taken, to rectify the situation;

d) a duty on employers to maintain a list of employees exposed to a Group 3 or Group 4 biological agent, together with specified details of each exposure, for at least ten years following the last known exposure;

e) a duty on employers to notify the HSE in writing at least 30 days in advance prior to the storage and use of biological agents in Groups 2, 3 or 4 at a particular premises; and

f) a duty on employers to notify the HSE in writing at least 30 days in advance prior to the consignment of biological agents specified in Part V of the Schedule, namely:

   i) all Group 4 biological agents;

   ii) rabies virus;

   iii) Simian herpes B virus;

   iv) Venezuelan equine encephalitis virus;

   v) tick-borne encephalitis group viruses in Group 3;

   vi) monkeypox virus; and

   vii) Mopeia virus.

See:

- *Hazardous substances*
- *Health risk assessment*
- *Health surveillance and health protection*
- *Occupational diseases and conditions*

C

Chains, ropes and lifting tackle

Ropes

Ropes may be constructed from natural fibre, wire or man-made fibre.

Natural fibre ropes are made from materials of vegetable origin, such as manila hemp, sisal, coir and cotton, and manufacturers do not normally provide a certificate stating the safe working load (SWL). However, it is normal for the breaking strength to be specified by the manufacturer from which the purchaser can ascertain the SWL.

It is common practice to designate a factor of safety for natural fibre ropes thus:

a)   new ropes used on a direct lift – not less than six

b)   ropes used as slings.

Fibre ropes are not legally required to have a test certificate before being taken into service, but they do require examination every six months and, therefore, should be capable of identification. They should be inspected regularly, and before use, for evidence of chemical attack, discolouration, weakness, reduced diameter or rot due to mildew, in which case they should be destroyed.

When lifting loads with sharp edges, the rope should be protected with packing.

Wire ropes are composed of strands of wire, the number of wires per strand being termed the 'construction' of the rope. Broken wires should require attention, the actual position of the breaks being significant. Where breaks occur over a short distance, or occur in one or two strands, the rope should be removed from service and the cause investigated.

Frequent lubrication of wire ropes is necessary to reduce wear, exclude moisture and delay corrosion. They should be stored in a clean dry place, cleaned after use, and hung on pegs to prevent corrosion and kinking.

Wire ropes should never be knotted as a means of joining ropes. They may be joined by the use of sockets, swaged ferrules, bulldog clips or by splicing.

Man-made fibre ropes are generally manufactured in nylon or Terylene. Compared with natural fibre ropes they have a higher tensile strength, greater capacity for absorbing shock loading, freedom from rotting and mildew formation, can be stored whilst still wet, and their performance is the same whether wet or dry. They are less liable to degradation due to contact with oil, petrol and solvents and are more resistant to acids and other corroding agents.

Chains

Chain is still extensively used, despite the increased use of wire rope. Chain does not kink or curl, grips the load better and possesses superior shock-absorbing properties. It is available in several grades, such as mild steel, high tensile steel and alloy steel.

Chain strengths vary considerably as shown in the table below.

TYPE	SWL (TONNES)	PROOF LOAD (TONNES)	MINIMUM BREAKING (TONNES)	MARKING
Wrought iron	1.5	3.0	6.75	–
Mild steel grade 30	1.5	3.0	7.15	3
HT steel grade 40	2.0	4.0	10.00	4 or 04
Alloy steel grade 60	3.0	6.0	15.00	06
Alloy steel grade 80	3.5	8.0	20.00	08

Table 1: Comparison of chain strengths

Generally, chains fail for several reasons:

a) a defect in a link;

b) the application of a static load in excess of the chain's breaking load (overloading); or

c) the sudden application of a load which, but for the shock, the chain would have been capable of withstanding (shock loading).

In no circumstances should nuts and bolts be used to replace broken links. Chains should never be knotted.

Lifting tackle

Lifting tackle includes slings, hooks, grips and eyebolts. The complete set of tackle in a lifting situation must be viewed as one specific unit, and the various parts should not be interchanged.

Slings are made from chains, wire, man-made or fibre ropes of adequate strength. Tables showing the maximum SWLs for slings at various leg angles must be displayed conspicuously and operators trained to adhere to the SWL specified in each case.

Slings showing evidence of cuts, distortion, excessive wear and stretching should be withdrawn. Wire rope slings should be well-lubricated and corners of loads should be packed. Even distribution of the load between the legs of a sling is essential.

Hooks used with lifting appliances are manufactured from forged steel or an equivalent material, and fitted with a safety catch shaped in such a way as to prevent the load from slipping or falling off.

Shackles used for joining lines should have a breaking strength of at least 1.5 times that of the lines joined.

Eyebolts are used for lifting loads which may be heavy and concentrated. The use of the wrong type of eyebolt is a common direct cause of lifting accidents.

Pulley blocks should be manufactured from shock-resistant metal e.g. mild steel. The diameter of the pulley should be at least 20 times the diameter of the rope to be used. The axle should be capable of lubrication and a suitable lubricating device provided. The sheaves and housing of blocks should be such that the rope cannot be damaged in the sheaf.

A **lifting beam (spreader bar)** is a special device which enables a particular load to be lifted in a particular way. They incorporate three basic components:

a) the beam, which is manufactured from rolled steel section or plate;

b) the means of attaching the beam to the lifting machine, such as a ring, shackle, eyebolt or hole in the main structure of the beam; and

c) the means of fixing the beam to the actual load to be raised, such as chain or wire rope slings which are attached to the beam with fittings at the ends for securing the load, such as shackles or locking pins.

The thickness of metal should not be less than 6mm, which can be reduced to 4.5mm with hollow sections provided they are adequately sealed against water penetration. Lifting beams are subject to weather corrosion and this factor should be considered in their design and fabrication.

See:

- *Lifting operations, machinery and equipment*

Children at work

The Children (Protection at Work) Regulations 1998 implement, with regard to children, the EC Directive on the Protection of Young People (94/33/EC).

The principal requirements of these regulations are:

- the minimum age at which a child may be employed in any work, other than as an employee of his parent or guardian in light agricultural or horticultural work on an occasional basis, is 14 years;

- anything other than light work is prohibited; *light work* is defined as work which does not jeopardize a child's safety, health, development, attendance at school or participation in work experience;

- the employment of children over the age of 13 years in categories of light work specified in local authority byelaws is permitted;

- the hours over which a child over the age of 14 years may work, and the rest periods which are required, are specified; a child must have at least one two week period in his school holidays free from any employment;

- the prohibition against a child going abroad for the purposes of performing for profit without a local authority licence covers a child going abroad for the purpose of taking part in sport or working as a model in circumstances where payment is made;

- where children take part in public performances, existing requirements for a local authority licence are extended to require such a licence to be obtained before a child may take part in sport or work as a model in circumstances where payment is made either to the child or to someone else.

See:

- *Young persons*

Common law liability

Duties of employers at common law

Common law is the body of case law of universal or common application formed by the judgements of the courts. Each judgement contains the judge's enunciation of the facts, a statement of the law applying to the case and the *ratio decidendi* or legal reasoning for the finding which he has arrived at. These various judgements are recorded in the series of Law Reports and have thus developed into the body of decided case law which we now have and continue to develop. Common law is, then, accumulated case law, recorded for the most part in the Law Reports, underpinned by the doctrine of precedent, under which a court is bound to follow earlier decisions of courts of its own level and of the decisions of superior courts.

The common law position is that employers must take reasonable care to protect their employees from risk of foreseeable injury, disease or death at work. The effect of this requirement is that if an employer knows of a health and safety risk to employees, or ought, in the light of the current state of the art, to have known of the existence of a hazard, he will be liable if an employee is injured or killed or suffers illness as a result of the risk, or if the employer failed to take reasonable care.

Reasonable care

The test of reasonable care is determined by the courts on the basis of what a reasonable man would do in the same circumstances as the defendant. If the existence of the duty of care is established as matter of law, then the breach of this duty is decided by the judge. There are five aspects to be considered in determining reasonable care:

Cost

The amount of money that it is necessary to spend against the slight possibility of risk is limited.

Obviousness of the risk

The more obvious the danger, the more liable the employer will be held for failing to prevent injury arising. A partial defence is that the employee may have been aware of the risk, in which case the employee can be sued for contributory negligence.

Inherent risk

All work carries with it some possibility of risk which is irreducible or irremovable for which the employer cannot be held responsible.

Likelihood of injury

The greater the risk, the greater the liability.

Severity of injury

The more serious the consequences, the greater the precautions required.

Employers' duties at common law

An employer's duties as common law were identified in general terms by the House of Lords in *Wilsons & Clyde Coal Co. Ltd. v English (1938) AC57*.

The common law requires that all employers provide and maintain:

a) a safe place of work with safe means of access and egress;

b) safe appliances and equipment and plant for doing the work;

c) a safe system for doing the work; and

d) competent and safety-conscious personnel.

These duties apply even though an employee may be working away on third party premises, or where an employee has been hired out to another employer, but where the control of the task he is performing remains with the permanent employer. The test of whether an employee has been temporarily 'employed' by another employer is one of 'control'.

Thus the common law governs the rights and duties of individuals towards each other.

Remedies

There are four remedies that are available to an individual:

Compensation

A cash value is placed upon the injury suffered or the loss experienced where an employer is found to be liable through failure to comply with the law.

Reparation

In this case an employer could be required to restore conditions so that they are the same as before the breach of the law.

Performance

Here an employer can be compelled to perform his obligations.

Injunction

Where an employer can be required to desist from an activity where it interferes with the common law rights of another.

See:

- *Duty of care*
- *Insurance*
- *Negligence*
- *Occupiers' liability*
- *Vicarious liability*

Competent persons

Many systems of work operate under the control of specifically trained operators or external specialists who understand the risks involved and, on the basis of their skill, knowledge and experience, know the precautions that must be taken. This may entail specific inspection, examination and testing of work equipment, or undertaking activities where there may be a high degree of foreseeable risk.

The expression 'competent person' occurs frequently in construction safety law. For example, under the Construction (Health, Safety and Welfare) Regulations 1996 certain inspections, examinations, operations and supervisory duties must be undertaken by competent persons.

Under the MHSWR, a person shall be regarded as competent (for the purpose of assisting the employer in undertaking the measures he needs to take to comply with the requirements and prohibitions imposed upon him by or under the relevant statutory provisions) where he has sufficient training and experience or knowledge and other qualities to enable him properly to assist in undertaking those measures. The onus is on the employer to decide whether persons are competent to undertake designated tasks and duties.

Specific duties and functions of competent persons

Noise at Work Regulations 1989

A competent person must make a noise assessment which is adequate for the purpose of:

 a)   identifying employees' noise exposure; and

b) providing the employer with appropriate information as to enable him to facilitate compliance with his duties.

Pressure Systems Safety Regulations 2000

The user of an installed pressure system and the owner of a mobile pressure system shall not operate the system or allow it to be operated unless he has a written scheme for the periodic examination, by a competent person, of the following parts of the system:

a) all protective devices;

b) every pressure vessel and every pipeline in which (in either case) a defect may give rise to danger; and

c) those parts of the pipework in which a defect may give rise to danger.

The user or owner shall:

a) ensure that the scheme has been drawn up, or certified as being suitable, by a competent person;

b) ensure that:

– the content of the scheme is reviewed at appropriate intervals by a competent person for the purpose of determining whether it is suitable in current conditions of use of the system; and

– the content of the scheme is modified in accordance with any recommendations made by that competent person arising out of that review.

Under these Regulations, the competent person:

a) advises the user or owner on the scope of the written scheme for periodic examination;

b) draws up or certifies the schemes of examination; and

c) undertakes examinations under the scheme.

A competent person is defined as a competent individual person (other than an employee) or a competent body of persons corporate or unincorporated;

and accordingly any reference in these regulations to a competent person performing a function includes a reference to his performing it through his employees.

Electricity at Work Regulations 1989

No person to carry out a work activity where technical knowledge or experience is necessary to prevent danger or injury, unless he has such knowledge or is under the appropriate degree of supervision. (Whilst the term does not appear, competence is implied.)

Management of Health and Safety at Work Regulations 1999

Competent persons must be appointed by an employer to assist him, firstly, in complying with legal requirements and, secondly, in implementing procedures for serious and imminent danger and for danger areas, thus:

Every employer shall appoint one or more competent persons to assist him in undertaking the measures he needs to take to comply with the requirements and prohibitions imposed upon him by or under the relevant statutory provisions.

Construction (Design and Management) Regulations 1994

Competence must be taken into account by:

a) a client when appointing a planning supervisor;

b) any person when arranging for a designer to prepare a design;

c) any person when arranging for a contractor to carry out or manage construction work.

Construction (Health, Safety and Welfare) Regulations 1996

Competent persons must be appointed by an employer for the supervision of:

a) the installation or erection of any scaffold and any substantial addition or alteration to a scaffold;

b) the installation or erection of any personal suspension equipment or any means of arresting falls;

c) erection or dismantling of any buttress, temporary support or temporary structure used to support a permanent structure;

d) demolition or dismantling of any structure, or any part of any structure, being demolition or dismantling which gives rise to a risk of danger to any person;

e) installation, alteration or dismantling of any support for an excavation;

f) construction, installation, alteration or dismantling of a cofferdam or caisson; and

g) the safe transport of any person conveyed by water to or from any place of work.

Competent persons are also required to inspect places of work as specified in Schedule 7 to the regulations opposite.

Construction (Health, Safety and Wedfare) Regulations 1996

SCHEDULE 7

Regulation 29(1)

PLACES OF WORK REQUIRING INSPECTION BY A COMPETENT PERSON

COLUMN 1 PLACE OF WORK	COLUMN 2 TIME OF INSPECTION
1. Any working platform or part thereof or any personal suspension equipment provided pursuant to paragraph (3)(b) or (c) of regulation 6	1. i) Before being taken into use for the first time; and ii) after any substantial addition, dismantling or other alteration; and iii) after any event likely to have affected its strength or stability; and iv) at regular intervals not exceeding seven days since the last inspection.
2. Any excavation which is supported pursuant to paragraphs (1), (2) or (3) of Regulation 12	2. i) Before any person carries out work at the start of every shift; and ii) after any event likely to have affected the strength or stability of the excavation or any part thereof; and iii) after any accidental fall of rock or earth or other material.
3. Cofferdams and caissons	3. i) Before any person carries out work at the start of every shift; and ii) after any event likely to have affected the strength or stability of the cofferdam or caisson or any part thereof.

See:

- *Construction safety*
- *Lifting operations, machinery and equipment*
- *Power presses*
- *Pressure systems*

Confined spaces

A confined space is defined in the Confined Spaces Regulations 1997 as a place which is substantially, though not always entirely, enclosed and where there is a risk that anyone who may enter the space could be:

a) injured due to fire or explosion;

b) overcome by gas, fumes, vapour, or the lack of oxygen;

c) drowned;

d) buried under free flowing solids, such as grain; or

e) overcome due to high temperature.

The principal hazards associated with work in confined spaces are the risk of asphyxiation, due to the presence of gas, fumes, mists, etc., and anoxia, oxygen deficiency, due to oxygen-depleted atmospheres.

There may be a secondary risk of explosion due to the use of, for instance, naked lights in flammable atmospheres, or to faulty electrical equipment.

Precautions necessary

A Permit to Work system should always be operated. However, a Permit to Work system would not normally be required if the risks are low and can easily be controlled, the system of work is simple and it has been established that other work activities being carried out will not prejudice safe working in the confined space (see **Permit to work systems**).

The legal requirements

General requirements with respect to the safety of employees must be considered, namely those under the HSWA and MHSWR.

In addition, an employer must take into account the requirements of the Confined Spaces Regulations 1997. These Regulations place a duty on employers to:

- avoid entry to confined spaces, for example, by carrying out the work from outside the space;

- follow a safe system of work, e.g. a Permit to Work system, if entry to a confined space is unavoidable; and

- put in place adequate emergency arrangements before work starts, which will also safeguard rescuers.

See:

- *Permit to Work systems*

Construction safety

Accidents in construction activities

Accidents are common in construction activities. The more common classes of accident are outlined below.

- Falls from ladders
- Falls from working platforms
- Falls of materials
- Falls from pitched roofs or through fragile roofs
- Falls through openings in flat roofs and floors
- Collapses of excavations
- On-site transport accidents
- Machinery and powered hand tools
- Machinery
- Fire
- Failure to use or wear personal protective equipment
- Work over water and transport over water
- Work involving hazardous substances
- Manual handling activities
- Underground services
- Confined spaces

Precautions necessary in construction activities

Work above ground

This entails the use of scaffolds, mobile access equipment and ladders. Falls from a height are one of the most common causes of fatal accidents in construction work (see *Work at height*).

The following factors should be considered in order to ensure safe working practices.

Scaffolds

Scaffolds may take the form of tied-in (or putlog) scaffolds or independent freestanding scaffolds. The use of movable access equipment, such as scaffold towers, must also be considered.

Basic safety requirements

- Safe means of access to and egress from working platforms must be provided
- All workplaces above ground must be kept safe
- Scaffolds should be provided at working heights above 2m
- Toe boards, hand rails and intermediate rails should be fitted and maintained
- Working areas should be adequately lit
- No materials should be thrown or tipped from working platforms
- Scaffolds must be constructed using approved materials and maintained in sound condition
- Scaffolds should be rigidly constructed as to prevent accidental displacement
- Standards should be vertical or leaning towards structure, securely fixed and braced
- Ledgers and transoms should be horizontal and securely fixed
- Putlogs should be straight, provided with flat ends and securely fixed

- Gangways should be adequate (minimum 0.44m wide)

- Working platforms should be adequate (minimum 0.64m for general work)

- Stairs should be fitted with handrails and toe boards installed on landings

- Warning notices should be displayed, and access blocked, to partly-erected scaffolds

- Careful lowering of items during dismantling

- Scaffolds should be rigidly connected to building unless constructed as an independent scaffold

- Scaffolds should be securely supported or suspended or strutted or braced

- A competent person must:
  - a) inspect scaffold materials; and
  - b) supervise modifications, additions and dismantling;
  - c) i) inspect every seven days;
    - ii) inspect after adverse weather;
  - d) record inspections in site register.

- Competent and experienced operators must be employed for the erection, modification and dismantling of a scaffold

Movable access equipment

This type of equipment commonly comprises a movable tower formed from scaffold tubes or pre-formed frames. In each case, the tower incorporates a working platform, access by means of an externally fixed ladder or internally-placed raking ladders, and caster wheels at the base, which permit the tower to be moved with ease.

This equipment is commonly used for high level maintenance work, painting and small-scale building work.

Basic safety requirements

The following requirements are necessary to ensure safe working:

- Working platform must be secure, completely boarded and fitted with toe boards, intermediate rails and hand rails.

- The height must not exceed three times the smaller base dimension.

- The installation of outriggers may be necessary to increase stability during windy conditions.

- Diagonal bracing should be installed on all four elevations and horizontally.

- Castors at the four corners must be securely fixed and fitted with a brake.

- Such scaffolds must be moved with great care by pushing/pulling at base level.

- No person, equipment or materials should be present on the platform during movement of same.

See further BS 5973:1981 – **Code of practice for access and working scaffolds and special scaffold structures in steel**.

Ladders

Safety precautions cover the actual construction and use of ladders.

Basic safety requirements

- Ladders must be of sound construction and adequately maintained.

- Defective ladders should never be used.

- Ladders should not be painted or treated as this may hide defects; treatment with clear preservative is acceptable.

- Wooden ladders must be fitted with reinforcing ties.

- During use, a ladder must:
  a) be equally and properly supported on each stile
  b) be securely fixed at or near its upper resting place or at the lower end, or footed
  c) rise at least 1m above the landing place.

- Landing places must be installed every 9.14m (30') of vertical distance and fitted with toe boards and hand rails.

- Openings in landings must be as small as possible.

- Folding ladders should have a level and firm footing.

Work below ground

The principal risks are collapse of an excavation, flooding and people, materials and vehicles falling into excavations.

Excavations

Factors for consideration in the support of an excavation are:

- the nature of the subsoil;

- projected life of the excavation;

- work to be undertaken, including equipment used;

- the possibility of flooding;

- the depth of the excavation; and

- the number of operators working in the excavation at any one time.

Basic safety requirements

- An adequate supply of timber and other materials must be available.

- Barriers must be installed as close as practicable to the edge and maintained in position.

- Adequate and suitable materials must be used for shoring.

- Timbering should be completed as early as practicable, and those involved in the work must be protected whilst undertaking this work

- Timbering must be of good construction, sound material, free from patent defect and of adequate strength.

- Struts and braces must be adequately secured.

- A competent person must be employed to:

  a) direct erection, alteration and dismantling of all timbering;

  b) inspect materials and other supports;

  c) inspect every part at least once per day;

  d) inspect face of every tunnel and base or crown of every shaft at the beginning of every shift;

  e) inspect the working end of every trench over 2m deep before each shift.

- Experienced operators must be employed for erection, alteration and dismantling.

- Excavations and approaches must be well-lit.

- No materials must be placed near the edge of an excavation.

- Steps must be taken to prevent premature collapse where excavations may affect the stability of a building.

- Means for reaching a place of safety, where there is risk of sudden flooding, must be provided.

- Means to prevent over-running of vehicles must be installed.

- The atmosphere must be well-ventilated.

Demolition operations

Demolition is the most hazardous operation undertaken in construction activities. The principal hazards are:

a) falls of men and materials;

b) collapse of structures;

c) overloading of floors with debris;

d) incorrect or unsafe demolition techniques;

e) explosions in tanks or other confined spaces;

f) the presence of live electric cables and gas mains;

g) the presence of dusty, corrosive and poisonous materials and/or atmospheres;

h) projecting nails, broken glass and cast iron fragments which can cause minor injuries.

Basic safety requirements

The principal precautions entail:

- a pre-demolition survey to identify, for instance, the nature and method of construction, previous use, location of services, presence of dangerous substances, cantilevered structures, etc;

- isolation of services;

- segregation of the area by barriers, control of access, display of warning notices, etc;

- installation of fans or catching platforms where necessary;

- ensuring the provision and use of correct personal protective equipment by operators: safety boots, hard hats, respiratory protection;

- use of temporary props where necessary;

- effective control when pulling arrangements, a demolition ball, pusher arm and/or explosives are being used;

- protection against falling items;

- control over access to dangerous areas;

- use of scaffolds where manual demolition is undertaken;

- protection against falling: safety harnesses, nets, sheets to be used;

- no work over open joisting;

- prior removal of glass in windows, doors and partitions;

- adequately lighting;

- competent person to oversee work and make continuing inspections;

- express measures to prevent premature collapse; and

- trained drivers/operators and banksmen to be employed whenever mechanical demolition is to be undertaken.

See:

- *Competent persons*
- *Contractors and visitors on site*
- *Lifting operations, machinery and equipment*
- *Method statements*
- *Passport schemes*
- *Shared workplaces*
- *Work at height*

Consultation on health and safety

Consultation between employers and employees is an important feature of the safety management process. This consultation may take place whereby managers meet with trade union appointed safety representatives, through the operation of a health and safety committee or as part of a normal employer/employee consultative process.

Safety representatives and safety committees regulations 1977

Objective of the regulations

The main objective of the Regulations is to provide a basic framework within which each undertaking can develop effective working relationships. As such, these working relationships must cover a wide range of situations, i.e. different forms of workplace and work activity.

Principal requirements of the regulations

- A recognized trade union may appoint safety representatives from amongst the employees in all cases where one or more employees are employed by an employer by whom it is recognized.

- The employer must be notified by the trade union of the names of the safety representatives.

- Each safety representative has certain prescribed functions as indicated below.

- Safety representatives have the following functions:

    a) to represent employees in consultation with employers;

    b) to co-operate effectively in promoting and developing health and safety measures;

    c) to make representations to the employer on any general or specific matter affecting the health and safety of their members;

    d) to make representations to the employer on general matters affecting the health and safety of other persons employed at the workplace;

    e) to carry out certain inspections;

    f) to represent members in consultations with the HSE;

    g) to receive information from Inspectors;

    h) to attend meetings of the safety committee if appropriate.

    None of these functions impose a duty on safety representatives, however.

- Employers must give safety representatives time off with pay for performing their functions and for any reasonable training they undergo.

- Safety representatives are entitled to carry out workplace inspections and employers to give reasonable assistance. Notice in writing must be given to the employer. The normal frequency of inspection is every three months although inspections may be undertaken at the scene of a reportable accident or dangerous occurrence and in other circumstances specified in the ACOP.

- Safety representatives are entitled to undertake inspections following any of the above events. An employer must provide reasonable facilities and assistance as safety representatives may reasonably require for the purpose of carrying out these inspections.

- Safety representatives can inspect any document which the employer has to maintain, other than documents relating to the health records of identifiable individuals.

Note: The ACOP to the regulations makes the following points:

Qualifications of safety representatives

So far as is reasonably practicable, representatives must have two years experience with the employer or in similar employment.

Functions of safety representatives

Representatives must keep themselves informed of legal requirements. They must encourage co-operation. They are entitled to carry out health and safety inspections and inform the employer of the outcome of inspections

Obligations of employers

Employers must provide safety representatives with information on:

a) health and safety plans and performance;

b) hazards and precautions;

c) the occurrence of accidents, dangerous occurrences and occupational disease; and

d) any other relevant information, including the results of any measurements taken.

Any two safety representatives can request in writing that their employer form a safety committee. The employer must consult with these representatives, post a notice indicating the composition of the committee and establish the committee no later than three months after such a request.

According to the ACOP, the following matters must be considered when establishing a safety committee:

Basic objectives

The basic objectives are to promote co-operation between employer and employees and to act as a focus for employee participation.

Functions

A safety committee should have a formally specified range of functions, including:

a) consideration of the circumstances of individual accidents and cases of reportable diseases, accident statistics and trends;

b) examination of safety audits and reports;

c) consideration of reports and information from inspectors;

d) assistance in the development of safety rules and procedures;

e) conducting periodic inspections of the workplace; and

f) monitoring the effectiveness of health and safety training, communications and safety propaganda.

Membership

Safety committees should be reasonably compact but allow for representation of management and all employees.

It should be appreciated that a trade union safety representative is not appointed by the safety committee and vice versa. Neither is responsible to or for the other. Management representation can include line managers, supervisors, engineers, HR specialists, medical advisers, occupational health nurses and health and safety advisers. Specialist knowledge should be available.

A committee must have authority to take action within its remit. Final responsibility for action, however, lies with the employer.

Conduct

Meetings should be held as often as is considered necessary. Agendas and minutes should be provided.

Arrangements at individual workplaces

The division of conduct of activities should be specified. There must be clear objectives and terms of reference for the committee, and the membership and structure defined in writing. The committee must publish matters notified by safety representatives.

Health and Safety (Consultation with Employees) Regulation 1996

- Under the Safety Representatives and Safety Committees Regulations employers must consult safety representatives appointed by any trade unions they recognize.

- Under these Regulations employers must consult any employees who are not covered by the above Regulations. This may be by direct consultation with employees or through representatives elected by the employees they are to represent.

- HSE Guidance accompanying the Regulations details:

  (a) which employees must be involved;

  (b) the information they must be provided with;

  (c) procedures for the election of representatives of employee safety;

  (d) the training, time off and facilities they must be provided with; and

  (e) their functions in office.

See:

- *Health and Safety at Work etc Act 1974*

Contractors and visitors on site

Under Section 3 of the HSWA, an employer must conduct his undertaking in such a way as to ensure, so far as is reasonably practicable, that persons not in his employment who may be affected are not thereby exposed to risks to their health or safety. This requirement is significant in the case of visitors, including contractors.

Visitors

Many people visit workplaces, such as sales representatives, clients, consultants and members of the public. A clearly established routine is necessary to safeguard the health and safety of all lawful visitors. This routine should include designation by signs of:

a) visitor parking areas and walkways from any parking area to a reception area; and

b) a specific reception area where visitors sign an attendance register indicating time of both arrival and departure.

Visitors should be advised of any hazards that they may be exposed to and the precautions necessary. In certain cases, they may need to be briefed of any safety procedures to be operated, such as those involving their participation in a Permit to Work system.

Where necessary they should be escorted to that part of the premises where they may be working.

Contractors

In terms of both criminal and civil liability, and of practical safety, the interface between the client (owner/occupier) of a premises or site and the principal contractor, contractors and other groups, such as designers, is of key importance.

Criminal liability

In this case, clients, main contractors and contractors are often said to be 'in joint occupation and control'. The principal contractor has the greatest liability under the Construction (Health, Safety and Welfare) Regulations 1996, as he has the greatest control. This relationship between clients, principal contractors and contractors has further practical implications with regard to Section 3 of the HSWA and the requirements of the Construction (Design and Management) (CDM) Regulations 1994 as far as criminal liability is concerned.

Civil liability

All three parties can be construed as being 'in occupation' for the purposes of the Occupiers Liability Act 1957 and can be proceeded against accordingly, including, if necessary, any architect, civil engineer or other professional person, if they have been negligent. It should be appreciated that for the purposes of liability, 'occupation' means managerial control, and a client may be just as much in control of a construction project as main and sub-contractors.

Regulating the activities of contractors

Organizations need to ensure effective regulation of contractors on their premises, particularly in view of the duties imposed on all parties under the CDM Regulations.

Contracting activities can cover a wide range of situations, from simple activities, such as window cleaning or maintenance of plant, to large-scale construction projects, such as extensions to premises. For projects to be undertaken safely, there must be co-operation, consultation, communication and co-ordination between the parties involved.

Important considerations

- Consultation between the parties concerned prior to commencement of project.

- Restrictions or controls on the use by the contractor of the client's equipment.

- Arrangements for the reporting, recording and investigation of injuries, diseases and dangerous occurrences.

- Methods for ensuring safe systems of work, including the use of Permit to Work systems and method statements.

- Measures to ensure safe operation of plant and machinery.

- Noise prevention and control.

- Fire prevention and protection.

- Measures to control hazardous substances on site.

- The provision and use of personal protective equipment.

- Control of contractors' vehicles.

- Site clearance arrangements.

- Demolition controls.

All the above factors must be considered prior to any project or construction activity taking place.

See:

- *Construction safety*
- *Occupiers' liability*
- *Passport schemes*
- *Traffic management on site*
- *Work at height*

Corporate liability and corporate manslaughter

Under the HSWA directors, managers, company secretaries and similar officers of the body corporate have both general and specific duties. Breaches of these duties can result in individuals being prosecuted.

Offences committed by companies

Where there has been a breach of one of the relevant statutory provisions on the part of a body corporate is proved to have been committed with the consent or connivance of, or to have been attributable to, any neglect on the part of, any director, manager, secretary or other similar officer of the body corporate or a person who was purporting to act in any such capacity, he as well as the body corporate shall be guilty of that offence and shall be liable to be proceeded against and punished accordingly.

Breach of this section has the following outcomes:

- Where an offence is committed through neglect by a board of directors, the company itself can be prosecuted as well as the directors individually who may have been to blame.

- Where an individual functional director is guilty of an offence, he can be prosecuted as well as the company.

- A company can be prosecuted even though the act or omission was committed by a junior official or executive or even a visitor to the company.

Generally, most prosecutions under Section 37(1) would be limited to that body of persons i.e. the board of directors and individual functional directors, as well as senior managers.

Offences committed by other corporate persons

Section 36 makes provision for dealing with offences committed by corporate officials e.g. personnel managers, health and safety specialists, training officers, etc. Thus:

Where the commission by any person of an offence under any of the relevant statutory provisions is due to the act or default of some other person, that other person shall be guilty of the offence, and a person may be charged with, and convicted of, the offence by virtue of this subsection whether or not proceedings are taken against the first mentioned person.

Corporate manslaughter

Manslaughter is of two kinds, that is, voluntary and involuntary. The former, which is essentially murder but reduced in severity owing to, say, diminished responsibility, is not relevant to health and safety. Involuntary manslaughter extends to all unlawful homicides where there is no malice aforethought or intent to kill.

There are two forms of involuntary manslaughter, that is, constructive manslaughter and reckless manslaughter. The former applies to situations where death results from an act unlawful at common law or by statute, amounting to more than mere negligence. Reckless manslaughter or gross negligence arises where death is caused by a reckless act or omission, and a person acts recklessly 'without having given any thought to the possibility of there being any such risk or, having recognized that there was some risk involved, has none the less gone on to take it. (*R v Caldwell [1981] 1 AER 961*)

See:

- *Common law liability*
- *Duty of care*
- *Insurance*
- *Negligence*

Courts and tribunals

There are two distinct systems whereby the courts deal with criminal cases and civil actions respectively. Some courts have both criminal and civil jurisdiction, however.

Criminal courts

Magistrates court

This is the lowest of the courts in England and Wales and deals mainly with summary offences, mainly criminal matters. Their jurisdiction is limited. Lay Justices of the Peace determine and sentence for many of the less serious offences. They also hold preliminary examinations into other offences to ascertain whether the prosecution can show a prima facie case on which the accused may be committed for trial at a higher court. The Sheriff Court performs a parallel function in Scotland, although procedures differ from those of the Magistrates Courts.

Crown courts

Serious indictable criminal charges and cases where the accused has the right to jury trial are heard on indictment in the Crown Court before a judge and jury. The court is empowered to impose unlimited fines and/or a maximum of two years imprisonment for health and safety-related offences. This court also hears appeals from Magistrates Courts.

Civil courts

County courts

These courts operate on an area basis and deal in the first instance with a wide range of civil matters. They are limited, however, in the remedies that can be applied. Cases are generally heard by circuit judges or registrars, the latter having limited jurisdiction. A judge can award compensation up to £50,000.

High court of justice

More important civil matters, because of the sums involved or legal complexity, will start in the High Court of Justice before a High Court judge. The High Court has three divisions:

1. Queen's Bench deals with contract and torts; claims in excess of that of the County Court's power.

2. Chancery deals with matters relating to, for instance, land, wills, bankruptcy, partnerships and companies.

3. Family deals with matters involving, for instance, adoption of children, marital property and disputes.

In addition, the Queen's Bench Division hears appeals on matters of law:

a) from the Magistrates Courts and from the Crown Court on a procedure called 'case stated', and

b) from some tribunals, for example, the finding of an industrial tribunal on an enforcement notice under the Health and Safety at Work Act.

It also has some supervisory functions over the lower courts and tribunals if they exceed their powers or fail to undertake their functions properly, or at all.

The High Court, the Crown Court and the Court of Appeal are known as the Supreme Court of Judicature.

The Court of Appeal

The Court of Appeal has two divisions:

a) the Civil Division, which hears appeals from the County Courts and the High Court; and

b) the Criminal Division, which hears appeals from the Crown Court.

The House of Lords

The Law Lords deal with important matters of law only, following appeal to the House of Lords from the Court of Appeal and in restricted circumstances from the High Court.

The European Court of Justice

This is the supreme law court, whose decisions on interpretation of European Community law are sacrosanct. Such decisions are enforceable through the network of courts and tribunals in all Member States.

Employment tribunals

Tribunals cover many employment matters, for example, industrial relations issues, and cases involving unfair dismissal, equal pay and sex discrimination.

Composition

Each tribunal consists of a legally qualified chairman appointed by the Lord Chancellor and two lay members, one from management and one from a trade union, selected from panels maintained by the Department of Employment following nominations from employers' organizations and trade unions.

Decisions

When all three members of a tribunal are sitting the majority view prevails.

Complaints relating to health and safety matters

Employment tribunals deal with the following employment-related health and safety issues:

a) appeals against improvement and prohibition notices served by enforcement officers; [HSWA 1974]

b) time off for the training of safety representatives; [Safety Representatives and Safety Committees Regulations 1977];

c) failure of an employer to pay a safety representative for time off for undertaking his functions and training [Safety Representatives and Safety Committees Regulations 1977];

d) failure of an employer to make a medical suspension payment [Employment Protection (Consolidation) Act 1978, Sec 22]; and

e) dismissal, actual or constructive, following a breach of health and safety law, regulation and/or term of employment contract.

Appeals against notices

Appeals are made against improvement and prohibition notices on the following grounds:

a) the time limit for compliance; and/or

b) substantive law involved.

Appeals on health and safety issues lie to the Divisional Court of the High Court. Like the Employment Appeals Tribunal, the latter can only interfere where the tribunal has erred in respect of the view of the law which it took.

Appeals from the Employment Appeals Tribunal and the High Court go to the Court of Appeal where litigants must be represented by counsel.

See:

- *Approved Codes of Practice and HSE Guidance Notes*
- *Disobedience and disregard for safety*
- *Duties, hierarchy of*
- *Duty of care*
- *Health and Safety at Work etc Act 1974*

D

Damage control

Asset protection is an important requirement for organizations. Assets include money, materials, manufactured goods, manpower and machinery (the 5 'M's). Damage control, as a management technique, is directly concerned with the protection of an organization's assets from accidental loss. This applies, in particular, to machinery, in order to maintain production, and to materials, manufactured goods and other finished products before they reach the consumer.

Within a total loss control framework, effective damage control indirectly protects assets through the elimination of damage to, for example, structural items, such as floors and walls, machinery and other items of work equipment, such as lift trucks, and finished products arising from poor storage arrangements. Planned preventive maintenance systems therefore form part of an effective damage control strategy.

The reporting, recording, investigation and costing of damage is an essential feature of a damage control programme. Moreover, evidence of damage to structures, work equipment, vehicles and final products is, in many cases, a clear indicator of poor standards of health and safety performance. The factors contributing to damage are similar in many respects to those leading to personal injury.

See:

- *Safety management systems*

Dermatitis

This term, fundamentally, means inflammation of the skin. Dermatitis is the most common form of occupational disease and prevention rests very much on levels of personal hygiene, the use of a range of skin protection agents and health surveillance procedures where people may be exposed to the risk of contact with certain physical, chemical and biological agents. Non-infective dermatitis is a prescribed disease in relation to exposure to dust, liquid, vapour or other skin irritant.

Dermatitis may be:

- exogenous, that is, caused by factors from outside the individual, such as acids and alkalis; or

- endogenous, namely, associated with factors from within the individual, such as allergies to a wide range of substances commonly encountered in everyday life.

In any consideration of the causes of dermatitis, therefore, the question of individual susceptibility to:

a) specific substances encountered in the workplace or at home; and

b) certain foods such as fish.

should be considered. Similarly, individuals may become sensitized to a wide range of agents whereby even the slightest contact with same will produce some form of skin response. For some people, dermatitis is a classic manifestation of stress which can be caused by a variety of circumstances.

The principal causes of dermatitis

Most case of dermatitis are exogenous in nature and are associated with exposure to a specific agent encountered at work. These agents can be classified as:

Physical factors

Exposure to heat can result in heat rash. Such rashes are common in people working on hot processes, such as foundry workers, metal workers and furnacemen. The secondary effects of burns should also be considered, together with possible exposure to ionising radiation.

Chemical agents

Contact with irritant and harmful chemical agents, such as acids, alkalis and sulphides of metals is, by far, the most common cause of dermatitis. The resistance of the skin to external irritants varies with age, sex, race, colour, diet and the state of health.

Biological agents

Many plants, in particular members of the *Liliaceae* and *Primulaceae* families, contain chemical compounds, exposure to which can lead to sensitivity to those compounds. Principal groups affected are nurserymen, florists and gardeners.

Similarly, exposure to certain woods, the dusts created during processing and the sap contained in, for instance, hardwoods, must be considered in the case of wood machinists, cabinet makers and carpenters. A small number of workers may become sensitized as a result of contact.

Grain itch, barley itch, grocer's itch and copra itch are varieties of dermatitis caused by mites found in these commodities. In the same way, scabies, may be contracted by people involved in animal handling, such as animal handlers, breeders and veterinary practitioners.

Endogenous dermatitis

Where there is clear evidence of endogenous dermatitis, the only solution may be the removal of the affected person from any future contact with the identified agent.

See:

- *Hazardous substances*
- *Health surveillance and health protection*
- *Occupational diseases and conditions*
- *Reportable and prescribed diseases*

Disobedience and disregard for safety

There are situations where employees disobey safety orders, disregard obvious dangers or fail to use equipment provided to ensure their safety whilst at work. It is essential that employers take disciplinary action in such situations including, in serious cases, dismissal for unsafe behaviour.

Disobedience

Where an **employee** disobeys orders and suffers damage as a result, any claim for injury may be reduced on the basis of contributory negligence on the part of that employee.

Where an employee disobeys safety instructions with the result that a fellow employee, a member of the public or an employee of a contractor is injured, his employer may be liable. In *Century Insurance Co. Ltd v Northern Ireland Road Transport Board (1942) AC 509* an employee of the respondent was employed to deliver petrol to garages. Whilst discharging petrol from a road tanker to an underground tank, the employee decided to smoke a cigarette. He lit a match and then discarded same whilst still alight, the lit match landing by the opening to the underground tank. This resulted in an explosion with injuries to people and damage to property. The Court of Appeal held that his employer was liable, since the employee was doing what he was employed to do, even though his was undertaking this task in a grossly negligent manner.

Rose v Plenty (1976) 1 AER 97 involved a milk roundsman employed by a Co-operative Society. The Society had paid considerable attention to the practice of roundsmen employing young children and paying them to deliver bottles of milk to doorsteps and collect empty bottles. They had forbidden roundsmen to carry on this practice and notices prohibiting same were displayed at retail depots. Contrary to this instruction, a young boy was injured when he rode on a milk float with one leg dangling over the side so that he could jump off quickly to deliver bottles of milk. Evidence indicated that the respondent drove negligently with the result that the boy's leg was trapped between the wheel and the kerb. The court ruled that the employee was 75% to blame and the boy 25%. At the Court of Appeal, however, it was held that the employer was liable. In this case, the employee was doing what he was employed to do but was doing it negligently.

In *National Coal Board v England (1954) 1 AER 546* an employee was injured whilst assisting a shotfirer to set up for shot blasting, contrary to instructions. In another case, *Smith v Chesterfield and District Co-operative Society Ltd (1953) 1 AER 447*, an employee disobeyed safety instructions by putting his hand under the guard of a pastry machine and suffered injury.

Disregard

Any disregard for obvious dangers features significantly in contributory negligence. In Rushton v Turner Bros Asbestos Co.Ltd. (1959) 3 AER 517 an employee was injured as a result of putting his hand up an exit chute to clear an obstruction in an asbestos fibre crushing machine. He had received extensive training in safe working practices and was aware of the dangers involved when cleaning the machine whilst it was in motion.

Failure to use safety equipment

An employee who fails to use safety equipment may be contributorily negligent. *Lewis v Denyer (1960) 3 AER 299* involved failure on the part of an employee to use push sticks, contrary to the requirements of the wood-working machinery regulations current at that time.

In *Bux v Slough Metals Ltd (1974) 1 AER 262* an employee sustained injury through failure to wear the goggles provided, contrary to the requirements of Non-Ferrous Metals (Melting and Founding) Regulations 1962.

See:

- *Common law liability*
- *Duty of care*
- *Gross misconduct (health and safety)*

Display screen equipment

The three principal risks to health associated with the use of display screen equipment are:

a) work-related upper limb disorders;

b) visual fatigue; and

c) postural fatigue.

Work-related upper limb disorders

In 1960, the International Labour Organization recognized RSI as an occupational disease, a condition caused by forceful, frequent, twisting and repetitive movements.

Repetitive strain injury covers some well-known conditions such as tennis elbow, flexor tenosynovitis and carpal tunnel syndrome. It is usually caused or aggravated by work, and is associated with repetitive and over-forceful movement, excessive workloads, inadequate rest periods and sustained or constrained postures, resulting in pain or soreness due to the inflammatory conditions of muscles and the synovial lining of the tendon sheath. Present approaches to treatment are largely effective, provided the condition is treated in its early stages. Tenosynovitis has been a prescribed industrial disease since 1975, and the HSE have proposed changing the name of the condition to 'work related upper limb disorder' on the grounds that the disorder does not always result from repetition or strain, and is not always a visible injury.

Many people, including assembly workers, supermarket checkout assistants and keyboard operators, are affected by RSI at some point in their lives.

Clinical signs and symptoms

These include local aching pain, tenderness, swelling and crepitus (a grating sensation in the joint) aggravated by pressure or movement. Tenosynovitis, affecting the hand or forearm, is the second most common prescribed industrial disease, the most common being dermatitis. True tenosynovitis, where inflammation of the synovial lining of the tendon sheath is evident, is rare and potentially serious. The more common and benign form is peritendinitis crepitans, which is associated with inflammation of the muscle-tendon joint that often extends well into the muscle.

Forms of RSI

Epicondylitis

Inflammation of the area where a muscle joins a bone.

Peritendinitis

Inflammation of the area where a tendon joins a muscle.

Carpal Tunnel Syndrome

A painful condition in the area where nerves and tendons pass through the carpal bone in the hand.

Tenosynovitis

Inflammation of the synovial lining of the tendon sheath.

Tendinitis

Inflammation of the tendons, particularly in the fingers.

Dupuytrens Contracture

A condition affecting the palm of the hand, where it is impossible to straighten the hand and fingers.

Writer's Cramp

Cramps in the hand, forearm and fingers.

Prevention of RSI

Injury can be prevented by:

a) improved design of working areas e.g. position of keyboard and VDU screens, heights of workbenches and chairs;

b) adjustments of workloads and rest periods;

c) provision of special tools;

d) health surveillance aimed at detecting early stages of the disorder; and

e) better training and supervision.

If untreated, RSI can be seriously disabling.

Operational stress

This can take the form of both visual fatigue and postural fatigue.

Visual fatigue

Visual fatigue (eye strain) is associated with glare from the display and the continual need to focus and refocus from screen to copy material and back again. The degree of individual fatigue will vary. Vision screening of staff on a regular basis, and as part of a pre-employment health screen, is recommended.

Postural fatigue

Postural fatigue, an outcome of operational stress, may take many forms. It can include backache, neck and shoulder pains associated with poor chair and workstation design and positioning in relation to controls and displays, insufficient leg room and the need to adjust body position.

Other causes of operational stress

Operational stress can also be created by noise from the unit and ancillary equipment, excessive heat and inadequate ventilation.

The degree of operator stress may vary according to age, sex, physical build, attitude to the task, current level of visual acuity, general health and the extent of time in tasks not involving attention to a display screen. Users should be encouraged to organize their work loads to permit frequent screen breaks.

Health and Safety (Display Screen Equipment) Regulations 1992

These Regulations should be read in conjunction with the MHSWR. The original regulations have been amended in light of the Health and Safety (Miscellaneous Amendments) Regulations 2002.

Important definitions

Display screen equipment means an alphanumeric or graphic display screen, regardless of the display process involved.

Operator means a self-employed person who habitually uses display screen equipment as a significant part of his normal work.

User means an employee who habitually uses display screen equipment as a significant part of his normal work.

Workstation means an assembly comprising:

a) display screen equipment (DSE) (whether provided with software determining the interface between the equipment and its operator or user, a keyboard or any other input device),

b) any optional accessories to the DSE,

c) any disk drive, modem, printer, document holder, work chair, work desk, work surface or other item peripheral to the DSE; and

d) the immediate environment around the DSE.

The terms 'habitual' and 'significant' in the definition of both 'user' and 'operator' are important in that many people who use DSE as a feature of their work activities may not necessarily be users as defined. Employers must decide which of their employees are defined 'users' by referring to the Guidance which accompanies the Regulations.

The Regulations do NOT apply to or are in relation to:

a) drivers' cabs or control cabs;

b) DSE on board a means of transport;

c) DSE mainly intended for public operation;

d) portable systems not in prolonged use;

e) calculators, cash registers or any equipment having a small data or measurement display required for direct use of the equipment; or

f) window typewriters.

Principal requirements

The principal requirements of the Regulations are:

- Every employer shall perform a suitable and sufficient analysis of those workstations which are used by both users and operators for the purpose of assessing the health and safety risks to which those persons are exposed in consequence of that use.

- Any assessment made by an employer shall be reviewed by him if:

  - there is reason to suspect that it is no longer valid; or

  - there has been a significant change in the matters to which it relates

  - and where, as a result of any such review, changes to the assessment are required, the employer concerned shall make them.

- The employer shall reduce the risks identified in consequence of an assessment to the lowest extent reasonably practicable.

- Every employer shall ensure that any workstation which may be used for the purposes of his undertaking meets the requirements laid down in the Schedule to these Regulations, to the extent specified in paragraph 1 thereof.

- Every employer shall so plan the activities of users at work in his undertaking that their daily work on DSE is periodically interrupted by such breaks or changes of activity as reduce their workload at that equipment.

- Where a person is a user or is to become a user, the employer who carries on the undertaking shall, if requested by that person, ensure that an appropriate eye and eyesight test is carried out on him by a competent person within the time specified in paragraph 2.

- The time specified above is:

  - in the case of a person who is a user, as soon as practicable after the request; or

  - in the case of a person who is to become a user, before he becomes a user.

- At regular intervals after an employee has been provided (whether before or after becoming an employee) with an eye and eyesight test, his employer shall, subject to paragraph 6, ensure that he is provided with a further eye and eyesight test of an appropriate nature, any such test to be carried out by a competent person.

- Where a user experiences visual difficulties which may reasonably be considered to be caused by work on DSE, his employer shall ensure that he is provided at his request with an appropriated eye and eyesight test, any such test to be carried out by a competent person as soon as practicable after being requested as aforesaid.

- Every employer shall ensure that each user employed by him is provided with special corrective appliances for the work being done by the user concerned where:
  - normal corrective appliances cannot be used; and
  - the result of any eye and eyesight test the user has been given in accordance with this regulation shows such provision to be necessary.

- Nothing in paragraph 3 shall require an employer to provide any employee with an eye and eyesight test against that employee's will.

- Where a person is a user or is to become a user, the employer shall ensure that he is provided with adequate health and safety training in the use of any workstation upon which he may be required to work. In the case of a person who is to become a user the training shall be provided before he becomes a user.

- Every employer shall ensure that operators and users at work in his undertaking are provided with adequate information about:
  - all aspects of health and safety relating to their workstations; and
  - such measures taken by him in compliance with his duties under Regulations 2 and 3 as relate to them and their work.

- Every employer shall ensure that users are provided with adequate information about such measures taken by him in compliance with his duties with respect to:
  a) the daily work routine of users;
  b) the provision of training prior to becoming a user;
  c) the provision of eye and eyesight tests; and
  d) the provision of training whenever the organization of his workstation is substantially modified.

DSE risk analysis

Risk analysis involves a consideration of the requirements laid down in the Schedule to the Regulations relating to:

a) the equipment;

b) the environment; and

c) the interface between the computer and operator/user.

See:

- *Ergonomics*
- *Occupational diseases and conditions*

Documentation requirements

Current health and safety legislation places considerable emphasis on the documentation of policies, procedures and systems of work and the maintenance of certain records.

The following are some of the documents and records that are required to be produced and maintained:

- Statement of Health and Safety Policy (Health and Safety at Work etc Act 1974).

- Risk assessments in respect of:
    - workplaces (Management of Health and Safety at Work Regulations 1999 and Workplace (Health, Safety at Welfare) Regulations 1992)

    - work activities (Management of Health and Safety at Work Regulations 1999 and Workplace (Health, Safety and Welfare) Regulations 1992)

    - work groups (Management of Health and Safety at Work Regulations)

    - new or expectant mothers (Management of Health and Safety at Work Regulations 1999)

    - young persons (Management of Health and Safety at Work Regulations 1999)

    - work equipment (Provision and Use of Work Equipment Regulations 1998)

    - personal protective equipment (Personal Protective Equipment Regulations 1992)

- manual handling operations (Manual Handling Operations Regulations 1992)

- display screen equipment (Health and Safety (Display Screen Equipment) Regulations 1992)

- substances hazardous to health (Control of Substances Hazardous to Health Regulations 2002)

- significant exposure to lead (Control of Lead at Work Regulations 1998)

- noise levels in excess of 85 dBA (Noise at Work Regulations 1989)

- before a radiation employer commences a new activity involving work with ionising radiation (Ionising Radiations Regulations 1999)

- the presence or otherwise of asbestos in non-domestic premises (Control of Asbestos at Work Regulations 2002)

- where a dangerous substance is or is liable to be present at the workplace (Dangerous Substances and Explosive Atmospheres Regulations 2002)

- work at height (Work at Height Regulations 2005).

- Safe systems of work, including permits to work and method statements.

- Pre-tender stage health and safety plan and construction phase health and safety plan (Construction (Design and Management) Regulations 1994.

- Planned preventive maintenance schedules (Workplace (Health, Safety and Welfare) Regulations 1992 and Provision and Use of Work Equipment Regulations 1998.

- Cleaning schedules (Workplace (Health, Safety and Welfare) Regulations 1992.

- Written scheme of examination for specific parts of an installed pressure system or of a mobile system and the last report relating to a system by a competent person (Pressure Systems Safety Regulations 2000).

- Written plan of work identifying those parts of the premises where asbestos is or is liable to be present in the premises and detailing how that work is to be carried out safely and without risk to health (Control of Asbestos at Work Regulations 2002).

- Records of examinations and tests of exhaust ventilation equipment and respiratory protective equipment and of repairs carried out as a result of those examinations and tests (Control of Lead at Work Regulations 2002, Control of Substances Hazardous to Health Regulations 2002 and Control of Asbestos at Work Regulations 2002).

- Record of air monitoring carried out in respect of:
  - specified substances or processes; and
  - lead
  - asbestos

  (Control of Substances Hazardous to Health Regulations 2002, Control of Lead at Work Regulations 2002 and Control of Asbestos at Work Regulations 2002).

- Record of examination of respiratory protective equipment (Ionising Radiations Regulations 1999).

- Records of air monitoring in cases where exposure to asbestos is such that a health record is required to be kept (Control of Asbestos at Work Regulations 2002).

- Personal health records (Control of Lead at Work Regulations 2002, Ionising Radiations Regulations 1999, Control of Substances Hazardous to Health Regulations 2002 and Control of Asbestos at Work Regulations 2002).

- Personal dose records (Ionising Radiations Regulations 1999).

- Record of quantity and location of radioactive substances (Ionising Radiations Regulations 1999).

- Record of investigation of certain notifiable occurrences involving release or spillage of a radioactive substance (Ionising Radiations Regulations 1999).

- Record of suspected overexposure to ionising radiation during medical exposure (Ionising Radiations Regulations 1999).

- Major Accident Prevention Policy (Control of Major Accident Hazards Regulations 1999).

- Off-Site Emergency Plan (Control of Major Accident Hazards Regulations 1999).

- Declaration of conformity by the installer of a lift and the manufacturer of a safety component for a lift together with any technical documentation or other information in relation to a lift or safety component required to be retained under the conformity assessment procedure (Lifts Regulations 1997).

- Declaration of conformity by the manufacturer of pressure equipment and assemblies (as defined) together with technical documentation or other information in relation to an item of pressure equipment and assemblies required to be retained under the conformity assessment procedure used (Pressure Equipment Regulations 1999).

- Any technical documentation or other information required to be retained under a conformity assessment procedure and a periodic inspection procedure (Transportable Pressure Vessels Regulations 2001).

- Procedures for serious and imminent danger and for danger areas (Management of Health and Safety at Work Regulations 1999).

- Emergency procedure to protect the safety of employees from an accident, incident or emergency related to the presence of a dangerous substance at the workplace (Dangerous Substances and Explosive Atmospheres Regulations 2001).

- Contingency plan in the event of a radiation accident (Ionising Radiations Regulations 1999).

- Local rules in respect of controlled areas and supervised areas (Ionising Radiations Regulations 1999).

- Written arrangements for non-classified persons (Ionising Radiations Regulations 1999).

See:

- *Electrical installations*

- *Health risk assessment*

- *Health surveillance and health protection*

- *Ionising radiation*

- *Lead at work*

- *Lifting operations, machinery and equipment*

- *Maintenance operations*

- *Manual handling operations*

- *Method statements*

- *Noise*

- *Permit to work systems*

- *Pressure systems*

- *Risk assessment*

- *Statements of health and safety policy*

- *Ventilation in the workplace*

Duties, hierarchy of

Statutory duties, such as those under the Health and Safety at Work etc Act 1974 and Regulations made under the Act, give rise to criminal liability. There are three distinct levels of duty which must be taken into account in interpreting the requirements of the law.

Absolute or strict requirements

Where risk of injury or disease is inevitable if safety requirements are not complied with, a statutory duty may well be absolute or strict, indicated by the terms 'shall' or 'must' in the text of the legislation. Absolute or strict duties imply a higher level of duty than those qualified by 'so far as is practicable' and 'so far as is reasonably practicable'.

Typical examples are:

Provision and Use of Work Equipment Regulations 1998

Every employer *shall* ensure that work equipment is maintained in an efficient state, in efficient working order and in good repair.

Workplace (Health, Safety and Welfare) Regulations 1992

Every workplace and the furniture, furnishings and fittings therein shall be kept sufficiently clean.

The majority of duties on employers under recent Regulations tend to be of an absolute nature e.g. Management of Health and Safety at Work Regulations 1999.

Duties qualified by 'so far as is practicable'

A duty qualified by "so far as is practicable" implies that if, in the light of current knowledge or invention or, in the light of the current state of the art, it is possible to comply with that requirement, irrespective of cost or sacrifice involved, then such a requirement must be complied with. *[Schwalb v Fass H & Son (1946) 175 LT 345]*

'So far as is practicable' means more than physically possible and implies a higher duty of care than a duty qualified by 'so far as is reasonably practicable'.

Duties qualified by 'so far as is reasonably practicable'

This implies a lesser level of duty than one qualified by 'so far as is practicable'. 'Reasonably practicable' is a narrower term than 'physically possible' (i.e. 'practicable'), and implies that a computation must be made in which the quantum of risk is placed in one scale and the sacrifice involved in the measures necessary for averting that risk are placed in the other. If it can be shown that there is a gross disproportion between these two factors, that is, the risk being insignificant in relation to the sacrifice, then a defendant discharges the onus upon himself. *[Edwards v National Coal Board (1949) 1 AER 743]*

The majority of the duties on persons under the Health and Safety at Work etc Act 1974 and many Regulations, such as the Noise at Work Regulations 1989, are qualified by the term 'so far as is reasonably practicable'.

See:

- *Health and Safety at Work etc Act 1974*

Duty of care

The duty of care at common law which is owed by an employer towards his employees is a personal one. Employers owe a general duty towards all their employees to take reasonable care so as to avoid injuries and diseases and deaths arising out of or in connection with work.

The duties of employers at common law were established in *Wilsons & Clyde Coal Co. Ltd. v English (1938) AC 57*. All employers must:

- provide a safe place of work, including safe access to, and egress from, that place of work;

- provide and maintain safe appliances and equipment and plant for doing the work;

- provide and maintain a safe system for doing the work; and

- provide competent and safety-conscious personnel.

See:

- *Common law liability*

- *Insurance*

- *Negligence*

- *Occupiers' liability*

- *Vicarious liability*

E

Electrical installations

What is electricity?

All atoms contain electrons which rotate around a nucleus in orbital layers like a system of sun and planets. The nucleus contains a positive charge and the rotating electrons are negatively charged. The outer layers of electrons are less closely bound to the nucleus than the inner layers and may, under certain conditions, move from atom to atom. Thus, a flow of electricity is really a rapid movement, or interchanging, of electrons in the atomic make-up of a substance. Electricity is, therefore, a form of energy.

Electrical circuits

For its energy to be utilized, electricity requires a means of conducting it to a load, such as lighting, heating or power, conducting it back from the load to the substation, and ultimately returning it to the alternator, which is the basic electrical circuit.

To make electricity flow in a circuit, it is necessary to apply sufficient pressure (volts) to force it to flow. The voltage applied to a circuit will force electricity around it, i.e. the current, which is measured in amps. An electrical circuit offers a resistance to the flow of electricity, depending on the nature of the material forming the electrical conductors, its cross-sectional area and length. The larger the cross-sectional area the lower will be the resistance, while the greater the length, the higher will be the resistance. Electrical resistance is measured in ohms.

Ohm's Law

Ohm's Law specifies the relationship between volts, amps and ohms thus:

$$\text{Amps} = \frac{\text{Volts}}{\text{Ohms}}$$

$$\text{Ohms} = \frac{\text{Volts}}{\text{Amps}}$$

$$\text{Volts} = \text{Amps} \times \text{Ohms}$$

The principal hazards

Hazards associated with the use of electricity can broadly be divided into two categories, namely the risk of injury to people and the risk of fire and/or explosion.

Injuries to people

Human injury is associated with shock, burns, physical injuries from explosions, microwaves, accumulators and batteries, and eye injuries.

Electric shock

This is the effect produced on the body and, in particular, the nervous system, by an electric current passing through it. The effect varies according to the strength of the current which, in turn, varies with the voltage and the electrical resistance of the body. The resistance of the body varies according to the points of entry and exit of the current and other factors, such as body weight and/or the presence of moisture.

VOLTAGE	RESPONSE	CURRENT
15 volts	Threshold of feeling	0.002-0.005 amps
20-25 volts	Threshold of pain	–
30 volts	Muscular spasm (non-release)	0.015 amps
70 volts	Minimum for death	0.1 amps
120 volts	Maximum for 'safety'	0.002 amps
200-240 volts	Most serious/fatal accidents	0.2 amps

Table 2: Typical responses to current/voltage

Common cause of death is ventricular fibrillation (spasm) of the heart muscle which occurs at 0.05 amps. The vascular system ceases to function and the victim dies of suffocation.

Remember. IT'S THE CURRENT THAT KILLS!

First aid

First Aid for a victim of electric shock must be cardiac massage plus mouth-to-mouth resuscitation until normal breathing and the heart action return. A victim who is 'locked on' to a live appliance must not be approached until the appliance is electrically dead.

Burns

A current passing through a conductor produces heat. Burns can be caused by contact with hot conductors or by the passage of a current through the body at the point of entry and exit. Electric arcing from short circuits may also cause burns.

Explosions

Electrical short circuit or sparking from the electrical contacts in switches or other equipment is a common cause of explosions and subsequent human injury or death. This presupposes the presence of a flammable atmosphere e.g. vapour, dust, gas.

Eye injuries

These can arise from exposure to ultraviolet rays from accidental arcing in a process such as welding.

Microwave apparatus

Microwaves can damage the soft tissues of the body.

Accumulators and batteries

Hydrogen gas may be produced as a by-product of battery charging which can cause explosive atmospheres with the risk of burns.

The risk of fire

Electricity is a common source of ignition for major fires. Some insulating materials and materials used for electrical connections may be flammable and can give rise to small fires in switchgear, distribution boxes or electricity sub-stations. The risk of losses from fire increases when these local fires go undetected and result in major fires.

Sources of electrical ignition include:

- **Sparks** between conductors or conductor and earth;

- **Arcs** are a larger and brighter discharge of electrical energy and are more likely to cause a fire;

- **Short circuits** arise when a current finds a path from live to return other than through apparatus, resulting in high current flow, heating of conductors to white heat and arcing;

- **Overloading** where too much current flows causing heating of conductors; and

- **Old and defective/damaged wiring** through breakdown of the insulation resulting in short circuit, or the use of progressively more equipment on an old circuit resulting in overloading.

Principles of electrical safety

The prime objective of electrical safety is to protect people from electric shock, and also from fire and burns, arising from contact with electricity. There are two basic preventive measures against electric shock, namely:

a) protection against **direct** contact e.g. by providing effective and sound insulation for parts of equipment liable to be charged with electricity; and

b) protection against **indirect** contact e.g. by providing effective earthing for metallic enclosures which are liable to be charged with electricity if the basic insulation fails for any reason.

When it is not possible to provide adequate insulation as protection against direct contact, a range of measures is available, including protection by the use of barriers or enclosures, and protection by position i.e. placing live parts out of reach.

Earthing

Earthing implies connection to the general mass of earth in such a manner as will ensure at all times an immediate discharge of electrical energy without danger. Earthing, to give protection against indirect contact with electricity can be achieved in a number of ways, including the connection of extraneous conductive parts of premises (radiators, taps, water pipes) to the main earthing terminal of the electrical installation. This creates an equipotential zone and eliminates the risk of shock that could occur if a person touched two different parts of the metalwork liable to be charged, under earth fault conditions, at different voltages.

When an earth fault exists, such as when a live part touches an enclosed conductive part, e.g. metalwork, it is vital to ensure that the electrical supply is automatically disconnected. This protection is brought about by the use of overcurrent devices i.e. correctly rated fuses or circuit breakers, or by correctly rated and placed residual current devices. The maintenance of earth continuity is vital.

Fuses

A fuse is basically a strip of metal of such size as would melt at a prede-termined value of current flow. It is placed in the electrical circuit and, on melting, cuts off the current to the circuit. Fuses should be of a type and rating appropriate to the circuit and the appliance it protects.

Circuit breakers

These devices incorporate a mechanism which trips a switch from the 'ON' to 'OFF' position if an excess current flows in the circuit. A circuit breaker should be of the type and rating for circuit and appliance it protects.

Earth leakage circuit breakers (residual current devices)

Fuses and circuit breakers do not necessarily provide total protection against electric shock. Earth leakage circuit breakers provide protection against earth leakage faults, particularly at those locations where effec-tive earthing cannot necessarily be achieved.

Reduced voltage

Reduced voltage systems are another form of protection against electric shock, the most commonly used being the 110 volt centre point earthed system. In this system the secondary winding of the transformer providing the 110 volt supply is centre tapped to earth, thereby ensuring that at no part of the 110 volt circuit can the voltage to earth exceed 55 volts.

Safe systems of work

When work is to be undertaken on electrical apparatus or a part of a circuit, a formally operated safe system of work should always be used. This normally takes the form of a Permit to Work system which ensures the following procedures:

a) switching out and locking off the electricity supply i.e. isolation;

b) checking by the use of an appropriate voltage detection instrument that the circuit, or part of same to be worked on, is dead before work commences;

c) high levels of supervision and control to ensure the work is undertaken correctly;

d) physical precautions, such as the erection of barriers to restrict access to the area, are implemented; and

e) formal cancellation of the Permit to Work once the work is completed satisfactorily and return to service of the plant or system in question.

See:

- *Competent persons*
- *Maintenance operations*
- *Permit to work systems*
- *Portable electrical appliances*

Emergency procedures

Management of Health and Safety at Work Regulations 1999

Regulation 7 of the MHSWR requires employers to establish 'procedures for serious and imminent danger and for danger areas'.

The duties under the Regulation are stated thus:

1. Every employer shall:

   a) establish and where necessary give effect to appropriate procedures to be followed in the event of serious and imminent danger to persons at work in his undertaking;

   b) nominate a sufficient number of competent persons to implement those procedures insofar as they relate to the evacuation from premises of persons at work in his undertaking; and

   c) ensure that none of his employees has access to any area occupied by him to which it is necessary to restrict access on grounds of health and safety unless the employee concerned has received adequate health and safety instruction.

2. Without prejudice to the generality of paragraph 1(a), the procedures referred to in that sub-paragraph shall:

   a) so far as is practicable, require any persons at work who are exposed to serious and imminent danger to be informed of the nature of the hazard and of the steps taken or to be taken to protect them from it;

   b) enable the persons concerned (if necessary by taking appropriate steps in the absence of guidance or instruction and in the light of their knowledge and the technical means at their disposal) to stop work and immediately proceed to a place of safety in the event of their being exposed to serious, imminent and unavoidable danger; and

(c) save in exceptional cases for reasons duly substantiated (which cases and reasons shall be specified in these procedures), require the persons concerned to be prevented from resuming work in any situation where there is still a serious and imminent danger.

3. A person shall be regarded as competent for the purposes of paragraph 1(b) where he has sufficient training and experience or knowledge and other qualities which enable him properly to implement the evacuation procedures referred to in that sub-paragraph.

A 'danger area' is defined in the ACOP as a work environment which must be entered by an employee where the level of risk is unacceptable without special precautions being taken.

Identifying the risks

The risk assessment required under Regulation 3 of the MHSWR should identify the significant risks arising out of work. These could include, for instance, the potential for a major escalating fire, explosion, building collapse, pollution incident, bomb threat and some of the scheduled dangerous occurrences listed in RIDDOR e.g. the explosion, collapse or bursting of any closed pressure vessel. All these events could result in a major incident, which can be defined as one that may:

a)   affect several departments within an undertaking;

b)   endanger the surrounding communities;

c)   be classed as a dangerous occurrence under RIDDOR; or

d)   result in adverse publicity for the organization with ensuing loss of public confidence and market place image.

Fundamentally, the question must be asked:

"What are the worst possible types of incident that could arise from the process or undertaking?"

Once these major risks, which could result in serious and imminent danger, have been identified, a formal emergency procedure must be produced.

Approved code of practice

The ACOP, which should be read in conjunction with the Regulations, raises a number of important points with regard to the establishment of emergency procedures.

Establishing the emergency procedure

The risk assessment undertaken to comply with the MHSWR should identify those highly significant risks where an emergency procedure is essential.

A properly conceived emergency procedure will take account of four phases or stages of an emergency.

Phase 1: Preliminary action

This refers to:

a) the preparation of a plan, tailored to meet the special requirements of the site, products and surroundings, including:

   i) a list of all key telephone numbers;

   ii) the system for the provision of emergency lighting e.g. hand lamps and torches;

   iii) the designation of exit routes;

   iv) a plan of the site layout identifying hydrant points and the location of shut-off valves to energy supplies e.g. gas; and

   v) notes on specific hazards on site for use by the emergency services;

b) the familiarization through training of every employee with the details of the plan, including the position of essential equipment;

c) the training of personnel involved, in particular, key personnel;

d) the initiation of a programme of inspection of potentially hazardous areas, testing of warning systems and evacuation procedures; and

e) stipulating specific periods at which the plan is to be re-examined and updated.

Phase 2: Action when emergency is imminent

There may be a warning of the emergency, in which case this period should be used to assemble key personnel, to review the standing arrangements in order to consider whether changes are necessary, to give advance warning to the external authorities, and to test all systems connected with the emergency procedure.

Phase 3: Action during emergency

If Phase 1 has been properly executed, and Phase 2, where applicable, Phase 3 proceeds according to plan. However, it is likely that unexpected variations in a predicted emergency will take place. The decision-making personnel, selected beforehand for this purpose, must be able to make precise and rapid judgements and see that the proper action follows their decisions.

Phase 4: Ending the emergency

There must be a procedure for declaring plant, systems and specific areas safe, together with an early reoccupation of buildings where possible.

Implementing the emergency procedure

The following matters must be taken into account when implementing an emergency procedure.

Liaison with external authorities and other companies

The closest contact must be maintained with the fire, police, ambulance and health authorities, together with the HSE and local authority. A mutual aid scheme involving neighbouring premises is best undertaken at this stage. A major emergency may involve a failure in the supply of gas, electricity, water and/or telephone communications. Discussions with the appropriate authority will help to determine priorities in re-establishing supply.

Emergency controller

A senior manager, with thorough knowledge of all processes and their associated hazards, should be nominated Emergency Controller, and a deputy appointed to cover absence, however brief this may be. Out of normal working hours, the senior member of management should take initial control until the Emergency Controller arrives.

Emergency control centre

A sound communication system is essential if a major emergency is to be handled effectively. A control centre should be established and equipped with means of receiving information from the forward control and assembly points, transmitting calls for assistance to external authorities, calling in essential personnel and transmitting information and instructions to personnel within the premises. Alternative means of communication must be available in the event of the main system being rendered inoperative e.g. field telephones. A fall-back control centre may be necessary in certain situations such as a rapidly-escalating fire.

Initiating the procedure

The special procedure for handling major emergencies must only be initiated when such an emergency is known to exist. A limited number of designated senior managers should be assigned the responsibility of deciding if a major emergency exists or is imminent. Only these persons should have authority to implement the procedure.

Notification to local authorities

Notification can be achieved by a predetermined short message, transmitted by an emergency line or by the British Telecom lines. The warning message should mention routes to the premises which may become impassable.

Call out of key personnel

A list of key personnel required in the event of a major emergency should be drawn up, together with the internal and home telephone numbers and addresses. The list should be available in control centres and constantly updated.

Immediate action on site

Any emergency would be dealt with by action by supervisors and operators designed to close down and make safe those parts which are affected or likely to be affected (danger areas). Preservation of human life and the protection of property are of prime importance, and injured persons should be conveyed to hospital with the least possible delay. This may require temporary facilities at points in a safe area accessible to ambulances.

Evacuation

Complete evacuation of non-essential personnel immediately the alarm is sounded is usually advisable, though it may not be necessary or advisable in large workplaces. In either situation, however, an evacuation alarm system should be installed and made known to all employees, for the purpose of evacuating the premises. Evacuation should be immediately followed by a roll call at a prescribed assembly point to ensure its success.

Access to records

Because relatives of injured and/or deceased employees will have to be informed by the police, each control centre should keep a list of names and addresses of all employees.

Public relations

As a major incident will attract the attention of the media, it is essential to make arrangements for official releases of information to the press and other news services. This is best achieved through a specifically designated Public Relations Officer. Other employees should be instructed not to release information, but to refer any enquiries to this officer, who should keep a record of any media enquiries dealt with during the emergency.

Catering and temporary shelter

Emergency teams will need refreshment and temporary shelter if the incident is of long duration. Where facilities on the premises cannot be used it may be possible for the local authority or neighbouring companies to provide facilities.

Contingency arrangements

A contingency plan should be drawn up covering arrangements for repairs to buildings, drying out and temporary waterproofing, replacement of raw materials, alternative storage and transport arrangements.

Training

Training is an important feature of any emergency procedure. Training exercises should include the participation of external services, such as the fire brigade, ambulance service and police. Where mutual aid schemes exist with neighbouring organizations, all possible participants should take part in any form of training exercise.

Statement of health and safety policy

Familiarization of all staff with the procedure, together with training exercises at regular intervals, will help reduce the risk of fatal and serious injuries following an emergency. For this reason the company emergency procedure should be linked to the Statement of Health and Safety Policy, perhaps as a specific Code of Practice referred to in the Statement.

See:

- *Accidents and accident prevention*
- *Competent persons*

Employee handbooks

Under the HSWA and various regulations, employers have a duty to provide information to employees on the hazards that could arise and the precautions that they must take. Under the MHSWR, any information provided to employees arising from the risk assessment process must be 'comprehensible and relevant' to the employees concerned.

One way of ensuring compliance with these requirements is through the issue to all employees of a Health and Safety Handbook indicating the hazards that could arise during their work and the precautions they must take. Such a document would be issued at induction training and it would be reasonable for new employees to signify to the effect that they have received this handbook.

> **See:**
>
> - *Information for employees*
> - *Information, instruction and training*

Enforcement procedures

The enforcing authorities for the HSWA and other health and safety legislation are:

a) the Health and Safety Executive (HSE) ;

b) local authorities, principally through their environmental health departments; and

c) fire authorities, for certain fire-related legislation.

Actual enforcement is undertaken by inspectors appointed under the Act and authorized by written warrant from the enforcing authority.

Powers of inspectors

Under Section 20 of the HSWA an inspector has the following powers:

a) to enter premises at any reasonable time and, where obstruction is anticipated, to enlist the support of a policed officer;

b) on entering a premises:

   i)   to take with him any person duly authorized by his enforcing authority; and

   ii) any equipment or materials required for any purpose for which the power of entry is being exercised;

c) to make such examination and investigation as may be necessary;

d) to direct that premises or any part of such premises, or anything therein, shall remain undisturbed for so long as is reasonably necessary for the purpose of examination or investigation;

e) to take such measurements and photographs and make such recordings as he considers necessary for the purposes of any examination or investigation;

f) to take samples of any articles or substances found in any premises, and of the atmosphere in or in the vicinity of such premises;

g) where it appears to him that an article of substance has caused or is likely to cause danger to health or safety, to cause it to be dismantled or subjected to any process or test;

h) to take possession of any article or substance and to detain same for so long as is necessary:

i) to examine same;

ii) to ensure it is not tampered with before his examination is completed;

iii) to ensure it is available for use as evidence in any proceedings for an offence under the relevant statutory provisions;

i) to require any person whom he has reasonable cause to believe to beable to give any information relevant to any examination or investigation to answer such questions as the inspector thinks fit and to sign a declaration of truth of his answers;

j) to require the production of, inspect and take copies of, any entry in:

i) any books or documents which by virtue of the relevant statutory provisions are required to be kept; and

ii) any other books or documents which it is necessary for him to see for the purposes of any examination or investigation;

k) to require any person to afford him such facilities and assistance with respect to any matter or things within that person's control or in relation to which that person has responsibilities as are necessary to enable the inspector to exercise any of the powers conferred on him by this section; and

l) any other power which is necessary for the purpose of carrying into effect the relevant statutory provisions.

After an inspector has completed an investigation or examination, he has a duty to inform safety representatives of the actual matters he has found (section 28(8)) and must give the employer similar information.

Notices

Enforcing officers may serve two types of notice:

Improvement notice

If an inspector is of the opinion that a breach of the relevant statutory provisions has, or is likely to, occur, he may serve an Improvement Notice on the employer, occupier or employee. The notice must state which statutory provision the inspector believes has been contravened and the reason for this belief. It should also state a time limit within which the contravention should be remedied (see Fig 4: **Improvement Notice**).

Health and Safety at Work, etc, Act 1974 Section 21, 23 and 24

IMPROVEMENT NOTICE

Name and address (See Section 46)	To _____ _____ _____
(a) Delete as necessary	(a) Trading as _____ _____
(b) Inspector's full name	(b) _____
(c) Inspector's official designation	one of (c) _____
(d) Official address	of (d) _____ _____ Telephone _____ hereby give you notice that I am of the opinion that at
(e) Location of premises or place and activity	(e) _____ _____

you, as (a) an employer/a self employed person/a person wholly or partly in control of the premises, or:-

(f) Other specified activity	(f)_____ (a) are contravening/have contravened in circumstances that make it likely that the __ contravention will continue or be repeated/or:-
(g) Provisions contravened	(g) _____ _____ _____

The reasons for my said opinion are:- _____
_____
_____
_____
_____
_____
_____
_____
_____

and I hereby require you to remedy the said contraventions, or as the case may be, the matters occasioned by them by:- (h) _____

(a) in the manner stated in the attached schedule which forms part of this notice.

Signature _____ Date _____

Being an Inspector appointed by an instrument in writing made pursuant to Section __ 19 of the said Act and entitled to issue this notice.

(a) An Improvement Notice is also being served on _____
of _____

related to the matters contained in this notice.

Figure 4: Improvement notice

Health and Safety at Work, etc, Act 1974 Section 22, 23 and 24

PROHIBITION NOTICE

Name and address (See Section 46)	To _____ _____ _____
(a) Delete as necessary	(a) Trading as _____ _____
(b) Inspector's full name	(b) _____
(c) Inspector's official designation	one of (c) _____
(d) Official address	of (d) _____ _____ Telephone _____ hereby give you notice that I am of the opinion that the following activities, namely:- _____ _____ _____ _____ _____
(e) Location of activity	Which are (a) being carried out by you/about to be carried out by you/under your control at (e) _____ involve, or will involve (a) a risk/an imminent risk, of serious personal injury. I am further of the opinion that the said matters involve contraventions of the following statutory provisions:- _____ _____ _____ because _____ _____ _____ _____
(f) Date	and I hereby direct that the said activities shall not be carried on by you or under your control (a) immediately/after (f)_____ unless the said contraventions and matters included in the schedule, which forms part of this notice, have been remedied. Signature _____ Date _____ being an Inspector appointed by an instrument in writing made pursuant to Section 19 of the said Act and entitled to issue this notice.

Figure 5: Prohibition notice

Where an inspector is of the opinion that a work activity involves or will involve a serious risk of personal injury, he may serve a Prohibition Notice on the owner and/or occupier of the premises or the person having control of that activity.

Such a notice will direct that the specified activities in the Notice shall not be carried on by, or under the control of, the person on whom the notice is served unless certain specified remedial measures have been complied with. It should be appreciated that it is not necessary for an inspector to believe that a legal provision is being or has been contravened. A Prohibition Notice is served where there is an immediate threat to life and in anticipation of danger.

A Prohibition Notice may have immediate effect after its service by an inspector. Alternatively, it may be deferred, thereby allowing the person time to remedy the situation, undertake works, etc. The duration of a deferred Prohibition Notice is stated on the Notice (see Fig 5: **Prohibition notice**).

Prosecution

Prosecution is frequently the outcome of a failure to comply with an Improvement Notice or Prohibition Notice. Conversely, an inspector may simply institute legal proceedings without service of a Notice. Cases are normally heard in a Magistrates Court, but there is also provision in the HSWA on indictment (in the Crown Court). Much depends upon the gravity of the offence.

Penalties

Magistrates can impose fines of up to £20,000 for a breach of Sections 2 to 6 of the Act, and for breach of an Improvement Notice or Prohibition Notice. The maximum fine for other offences is £5000.

The higher courts can impose prison sentences for offences concerning explosives, licensing regimes and breach of both a Prohibition Notice and an Improvement Notice.

See:

- *Corporate liability and corporate manslaughter*

- *Courts and tribunals*

- *Health and Safety at Work etc Act 1974*

Ergonomics

Ergonomics is the scientific study of the interrelationships between people, their jobs, the working environment, the equipment used and the working systems operated. Ergonomics, sometimes defined as 'human factors engineering' or 'the scientific study of work', seeks to create working environments in which people receive prime consideration.

It is also defined as 'the study of the man-machine interface'. This interface is significant in the design of work layouts and safe systems of work, and in the setting of work rates.

Areas of ergonomic study

The human system

This area is concerned with the study of the principal characteristics of people, in particular the physical elements of body dimensions, strength and stamina, coupled with the psychological elements of learning, perception and reaction to given situations.

Environmental factors

This area covers the effects on the human system of the working environment, in particular the effects of environmental stressors, such as noise, temperature and humidity extremes, inadequate lighting and ventilation, feature in this area of study.

The man-machine interface

This involves the study of controls and displays and other design features of machinery, vehicles, automation and communication systems with a view to reducing operator error and stress on the operator.

The total working system

In this case, consideration is given to the potential for fatigue and other manifestations of stress, work rate, productivity, system effectiveness and the related aspects of occupational health and safety. This area would take into account, for instance, manual handling procedures and the effects of poor manual handling techniques on posture and the potential for muscle fatigue and muscular disorders.

The influence of equipment and system design on human performance

In the design of work layouts, systems and equipment the following matters should be considered.

Layout

Layout of working areas and operating positions should allow for free movement, safe access to and egress from same, and unhindered visual and oral communication. Congested, badly-planned layouts result in operator fatigue and increase the potential for accidents.

Vision

The operator should be able to set controls and read dials and displays with ease. This reduces fatigue and the potential for accidents arising from faulty or incorrect perception.

Posture

The more abnormal the operating posture, the greater is the potential for fatigue and long-term injury. Work processes and systems should be designed to permit a comfortable posture which reduces excessive job movements. This requirement should be considered in the siting of controls e.g. levers, gear sticks, and in the organization of working systems, such as assembly and inspection tasks.

Comfort

The comfort of the operator, whether driving a vehicle or operating machinery, is essential for his physical and mental well-being. Environmental factors, such as temperature, lighting and humidity, directly affect comfort and should be given priority.

Principles of interface design

Separation

Physical controls should be separated from visual displays. The safest routine is achieved where there is no relationship between them.

Comfort

Where separation cannot be achieved, control and display elements should be mixed to produce a system which can be operated with ease.

Order of use

Controls and displays should be located in the order in which they are used, e.g. left to right for starting up a machine or process and the reverse direction for closing down or stopping same.

Priority

Where there is no competition for space, the controls most frequently used should be sited in key positions. Important controls, such as emergency stop buttons, should be sited in a position which is most easily seen and reached.

Function

With large operating consoles, the controls can be divided according to the various functions. Such division of controls is common in power stations and highly automated manufacturing processes. This layout relies heavily on the skills of the operator and, in particular, his speed of reaction. A well-trained operator, however, benefits from such functional division and the potential for human error is greatly reduced.

Fatigue

The convenient siting of controls is paramount. In designing the layout for an operating position, the hand movements of body positions of the operator can be studied (Cyclogram Torque technique) with a view to reducing or minimizing excessive movements.

Anthropometry

This is the study and measurement of human body dimensions, the orderly treatment of resulting data and the application of this data in the design of workspace layouts and equipment.

The need to match the physical dimensions of people to the equipment they use was aptly demonstrated by the Cranfield Institute of Technology who created 'Cranfield Man'. Using a horizontal lathe, researchers examined the positions of controls and compared the locations of these controls with the physical dimensions of the average operator. The Table below shows the wide differences between the two sets of dimensions, which clearly result in fatigue and an increased potential for error on the part of the operator.

AVERAGE OPERATOR DIMENSIONS	DIMENSIONS	OPERATOR WHO WOULD SUIT THESE CONTROLS
1.75m	Height	1.35m
0.48m	Shoulder width	0.61m
1.83m	Arm span	2.44m
1.07m	Elbow height	0.76m

Table 3: Physical dimensions of the average operator compared with those of 'Cranfield Man'

The study showed that the ideal operator would be a dwarf with a 2.44m arm span.

There is a need, therefore, for organizations to consider these factors, many of which could be significant in preventing human error and certainly in reducing the potential for accidents.

See:

- *Display screen equipment*
- *Human error*
- *Human factors and safety*

F

Fire prevention

Every year fire and its effects represent substantial losses to organizations. It is essential, therefore, that everyone is familiar with fire procedures and the measures to prevent fire.

What is fire?

'Fire' can be defined in several ways:

- A spectacular example of a fast chemical reaction between a combustible substance and oxygen accompanied by the evolution of heat.

- A mixture in gaseous form of a combustible substance and oxygen with sufficient energy put into the mixture to start a fire.

- An unexpected combustion generating sufficient heat or smoke resulting in damage to plant, equipment, goods and/or buildings.

Principles of combustion

In order to appreciate the principles of fire prevention, it is necessary to have a broad understanding of the principles of combustion. The three requirements for a fire to start and continue are the presence of fuel to burn, an ignition source of sufficient energy to set the fuel alight and air or oxygen to maintain combustion. If one of these three components is removed, combustion cannot take place.

Heat may be transferred by convection, conduction and radiation.

The main causes of fire and fire spread

Past studies by the Fire Protection Association into the causes of a range of industrial fires have indicated the following as the principal sources of fire in production and storage areas:

Production areas

1. Heat-producing plant and equipment
2. Frictional heat and sparks
3. Refrigeration plant
4. Electrical equipment – setting fire to:
   a) materials being processed;
   b) dust; and
   c) waste and packing materials.

Storage areas

1. Intruders, including children
2. Cigarettes and matches
3. Refuse burning
4. Electrical equipment – setting fire to:
   a) stored goods; and
   b) packing materials.

Fire instructions

A fire instruction is a notice informing people of the action they should take on either:

a) hearing the alarm; or
b) discovering a fire.

Other requirements

In addition to displaying fire instructions, people:

a) should receive training in evacuation procedures i.e. fire drills, at least quarterly; and

b) the alarm should be sounded weekly.

It is advantageous to have key personnel trained in the correct use of fire appliances.

Grouping and coding of fire appliances

All fire appliances must be painted red and incorporate a colour-coded label or band thus:

EXTINGUISHER	COLOUR CODE
Water	Red
Foam	Cream
Carbon dioxide	Black
Dry chemical powder	Blue
Vaporizing liquid	Green

Table 4: Colour coding of fire appliances

Fire alarm systems

A method of giving warning of fire is required in commercial, industrial and public buildings. The purpose of a fire alarm is to give an early warning of a fire in a building:

a) to increase the safety of occupants by encouraging them to escape to a place of safety;

b) to increase the possibility of early extinction of the fire thus reducing the loss of or damage to the property.

BS 5839: Part 1:1988 lays down guidelines to be followed for the installation of fire alarm systems.

In larger buildings this may take the form of a mains operated system with breakglass alarm call points, an automatic control unit and electrically-operated bells or sirens.

In small buildings it would be reasonable to accept a manually operated, dry battery or compressed air-operated gong, klaxon or bell. To avoid the alarm point being close to the seat of a fire, duplicate facilities are necessary.

Storage and use of flammable substances

The following points need consideration:

1. Flammable liquids

Separate storage; storage of smallest quantities in the work area; transport in closed containers; correct labelling; safe dispensing; fire appliances available during use and dispensing; adequate ventilation; no smoking or naked lights.

2. Liquefied and compressed gases

Store and transport in upright position; store in open well-ventilated area out of direct sunlight; secure with walls chains or racks; oxygen cylinders stored separately; no handling by the valves; no dropping or rolling of cylinders; turn off at bottle valve when not in use.

Regulatory reform (Fire Safety) Order 2005

This Order is made under the Regulatory Reform Act 2004 and is enforced by the Area Fire Authority except in the following cases:

- HSE, in the case of nuclear installations, ships of HM Navy and construction sites;

- fire service maintained by Secretary of State for Defence;
- the relevant local authority in the case of sports grounds and regulated stands;
- fire inspectors in the case of Crown premises and UKAEA premises.

The Order either revokes or repeals all previous fire safety legislation.

Level of duty

The level of duty in most cases is absolute although, in some cases, it is qualified by 'so far as is reasonably practicable' (SFARP).

Defence

Where charged with an offence, a person may submit the defence that he had taken all reasonable precautions and exercised all due diligence.

Reasonably practicable measures

The onus of proving the limits of what is *reasonably practicable* rests with the accused thus:

In any proceedings for an offence consisting of a duty or requirement so far as is reasonably practicable, it is for the accused to prove that it was not reasonably practicable to do more than was in fact done to satisfy the duty of requirement.

Responsible persons

A responsible person is defined thus:

a) in relation to a workplace, the employer, if the workplace is to any extent under his control;

b) in relation to any premises not falling within (a) above:

i) the person who has control of the premises (as occupier or otherwise) in connection with the carrying on by him of a trade, business is undertaking (whether for profit is not); or

ii) the owner, where the person in control of the premises does not have control in connection with the carrying on by him of a trade business or other undertaking.

Relevant persons

A 'relevant person' is defined as:

a) any person (including the responsible person) who may be lawfully on the premises; and

b) any person in the immediate vicinity of the premises who is at risk from fire on the premises,

but does not include a firefighter who is carrying out his duties in relation to the functions of a fire authority.

Duties of responsible persons

- Take such general fire precautions (as defined) as will ensure safety of any of his employees (SFARP).

- In relation to relevant persons who are not his employees, take such general fire precautions as may reasonably be required in the circumstances of the case to ensure that the premises are safe.

- Make a suitable and sufficient assessment of the risks to which relevant persons are exposed for the purpose of identifying the general fire precautions he needs to take to comply with the requirements and prohibitions imposed upon him by or under this Order.

- Consider implications of presence of dangerous substances in the risk assessment process.

- Review risk assessment if no longer valid or there has been a significant change in the matters to which it relates.

- Not employ a young person unless he has considered matters to be taken into particular account set out in Part 2 of Schedule 1.

- Record the significant findings of the risk assessment and details of any group being especially at risk.

- Not to commence a new work activity involving a dangerous substance unless a risk assessment has been made and measures required by the Order have been implemented.

- When implementing preventive and protective measures do so on the basis of the principles specified in Part 3 of Schedule 1.

- Make and give effect to arrangements for the effective planning, organization, control, monitoring and review of preventive and protective measures.

- Record the arrangements in specified cases.

- Where a dangerous substance is present, eliminate or reduce risks (SFARP).

- Replace a dangerous substance or use of a dangerous substance with a substance or process which eliminates or reduces risks (SFARP).

- Where not reasonably practical (RP) to reduce above risks, apply measures to control the risk and mitigate the detrimental effects of fire.

- Arrange safe handling, storage and transport of dangerous substances and wastes.

- Ensure any conditions necessary for eliminating or reducing risk are maintained.

- Ensure premises are equipped with appropriate fire-fighting equipment and with fire detectors and alarms and that non-automatic fire-fighting equipment is easily accessible, simple to use and indicated by signs.

- Take measures for fire-fighting in the premises, nominate competent persons to implement these measures and arrange any necessary contact with external services.

- Ensure routes to emergency exits and the exits themselves are kept clear at all times.

- Comply with specific requirements dealing with emergency routes, exits and doors and the illumination of emergency routes and exits in respect of premises.

- Establish and, where necessary, give effect to appropriate procedures for serious and imminent danger and for danger zones, including safety drills, nomination of competent persons to implement the procedures and restriction of access to areas on the grounds of safety.

- Ensure additional emergency measures are taken in respect of dangerous substances, including provision of information on emergency arrangements, suitable warnings and other communication systems, before any explosion conditions are reached, visual and audible warnings, and escape facilities.

- Ensure relevant information is made available to emergency services and displayed at the premises.

- In the event of an accident, incident or emergency related to the presence of a dangerous substance, take immediate steps to mitigate the effects of fire, restore the situation to normal, and inform relevant persons.

- Ensure only those persons essential for the carrying out of repairs and other necessary work are permitted in an affected area.

- Ensure that premises and any facilities, equipment and devices are subject to a suitable system of maintenance and are maintained in an efficient state, in efficient working order and in good repair.

- Appoint one or more competent persons to assist him in undertaking the preventive and protective measures, ensuring adequate co-operation between competent persons.

- Ensure that competent persons have sufficient time to fulfil their functions and the means at their disposal are adequate having regard to the size of the premises, the risks and the distribution of those risks.

- Ensure competent persons not in his employment are informed of factors affecting the safety of any person and are provided with the same information as employees.

- Provide employees with comprehensible and relevant information on the risks identified in the risk assessment, preventive and protective measures, the identities of competent persons for the purposes of evacuation of premises and the notified risks arising in shared workplaces.

- Before employing a child, provide the parent with comprehensible and relevant information on the risks to that child, the preventive and protective measures and the notified risks arising in shared workplaces.

- Where a dangerous substance is on the premises, provide employees with the details of any such substance and the significant findings of the risk assessment.

- Provide information to employers and the self-employed from outside undertakings with respect to the risks to those employees and the preventive and protective measures taken.

- Provide non-employees working in his undertaking with appropriate instructions and comprehensible and relevant information regarding any risks to those persons.

- Ensure the employer of any employees from an outside undertaking working in or on the premises is provided with sufficient information with respect to evacuation procedures and the competent persons nominated to undertake evacuation procedures.

- Ensure employees are provided with adequate safety training at the time of first employment, and on being exposed to new or increased risks arising from transfer or change of responsibilities, introduction of, or change in, work equipment, the introduction of new technology and the introduction of a new system of work or a change respecting an existing system of work.

- In the case of shared workplaces, co-operate with other responsible person(s), take all reasonable steps to co-ordinate the measures he takes to comply with this Order with the measures taken by other responsible persons, and take all reasonable steps to inform other responsible persons

Duties of employees

Every employee must:

- take reasonable care for the safety of himself and others who may be affected by his acts or omissions while at work;

- co-operate with his employer to enable him to comply with any duty or requirement imposed by this Order;

- inform his employer or any other employee with the specific responsibility for the safety of his fellow employees of any work situation which represents a serious and immediate danger to safety, and any other matter which represents a shortcoming in the employer's protection arrangements for safety.

Powers of the secretary of state

- The Secretary of State may by regulations make provision as to the precautions which are to be taken or observed in relation to the risk to relevant persons as regards premises to which this Order applies.

Enforcement of the order

- Every enforcing authority must enforce the provisions of this Order and any regulations made under it.

- The enforcing authority must have regard to such guidance as the Secretary of State may give.

Enforcing authorities – powers of inspectors

- An inspector may do anything necessary for the purpose of carrying out this Order and any regulations made under it into effect and, in particular, so far as may be necessary for that purpose, shall have the power to do at any reasonable time the following:
  - to enter premises and to inspect the whole or part of that premises;
  - to make such inquiry as may be necessary

- to ascertain as regards the premises, whether the provisions of this Order or regulations made under it apply or have been complied with; and

- to identify the person responsible in relation to the premises;

- to require the production of any records;

- to require any person having responsibilities in relation to any premises to give him such reasonable facilities and assistance;

- to take samples of articles and substances found in any premises for the purpose of ascertaining their fire resistance or flammability; and

- to cause any article or substance found in any premises to be dismantled or subjected to any process or test.

- An inspector must, if so required, produce evidence of his authority.

- Where intending to cause any article or substance to be dismantled or subjected to any process or test, at the request of a person present at the time, to cause anything which is to be done in the presence of that person.

- An inspector must consult the above person(s) for the purposes of ascertaining what dangers, if any, there may be in doing anything which he proposes to do under that power.

- The above powers conferred on a fire inspector, or any other person authorized by the Secretary of State, are also exercisable by an officer of the fire brigade maintained by the fire authority when authorized in writing by such an inspector.

Alterations notices

- Where premises constitute a serious risk to relevant persons or may constitute such a risk if any change is made to them or the use to which they are put, the enforcing authority (EA) may serve on the responsible person an Alterations Notice.

- Where an Alterations Notice has been served, before making any of the following changes which may result in a significant increase in risk, namely:

- a change to the premises;

- a change to the services, fittings or equipment in or on the premises;

- an increase in the quantities of dangerous substances which are present in or on the premises;

- a change to the use of the premises,

- the responsible person must notify the EA of the proposed changes.

Enforcement notices

- If the EA is of the opinion that the responsible person has failed to comply with any provision of this Order or of any regulations made under it, the enforcing authority may serve on that person an Enforcement Notice.

- An Enforcement Notice may include directions as to the measures which the EA consider are necessary to remedy the above failure, including a choice between different ways of remedying the contravention.

- A court may cancel or modify an Enforcement Notice.

- An EA may withdraw a notice at any time before the end of the period specified, or extend or further extend the period of the notice.

Prohibition notices

- If the EA is of the opinion that use of premises involves, or will involve, a risk to relevant persons so serious that use of the premises ought to be prohibited or restricted, the authority may serve on the responsible person a Prohibition Notice, such a Notice to include anything affecting the escape of relevant persons from the premises.

- A Prohibition Notice must:
  - state that EA is of the opinion referred to above;
  - specify the matters which give or will give rise to that risk; and
  - direct that the use to which the notice relates is prohibited or restricted to such extent as may be specified until the specified matters have been remedied.

- A Prohibition Notice may take immediate effect or be deferred for a period specified in the notice.

- Before serving a Prohibition Notice in relation to a house in multiple occupation the EA shall, where practicable, notify the local housing authority.

Appeals

- A person on whom an Alterations Notice, an Enforcement Notice, a Prohibition Notice or a notice given by the fire authority respecting fire-fighter's switches for luminous signs is served may, within 21 days, appeal to a Magistrates Court.

- On appeal, the court may either cancel or affirm the notice in its original form or with modifications.

- Where an appeal is brought against an Alterations Notice or an Enforcement Notice, such appeal has the effect of suspending the operation of the notice.

- Where an appeal is brought against a Prohibition Notice, such appeal does not have the effect of suspending the notice, unless the court so directs.

- A person, and the EA, if aggrieved by an order made by a Magistrates Court may appeal to the Crown Court.

Miscellaneous

- Certain luminous tube signs designed to work at a voltage normally exceeding the prescribed voltage, or other equipment so designed, must be provided with a cut-off switch so placed and coloured or marked as to be readily recognizable and accessible to fire-fighters.

- The responsible person must ensure that the premises and any facilities, equipment and devices for the use by or protection of fire-fighters are subject to a suitable system of maintenance and are maintained in an efficient state, in efficient working order and in good repair.

- Nothing in this Order is to be construed as conferring a right of action in any civil proceedings (other than proceedings for the recovery of a fine).

- Breach of a duty imposed on an employer by or under this Order, so far as it causes damage to an employee, confers a right of action on that employee in any civil proceedings.

- No employer must levy or permit to be levied on any employee of his any charge in respect of anything done or provided in pursuance of any requirement of this Order or regulations made under this Order.

- In the case of licensed premises:
  - the licensing authority must consult the EA before issuing the licence;
  - the EA must notify the licensing authority of any action that the EA takes.

Where it is proposed to erect a building, or make any extension of, or structural alteration to, a building to which the Order applies, the local authority must consult the EA before passing those plans.

Service of notices

Similar provisions as those for the HSWA apply with respect to the Service of Notices.

Schedule 1

Part I – Matters to be considered in risk assessment in respect of dangerous substances

The matters are:

- the hazardous properties of the substance;
- information on safety provided by the supplier, including information contained in any relevant safety data sheet;

- the circumstances of the work including:
  - the special, technical and organizational measures and the substances used and their possible interactions;
  - the amount of the substance involved;
  - where the work will involve more than one dangerous substance, the risk presented by such substances in combination; and
  - the arrangements for the safe handling, storage and transport of dangerous substances and of waste containing dangerous substances;
- activities, such as maintenance, where there is the potential for a high level of risk;
- the effect of measures which have been or will be taken pursuant to this Order;
- the likelihood that an explosive atmosphere will occur and its persistence;
- the likelihood that ignition sources, including electrostatic discharges, will be present and become active and effective;
- the scale of the anticipated effects;
- any places which are, or can be connected via openings to, places in which explosive atmospheres may occur; and
- such additional safety information as the responsible person may need in order to complete the assessment.

Part 2 – Matters to be taken into particular account in risk assessment in respect of young persons

The matters are:

- the inexperience, lack of awareness of risks and immaturity of young persons;
- the fitting-out and layout of the premises;
- the nature, degree and duration of exposure to physical and chemical agents;

- the form, range and use of work equipment and the way in which it is handled;

- the organization of processes and activities;

- the extent of the safety training provided or to be provided to young persons; and

- risks from agents, processes and work listed in the Annex to Council Directive 94/33/EC on the protection of young people at work.

Part 3 – Principles of prevention

These principles are:

- avoiding risks;

- evaluating the risks which cannot be avoided;

- combating the risks at source;

- adapting to technical progress;

- replacing the dangerous by the non-dangerous or less-dangerous;

- developing a coherent overall prevention policy which covers technology, organization of work and the influence of factors relating to the working environment;

- giving collective protective measures priority over individual protective measures; and

- giving appropriate instructions to employees.

Part 4 – Measures to be taken in respect of dangerous substances

- In applying measures to control risks the responsible person must, in order of priority:
    - reduce the quantity of dangerous substances to a minimum;
    - avoid or minimize the release of a dangerous substance;
    - control the release of a dangerous substance at source;
    - prevent the formation of an explosive atmosphere, including the application of appropriate ventilation;

– ensure that any release of a dangerous substance which may give rise to risk is suitably collected, safely contained, removed to a safe place or otherwise rendered safe, as appropriate;

– avoid:

i) ignition sources including electrostatic discharges; and

ii) such other adverse conditions as could result in harmful physical effects from a dangerous substance; and segregate incompatible dangerous materials.

• The responsible person must ensure that mitigation measures applied in accordance with article 12(3)(b) include:

– reducing to a minimum the number of persons exposed;

– measures to avoid the propagation of fires or explosions;

– providing explosion pressure relief arrangements;

– providing explosion suppression equipment;

– providing plant which is constructed so as to withstand the pressure likely to be produced by an explosion; and

– providing personal protective equipment.

• The responsible person must:

– ensure that the premises are designed, constructed and maintained so as to reduce risk;

– ensure that suitable special, technical and organizational measures are designed, constructed, assembled, installed, provided and used so as to reduce risk;

– ensure that special, technical and organizational measures are maintained in an efficient state, in efficient working order and in good repair;

– ensure that equipment and protective systems meet the following requirements:

i) where power failure can give rise to the spread of additional risk, equipment and protective systems must be able to be maintained in a safe state of operation independently of the rest of the plant in the event of power failure;

ii) means for manual override must be possible, operated by employees competent to do so, for shutting down equipment and protective systems incorporated within automatic processes which deviate from the intended operating conditions, provided that the provision or use of such means does not compromise safety;

iii) on operation of emergency shutdown, accumulated energy must be dissipated as quickly and as safely as possible or isolated so that it no longer constitutes a hazard; and

iv) necessary measures must be taken to prevent confusion between connecting devices;

- where the work is carried out in hazardous places or involves hazardous activities, ensure that appropriate systems of work are applied including:

  i) the issuing of written instructions for carrying out the work; and

  ii) a system of permits to work, with such permits being issued by a person with responsibility for this function prior to commencement of the work concerned.

Management of fire procedures

It is essential that formal fire procedures are established and maintained. Fire prevention and protection is a key function of the competent persons appointed under the MHSWR.

In addition, the advice and guidance of the local Fire and Rescue Authority and its officers should always be sought, particularly where any work or alterations may require a change to the structure and layout of the workplace.

First aid

First aid is defined as 'the skilled application of accepted principles of treatment on the occurrence of an accident or in the case of sudden illness, using facilities and materials available at the time'.

First aid is rendered:

a) to sustain life;

b) to prevent deterioration in an existing condition; and

c) to promote recovery.

The significant areas of first aid treatment are:

a) restoration of breathing (resuscitation);

b) control of bleeding; and

c) prevention of collapse.

Health and Safety (First Aid) Regulations 1981

These Regulations apply to nearly all workplaces in the UK. Under the Regulations *first aid* means:

a) in cases where a person will need help from a medical practitioner or nurse, treatment for the purpose of preserving life and minimizing the consequences of injury or illness until such help is obtained; and

b) treatment of minor injuries which would otherwise receive no treatment or which do not need treatment by a medical practitioner or nurse.

Duties of employers

An employer must provide, or ensure that there are provided, such equipment and facilities as are adequate and appropriate in the circumstances for enabling first aid to be rendered to his employees if they are injured or become ill at work.

Two main duties are imposed on employers by the Regulations:

a) to provide first aid; and

b) to inform employees of the first aid arrangements.

Self-employed persons must provide first aid equipment for their own use.

Approved code of practice

This ACOP emphasizes the duty of employers to consider a number of factors and determine for themselves what is adequate and appropriate in all the circumstances. Furthermore, where there are particular risks associated with the operation of an enterprise, the employer must ensure that first aiders receive training to deal with these specific risks.

Factors to be considered in assessing first aid provision include:

a) the number of employees;

b) the nature of the undertaking;

c) the size of the establishment and the distribution of employees;

d) the location of the establishment and the locations to which employees go in the course of their employment;

e) use of shift working; (each shift should have the same level of first aid cover/protection); and

f) the distance from external medical services e.g. local casualty department.

The general guidance suggests that even in a simple office there ought to be a first aider for every 50 persons.

First aid boxes

There should be at least one first aid box, the contents being listed in the HSE Guidance.

HSE guidance 1990

Contents of first aid boxes

A first aid box should contain the following items:

- 1 x Guidance Card
- 20 x assorted individually wrapped sterile adhesive dressings
- 2 x sterile eye pads with attachment
- 6 x individually wrapped triangular bandages
- 6 x safety pins
- 6 x medium sized individually wrapped sterile unmedicated wound dressings
- 2 x large individually wrapped sterile unmedicated wound dressings
- 3 x extra large individually wrapped sterile unmedicated wound dressings and NOTHING ELSE.

A minimum 300ml sterile water container should be provided where mains water is not available.

Equipment etc. for first aid rooms

The following equipment and other items are recommended for first aid rooms:

a) a sink with running hot and cold water always available;

b) drinking water when not available on tap, together with disposable cups;

c) soap;

d) paper towels;

e) smooth topped work surfaces;

f) a suitable store for first aid materials;

g) suitable refuse containers lined with a disposable plastic bag;

h) a couch with waterproof surface, together with frequently cleaned pillows and blankets;

i) clean protective garments;

j) a chair;

k) an appropriate record (Form BI 510); and

l) a bowl.

Travelling first aid kits

The minimum contents for a travelling first aid kit are:

- 1 x Guidance card
- 6 x individually wrapped sterile adhesive dressings
- 1 x large sterile unmedicated dressing
- 2 x triangular bandages
- 2 x safety pins; and

individually wrapped moist cleansing wipes.

G

Gross misconduct (health and safety)

'Gross misconduct' from a health and safety viewpoint implies the flagrant and/or continuous disregard for health and safety requirements and established precautions in a workplace or work activity by an employee. Typical examples are:

- smoking in an area where there may be a fire hazard;
- continuous failure to wear an item of personal protective equipment;
- blatant disregard for workplace safety rules and procedures;
- vandalism of company property;
- breach of specific duties on employees under health and safety law;
- dangerous driving on site; and
- removal of machinery guards and/or nullification of safety devices to machinery.

It is important that organizations specific clearly certain offences constituting gross misconduct in their information and instructions to employees and during any health and safety training undertaken for employees.

Dismissal

Whilst dismissal may be the ultimate sanction an employer can impose, other alternatives, such as suspension for a short period, with or without pay, should be considered. Details of such a procedure should be specified in any contract of employment.

> **See:**
>
> • *Disobedience and disregards for safety*

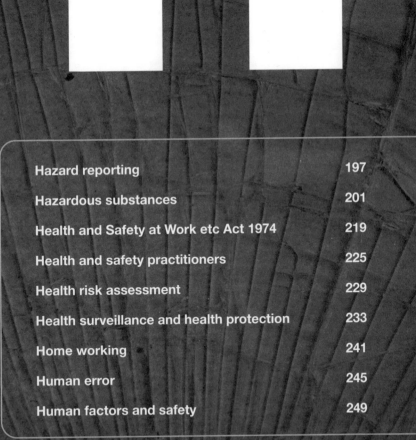

H

Hazard reporting

Under the MHSWR employees have a duty to inform their employer of:

- any work situation which represents a serious and immediate danger to health and safety; and

- any matter which represents a shortcoming in the employer's protection arrangements for health and safety.

A typical hazard report form is shown in Figure 6.

HAZARD REPORT

Report No.

REPORT (to be completed by the person identifying the hazard, situation of serious and imme-diate danger and/or shortcoming in the employer's protection arrangements)

Date _____ Time _____

Location _____

Reported to:

Verbal _____ Written _____(Names)

Description of hazard/danger/ shortcoming in protection arrangements

_____

_____

_____

_____

Signature _____ Position _____

ACTION (to be completed by manager/supervisor)

Danger/hazard/shortcoming identified YES/NO   Time_____

Remedial action (including changes in the system of work)_____

_____

_____

Action to be taken by:

Name _____

Estimated cost _____

*Priority Rating: 1 2 3 4 5 (See below)

Completion: Completion date _____Time _____

Interim precautions _____

_____

Signature _____ (Departmental Manager)

FINANCIAL APPROVAL (to be completed by the authorizing manager)

The expenditure necessary to eliminate or control the above hazard is approved.

Signature _____ (Manager)

Date _____

COMPLETION

The remedial action described above is complete. Actual cost £ _____

Signature of person responsible for completing work_____

SAFETY ADVISER CHECK

I have checked implementation of the above precautions and the hazard has been elim-inated/controlled.

Signature _____(Safety Adviser) Date _____

*PRIORITY RATINGS

1 – Immediate action. 2 – Within 48 hours. 3 – Within 1 week. 4 – Within 1 month
5 – Within 3 months

Fig 6: Hazard report

See:

- *Employee handbooks*
- *Information for employees*
- *Information, instruction and training*

Hazardous substances

Hazardous substances can be encountered to varying degrees in the majority of workplaces.

Control of substances hazardous to health (COSHH) Regulations 2002

The COSSH Regulations apply to every form of workplace and every type of work activity involving the use of substances which may be hazardous to health to people at work. The regulations are supported by a number of ACOPs, including *Control of substances hazardous to health, Control of carcinogenic substances and Control of biological agents.*

Important definitions

Biological agent means any micro-organism, cell, culture or human endoparasite, including any which have been genetically modified, which may cause any infection, allergy, toxicity or otherwise create a hazard to human health.

Carcinogen means:

    a)   a substance or preparation which is classified in accordance with the classification provided for by Regulation 4 of the CHIP Regulations would be in the category of danger, carcinogenic (category 1) or carcinogenic (category 2) whether or not the substance or preparation would be required to be classified under those Regulations; or

b) a substance or preparation:

    i) listed in Schedule 1; or

    ii) arising from a process specified in Schedule 1 which is a substance hazardous to health.

Control measure means a measure taken to reduce exposure to a substance hazardous to health (including the provision of systems of work and supervision, the cleaning of workplaces, premises, plant and equipment, the provision and use of engineering controls and personal protective equipment).

Health surveillance means the assessment of the state of health of an employee, as related to exposure to substances hazardous to health, and includes biological monitoring.

Inhalable dust means airborne material which is capable of entering the nose and mouth during breathing, as defined by BS EN 481 1993.

Micro-organism means a microbiological entity, cellular or non-cellular, which is capable of replication or of transferring genetic material.

Preparation means a mixture or solution of two or more substances.

Respirable dust means airborne material which is capable of penetrating the gas exchange region of the lung, as defined by BS EN 481 1993.

Substance hazardous to health means a substance (including any preparation):

a) which is listed for supply in Part 1 of the Approved Supply List as dangerous for supply within the meaning of the CHIP Regulations and for which an indication of danger specified for the substance is very toxic, toxic, harmful, corrosive or irritant;

b) for which the HSC has approved a maximum exposure limit or an occupational exposure standard;

c) which is a biological agent;

d) which is dust of any kind, except dust which is a substance within paragraph (a) or (b) above, when present at a concentration in air equal to or greater than:

    i) 10mg/m3, as a time-weighted average over an eight hour period, of inhalable dust; or

    ii) 4mg/m3, as a time-weighted average over an eight hour period, of respirable dust

e) which, not being a substance falling within sub-paragraphs (a) to (d), because of its chemical or toxicological properties and the way it is used or is present at the workplace creates a risk to health.

The principal requirements of the Regulations are:

- Where a duty is placed by these regulations on an employer in respect of his employees, he shall, so far as is reasonably practicable, be under a like duty in respect of any other person, whether at work or not, who may be affected by the work carried out by the employer except that the duties of the employer:

    – under Regulations 11 (health surveillance) shall not extend to persons who are not his employees; and

    – under Regulations 10, 12(1) and (2) and 13 (which relate respectively to monitoring, information and training and dealing with accidents) shall not extend to persons who are not his employees, unless those persons are on the premises where the work is being carried out.

- Those substances described in column 1 of Schedule 2 are prohibited to the extent set out in the corresponding entry in column 2 of that Schedule.

- An employer shall not carry out work which is liable to expose any employees to any substance hazardous to health unless he has:

    – made a suitable and sufficient assessment of the risk created by that work to the health of those employees and of the steps that need to be taken to meet the requirements of these Regulations; and

    – implemented the steps referred to in sub-paragraph (a) above.

The risk assessment shall include consideration of:

- the hazardous properties of the substance;

- information on health effects provided by the supplier, including information contained in any relevant safety data sheet;

- the level, type and duration of exposure;

- the circumstances of the work, including the amount of the substance involved;

- activities, such as maintenance, where there is a potential for a high level of exposure;

- any relevant occupational exposure standard, maximum exposure limit or similar occupational exposure limit;

- the effect of preventive and control measures which have been, or will be, taken in accordance with Regulation 7;

- the results of relevant health surveillance;

- the results of monitoring of exposure in accordance with Regulation 10;

- in circumstances where the work will involve exposure to more than one substance hazardous to health, the risk presented by exposure to such substances in combination;

- the approved classification of any biological agent; and

- such additional information as the employer may need in order to complete the risk assessment.

The risk assessment shall be reviewed regularly and forthwith if:

- there is reason to suspect that the risk assessment is no longer valid;

- there has been a significant change in the work to which the assessment relates; or

- the results of any monitoring carried out in accordance with Regulation 10 show it to be necessary,

and where, as a result of the review, changes to the risk assessment are required, those changes shall be made.

Where the employer employs five or more employees, he shall record:

- the significant findings of the risk assessment as soon as is practicable after the risk assessment is made; and

- the steps he has taken to meet the requirements of Regulation 7 below. Additionally:

  - every employer shall ensure that the exposure of his employees to substances hazardous to health is either prevented or, where this is not reasonably practicable, adequately controlled;

  - in complying with his duty under the above paragraph, substitution shall by preference be undertaken, whereby the employer shall avoid, so far as is reasonably practicable, the use of a substance hazardous to health at the workplace by replacing it with a substance or process which, under the conditions of its use, either eliminates or reduces the risk to the health of his employees;

- where it is not reasonably practicable to prevent exposure to a substance hazardous to health, the employer shall comply with his duty of control under paragraph 1 by applying protection measures appropriate to the activity and consistent with the risk assessment, including in order of priority:

  - the design and use of appropriate work processes, systems and engineering controls and the provision and use of suitable work equipment and materials;

  - the control of exposure at source, including adequate ventilation systems and appropriate organizational measures; and

  - where adequate control of exposure cannot be achieved by other means, the provision of suitable personal protective equipment in addition to the measures required by the above sub-paragraphs.

The measures referred to in the above paragraph shall include:

- arrangements for the safe handling, storage and transport of substances hazardous to health, and waste containing such substances, at the workplace;

- the adoption of suitable maintenance procedures;

- reducing, to the minimum required for the work concerned:

    - the number of employees subject to exposure;

    - the level and duration of exposure; and

    - the quantity of substances hazardous to health present at the workplace;

- the control of the working environment, including appropriate general ventilation; and

- appropriate hygiene measures including adequate washing facilities.

Where it is not reasonably practicable to prevent exposure to a carcinogen, the employer shall apply the following measures in addition to those required by paragraph 3 above:

- totally enclosing the process and handling systems, unless this is not reasonably practicable;

- the prohibition of eating, drinking and smoking in areas that may be contaminated by carcinogens;

- cleaning floors, walls and other surfaces at regular intervals and whenever necessary;

- designating those areas and installations which may be contaminated by carcinogens and using suitable and sufficient warning signs; and

- storing, handling and disposing of carcinogens safely, including closed and clearly labelled containers.

Without prejudice to the generality of paragraph 1, where it is not reasonably practicable to prevent exposure to a biological agent, the employer shall apply the following measures in addition to those required by paragraph 3 above:

- displaying suitable and sufficient warning signs, including the biohazard sign shown in Part IV of Schedule 3;

- specifying appropriate decontamination and disinfection procedures;

- instituting means for the safe collection, storage and disposal of contaminated waste, including the use of secure and identifiable containers, after suitable treatment where appropriate;

- testing, where it is necessary and technically possible, for the presence, outside the primary physical confinement, of biological agents used at work;

- specifying procedures for working with, and transporting at the workplace, a biological agent or material that may contain such an agent;

- where appropriates, making available effective vaccines for those employees who are not already immune to the biological agent to which they are exposed or are liable to be exposed;

- instituting hygiene measures compatible with the aim of preventing or reducing the accidental transfer or release of a biological agent from the workplace, including:

    - the provision of appropriate and adequate washing and toilet facilities; and

    - where appropriate, the prohibition of eating, drinking, smoking and the application of cosmetics in working areas where there is a risk of contamination by biological agents; and

    - where there are human patients or animals which are, or are suspected of being, infected with a Group 3 or 4 biological agent, the employer shall select the most suitable control and containment measures from those listed in Part II of Schedule 3 with a view to controlling adequately the risk of infection.

- Where there is exposure to a substance for which a maximum exposure limit has been approved, control of exposure shall, so far as the inhalation of that substance is concerned, only be treated as being adequate if the level of exposure is reduced so far as is reasonably practicable and in any case below the maximum exposure limit.

- Where there is exposure to a substance for which an occupational exposure standard has been approved, control of exposure shall, so far as the inhalation of that substance is concerned, only be treated as being adequate if:
  - that occupational exposure standard is not exceeded; or
  - where that occupational exposure standard is exceeded, the employer identifies the reasons for the standard being exceeded and takes appropriate action to remedy the situation as soon as is reasonably practicable.
- Personal protective equipment provided by an employer in accordance with this Regulation shall be suitable for the purpose and shall:
  - comply with any provision in the Personal Protective Equipment Regulations 2002 which is applicable to that item of personal protective equipment; or
  - in the case of respiratory protective equipment, where no provision referred to in the above sub-paragraph applies, be of a type approved or shall conform to a standard approved, in either case, by the HSE.
- Without prejudice to the provisions of this Regulation, Schedule 3 shall have effect in relation to work with biological agents.
- In this regulation 'adequate' means adequate having regard only to the nature of the substance and the nature and degree of exposure to substances hazardous to health.
- Every employer who provides any control measure, other thing or facility in accordance with these Regulations shall take all reasonable steps to ensure that it is properly used or applied as the case may be.
- Every employee shall make full and proper use of any control measure, other thing or facility provided in accordance with these Regulations and, where relevant, shall:
  - take all reasonable steps to ensure it is returned after use to any accommodation provided for it; and

- if he discovers a defect therein, report it forthwith to his employer.

- Every employer who provides any control measure to meet the requirements of Regulation 7 shall ensure that, where relevant, it is maintained in efficient state, in efficient working order and in good repair and in a clean condition.

- Where engineering controls are provided to meet the requirements of Regulation 7, the employer shall ensure that thorough examination and testing of those controls is carried out:

  - in the case of local exhaust ventilation plant, at least once every 14 months, or for local exhaust ventilation plant used in conjunction with a process specified in column 1 of Schedule 4, at not more than the interval specified in the corresponding entry in column 2 of that Schedule; or

  - in any other case, at suitable intervals.

- Where respiratory protective equipment (other than disposable respiratory protective equipment) is provided to meet the requirements of Regulation 7, the employer shall ensure that through examination and, where appropriate, testing of that equipment is carried out at suitable intervals.

- Every employer shall keep a suitable record of the examination and tests carried out in accordance with paragraphs 2 and 3 above and of repairs carried out as a result of those examinations and tests, and that record or a suitable summary thereof shall be kept for at least five years from the date on which it was made.

- Every employer shall ensure that personal protective equipment, including protective clothing, is:

  - properly stored in a well-defined place;

  - checked at suitable intervals; and

  - when discovered to be defective, repaired or replaced before further use.

- Personal protective equipment which may be contaminated by a substance hazardous to health shall be removed on leaving the working area and kept apart from uncontaminated clothing and equipment.

- The employer shall ensure that the equipment referred to in paragraph 6 is subsequently decontaminated and cleaned or, if necessary, destroyed.

- Where the risk assessment indicates:

    – it is a requisite for ensuring the maintenance of adequate control of the exposure of employees to substances hazardous to health; or

    – it is otherwise requisite for protecting the health of employees,

    – the employer shall ensure the exposure of employees to substances hazardous to health is monitored in accordance with a suitable procedure.

- Paragraph 1 shall not apply where the employer is able to demonstrate by another method of evaluation that the requirements of Regulation 7(1) have been complied with.

- The monitoring referred to in paragraph 1 shall take place:

    – at regular intervals; and

    – when any change occurs which may affect that exposure.

- Where a substance or process is specified in column 1 of Schedule 5, monitoring shall be carried out at least at the frequency specified in the corresponding entry in column 2 of that Schedule.

- The employer shall ensure that a suitable record of monitoring carried out for the purpose of this regulation is made and maintained and that that record or a suitable summary thereof is kept available:

    – where the record is representative of the personal exposures of identifiable employees, for at least 40 years; or

    – in any other case, for at least five years, from the date of the last entry made in it

- The employer shall:

    - on reasonable notice being given, allow an employee access to his personal monitoring record;

    - provide the HSE with copies of such monitoring records as the HSE may require; and

    - if he ceases to trade, notify the HSE forthwith in writing and make available to the HSE all monitoring records kept by him.

- Where it is appropriate for the protection of the health of his employees who are, or are liable to be exposed to a substance hazardous to health, the employer shall ensure that such employees are under suitable health surveillance.

- Health surveillance shall be treated as being appropriate where:

    - the employee is exposed to one of the substances specified in column 1 of Schedule 6 and is engaged in a process specified in column 2 of that Schedule, and there is a reasonable likelihood that an identifiable disease or adverse health effect will result from that exposure; or

    - the exposure of the employee to a substance hazardous to health is such that:

        - an identifiable disease or adverse health effect may be related to the exposure;

        - there is a reasonable likelihood that the disease or effect may occur under the particular conditions of his work; and

        - there are valid techniques for detecting indications of the disease or effect,

        - and the technique of investigation is of low risk to the employee.

- The employer shall ensure that a health record, containing particulars approved by the HSE, in respect of each of his employees to whom paragraph 1 applies, is made and maintained and that that record or a copy thereof is kept available in a suitable form for at least 40 years from the date of the last entry made in it.

- The employer shall:

    - on reasonable notice being given, allow an employee access to his personal health record;

    - provide the HSE with copies of such health records as the HSE may require; and

    - if he ceases to trade, notify the HSE forthwith in writing and make available to the HSE all health records kept by him.

- If an employee is exposed to a substance specified in Schedule 6 and is engaged in a process specified therein, the health surveillance required under paragraph 1 shall include medical surveillance under the supervision of a relevant doctor at intervals of not more than 12 months or at such shorter intervals as the relevant doctor may require.

- Where an employee is subject to medical surveillance and a relevant doctor has certified by an entry in the health record of that employee that in his professional opinion that employee should not be engaged in work which exposes him to that substance or that he should only be so engaged under conditions specified in the record, the employer shall not permit the employee to be engaged in such work except in accordance with the conditions, in any, specified in the health record, unless that entry has been cancelled by a relevant doctor.

- An employee to whom this Regulation applies shall, when required by his employer and at the cost of the employer, present himself during his working hours for such health surveillance procedures as may be required for the purposes of paragraph 1 and, in the case of an employee who is subject to medical surveillance in accordance with paragraph 5, shall furnish the relevant doctor with such information concerning his health as the relevant doctor may reasonably require.

- Where, as a result of health surveillance, an employee is found to have an identifiable disease or adverse health effect which is considered by a relevant doctor or other occupational health professional to be the result of exposure to a substance hazardous to health the employer of that employee shall:

  - ensure that a suitably qualified person informs the employee accordingly and provides the employee with information and advice regarding further health surveillance;

  - review the risk assessment;

  - review any measures taken to comply with Regulation 7, taking into account any advice given by a relevant doctor, occupational health professional or by the HSE;

  - consider assigning the employee to alternative work where there is no risk of further exposure to that substance, taking into account any advice given by a relevant doctor or occupational health professional; and

  - provide for a review of the health of any employee who has been similarly exposed, including a medical examination where such an examination is recommended by a relevant doctor, occupational health professional or by the HSE.

- Where, for the purpose of carrying out his functions under these Regulations, a relevant doctor requires to inspect any workplace or any record kept for the purposes of these Regulations, the employer shall permit him to do so.

- Where an employee or an employer is aggrieved by a decision recorded in the health record by a relevant doctor to suspend an employee from work which exposes him to a substance hazardous to health (or to impose conditions on such work), he may, by an application in writing to the HSE within 28 days of the date on which he was notified of the decision, apply for that decision to be reviewed in accordance with a procedure approved for the purposes of this paragraph by the HSC, and the result of that review shall be notified to the employee and employer and entered in the health record in accordance with the approved procedure.

- Every employer who undertakes work which is liable to expose an employee to a substance hazardous to health shall provide that employee with suitable and sufficient information, instruction and training.

- Without prejudice to the generality of the above paragraph, the information, instruction and training provided under that paragraph shall include:

  - details of the substances hazardous to health to which the employee is liable to be exposed including:

    - the names of those substances and the risk which they present to health;

    - any relevant occupational exposure standard, maximum exposure limit or similar occupational exposure limit;

    - access to any relevant safety data sheet; and

    - other legislative provisions which concern the hazardous properties of those

  - substances;

  - the significant findings of the risk assessment;

  - the appropriate precautions and action to be taken by the employee in order to safeguard himself and other employees at the workplace;

  - the results of any monitoring of exposure in accordance with Regulation 10 and, in particular, in the case of a substance hazardous to health for which a maximum exposure limit has been approved, the employee or his representatives shall be informed forthwith, if the results of such monitoring show that the maximum exposure limit has been exceeded;

  - the collective results of any health surveillance undertaken in a form calculated to prevent those results from being identified as relating to a particular person; and

  - where employees are working with a Group 4 biological agent or material that may contain such an agent, the provision of written instructions and, if appropriate, the display of notices which outline the procedures for handling such an agent or material.

- The information, instruction and training required by paragraph 1 shall be:

  - adapted to take account of significant changes in the type of work carried out or methods of work used by the employer; and

  - provided in a manner appropriate to the level, type and duration of exposure identified by the risk assessment.

- Every employer shall ensure that any person (whether or not his employee) who carries out work in connection with the employer's duties under these Regulations has suitable and sufficient information, instruction and training.

- Where containers and pipes for substances hazardous to health used at work are not marked in accordance with any relevant legislation listed in Schedule 7, the employer shall, without prejudice to any derogations provided for in that legislation, ensure that the contents of those containers and pipes, together with the nature of those contents and any associated hazards, are clearly identifiable.

- Subject to paragraph 4 below and without prejudice to the relevant provisions of the MHSWR, in order to protect the health of his employees from an accident, incident or emergency related to the presence of a substance hazardous to health at the workplace, the employer shall ensure that:

  - procedures, including the provision of appropriate first aid facilities and relevant safety drills (which shall be tested at regular intervals), have been prepared which can be put into effect when such an event occurs;

  - information on emergency arrangements, including:

    - details of relevant work hazards and hazard identification arrangements; and

    - specific hazards likely to arise at the time of an accident, incident or emergency,

  - is available;

- suitable warning and other communication systems are established to enable an appropriate response, including remedial actions and rescue operations, to be made immediately when such an event occurs.

- The employer shall ensure that information on the procedures and systems and on the information required is:

  - made available to relevant accident and emergency services to enable those services, whether internal or external to the workplace, to prepare their own response procedures and precautionary measures; and

  - displayed at the workplace, if this is appropriate.

- Subject to paragraph 4 below, in the event of an accident, incident or emergency related to the presence of a substance hazardous to health at the workplace, the employer shall ensure that:

  - immediate steps are taken to:

    - mitigate the effects of the event;

    - restore the situation to normal; and

    - inform those of his employees who may be affected.

  - only those persons who are essential for the carrying out of repairs and other necessary work are permitted in the affected area and they are provided with:

    - appropriate personal protective equipment; and

    - any necessary specialized safety equipment and plant;

    - which shall be used until the situation is restored to normal; and

  - in the case of an incident or accident which has or may have resulted in the release of a biological agent which could cause severe human disease, as soon as practicable thereafter his employees or their representatives are informed of:

    - the causes of the incident or accident; and

    - the measures taken or to be taken to rectify the situation.

- Paragraph 1 and, provided the substance hazardous to health is not a carcinogen or biological agent, paragraph 3 above shall not apply where:

  - the results of the risk assessment show that, because of the quantity of each substance hazardous to health present at the workplace, there is only a slight risk to the health of employees; and

  - the measures taken by the employer to comply with the duty under Regulation 7(1) are sufficient to control that risk.

- An employee shall report forthwith to his employer or to any other employee of that employer with specific responsibility for the health and safety of his fellow employees, any accident or incident which has or may have resulted in the release of a biological agent which could cause severe human disease.

- Specific requirements apply with respect to fumigations in which the fumigant used or intended to be used is hydrogen cyanide, phosphine or methyl bromide. It should be read in conjunction with Schedule 8 (Fumigations excepted from Regulation 14) and Schedule 9 (Notification of certain fumigations).

- For the purposes of Part I of the HSWA, the meaning of 'work' shall be extended to include any activity involving the consignment, storage or use of a Group 2, 3 or 4 biological agent and the meaning of "at work" shall be extended accordingly, and in that connection the references to employer in paragraphs 5 and 6 of Schedule 3 include references to any persons carrying out such an activity.

- Subject to Regulation 21 of the MHSWR 1999, in any proceedings for an offence consisting of a contravention of these Regulations, it shall be a defence for any person to prove that he took all reasonable precautions and exercised all due diligence to avoid the commission of that offence.

See:

- *Biological agents*
- *Dermatitis*
- *Health risk assessment*
- *Health surveillance and health protection*
- *Occupational diseases and conditions*
- *Ventilation in the workplace*

Health and Safety at Work etc Act 1974

The Health and Safety at Work etc Act 1974 (HSWA) brought in a radically new approach to dealing with the risks to people at work. The Act covers all people at work, except domestic workers in private employment. It is aimed at people and their activities, sooner than premises and processes. It covers 'all persons at work' whether they be employers, employees or the self-employed.

The legislation includes provisions for both the protection of people at work and the prevention of risks to the health and safety of the general public which may arise from work activities.

Objectives of HSWA

- To secure the health, safety and welfare of all persons at work.

- To protect others against the risks arising from workplace activities.

- To control the obtaining, keeping and use of explosive or highly flammable substances.

- To control emissions into the atmosphere of noxious or offensive substances.

Under the HSWA various groups of people, for instance, employers, employees, occupiers of premises and people who manufacture and design articles and substances for use at work, have both specific and general duties, which are outlined below. All these duties are of a 'reasonably practicable' nature.

Section 2: General duties of employers to their employees

It is the duty of every employer, so far as is reasonably practicable, to ensure the health, safety and welfare at work of all his employees.

More particularly, this includes:

a) the provision and maintenance of plant and systems of work that are, so far as is reasonably practicable, safe and without risks to health;

b) arrangements for ensuring, so far as is reasonably practicable, safety and absence of risks to health in connection with the use, handling, storage and transport of articles and substances;

c) the provision of such information, instruction training and supervision as is necessary to ensure, so far as is reasonably practicable, the health and safety at work of employees;

d) so far as is reasonably practicable as regards any place of work under the employer's control, the maintenance of it in a condition that is safe and without risks to health and the provision and maintenance of means of access to, and egress from, it that are safe and without such risks;

e) the provision and maintenance of a working environment for his employees that is, so far as is reasonably practicable, safe, without risks to health, and adequate as regards facilities and arrangements for their welfare at work.

Statements of health and safety policy

Employers must prepare and, as often as is necessary, revise a written Statement of Health and Safety Policy, and bring the Statement and any revision of it to the notice of all his employees.

Joint consultation

Every employer must consult appointed safety representatives with a view to making and maintaining arrangements which will enable him and his employees to co-operate effectively in promoting and developing measures to ensure the health and safety at work of the employees, and in checking the effectiveness of such measures.

Section 3: General duties of employers and self-employed to persons other than their employees

Every employer must conduct his undertaking in such a way as to ensure, so far as is reasonably practicable, that persons not in his employment who may be affected thereby are not thereby exposed to risks to their health or safety. (Similar duties are imposed on self-employed persons.)

Every employer and self-employed person must give to persons (not being his employees) who may be affected by the way in which he conducts his information the prescribed information about such aspects of the way in which he conducts his undertaking as might affect their health and safety.

Section 4: General duties of persons concerned with premises to persons other than their employees

This section has effect for imposing on persons duties in relation to those who:

   a) are not their employees; but

   b) use non-domestic premises made available to them as a place of work.

Every person who has, to any extent control of premises must ensure, so far as is reasonably practicable, that the premises, all means of access thereto or egress there from, and any plant or substances in the premises or provided for use there, is or are safe and without risks to health.

Section 5: General duty of persons in control of certain premises in relation to harmful emissions into atmosphere

Any person having control of any premises of a class prescribed for the purposes of section 1(1)(d) must use the best practicable means for preventing the emission into the atmosphere from the premises of noxious or offensive substances and for rendering harmless and inoffensive such substances as may be so emitted.

Section 6: General duties of manufacturers, etc. as regards articles and substances for use at work

Any person who designs, manufactures, imports or supplies any article for use at work:

a) must ensure, so far as is reasonably practicable, that the article is so designed and constructed as to be safe and without risks to health when properly used;

b) must carry out or arrange for the carrying out of such testing and examination as may be necessary to comply with the above duty; and

c) must provide adequate information about the use for which it is designed and has been tested to ensure that, when put to that use, it will be safe and without risks to health.

Any person who undertakes the design or manufacture of any article for use at work must carry out or arrange for the carrying out of any necessary research with a view to the discovery and, so far as is reasonably practicable, the elimination or minimization of any risks to health or safety to which the design or article may give rise.

Any person who erects or installs any article for use at work must ensure, so far as is reasonably practicable, that nothing about the way it is erected or installed makes it unsafe or a risk to health when properly used.

Any person who manufactures, imports or supplies any substance for use at work:

a) must ensure, so far as is reasonably practicable, that the substance is safe and without risks to health when properly used;

b) must carry out or arrange for the carrying out of such testing and examination as may be necessary; and

c) must take such steps as are necessary to ensure adequate information about the results of any relevant tests is available in connection with the use of the substance at work.

Section 7: General duties of employees at work

It is the duty of every employee while at work:

a) to take reasonable care for the health and safety of himself and of other persons who may be affected by his acts or omissions at work; and

b) as regards any duty or requirement imposed on his employer, to co-operate with him so far as is necessary to enable that duty or requirement to be performed or complied with.

Section 8: Duty not to interfere with or misuse things provided pursuant to certain provisions

No person shall intentionally or recklessly interfere with or misuse anything provided in the interests of health, safety or welfare in pursuance of any of the relevant statutory provisions.

Section 9: Duty not to charge employees for things done or provided pursuant to certain specific requirements

No employer shall levy or permit to be levied on any employee of his any charge in respect of anything done or provided in pursuance of any specific requirement of the relevant statutory provisions.

See:

- *Courts and tribunals*
- *Enforcement procedures*
- *Information, instruction and training*
- *Statements of health and safety Policy*

Health and safety practitioners

Health and safety practitioners may carry a range of titles – health and safety manager, safety officer, health and safety adviser, etc. Most organizations use the term adviser, however.

The HSE publication *Successful Health and Safety Management* (HS(G)65) outlines the role and functions of health and safety advisers thus:

Organizations that successfully manage health and safety give health and safety advisers the status and ensure they have the competence to advise management and workers with authority and independence. Subjects on which they advise include:

- health and safety policy formulation and development;

- structuring and operating all parts of the organization (including the supporting Systems) in order to promote a positive health and safety culture and to secure the effective implementation of policy;

- planning for health and safety, including the setting of realistic short and long-term objectives, deciding priorities and establishing adequate performance standards;

- day-to-day implementation and monitoring of policy and plans; including accident and incident investigation, reporting and analysis;

- reviewing performance and auditing the whole safety management system.

To fulfil these functions they have to:

- maintain adequate information systems on relevant law (civil and criminal) and on guidance and developments in general and safety management practice;

- be able to interpret the law and understand how it applies to the organization;

- establish and keep up-to-date organizational and risk control standards relating to both 'hardware' (such as the place of work and the plant, substances and equipment in use) and 'software' (such as procedures, systems and people); this task is likely to involve contributions from specialists, for example, architects, engineers, doctors and occupational hygienists;

- establish and maintain procedures for the reporting, investigating and recording and analysis of accidents and incidents;

- establish and maintain adequate and appropriate monitoring and auditing systems;

- present themselves and their advice in an independent and effective manner, safeguarding the confidentiality of personal information such as medical records.

Relationships

Within the organization

- The position of health and safety advisers within the organization is such that they support the provision of authoritative and independent advice.

- The post holder has a direct reporting line to directors on matters of policy and authority to stop work which is being carried out in contravention of agreed standards and which puts people at risk of injury.

- Health and safety advisers have responsibility for professional standards and systems and on a large site or in a group of companies may also have line management responsibility for junior health and safety professionals.

Outside the organization

Health and safety advisers are involved in liaison with a wide range of outside bodies and individuals including local authority environmental health officers and licensing officials, architects and consultants, etc, the fire service, contractors, insurance companies, clients and customers, the Health and Safety Executive, the public, equipment suppliers, HM Coroner or Procurator Fiscal, the media, the police, general practitioners and hospital staff.

See:

- *Competent persons*
- *Safety budgets*
- *Safety management systems*
- *Safety monitoring systems*

Health risk assessment

Under the COSHH Regulations an employer shall not carry out work which is liable to expose any employees to any substance hazardous to health unless he has:

- made a suitable and sufficient assessment of the risk created by that work to the health of those employees and of the steps that need to be taken to meet the requirements of these Regulations; and

- implemented the steps referred to in sub-paragraph (a).

The risk assessment shall include consideration of:

- the hazardous properties of the substance;

- information on health effects provided by the supplier, including information contained in any relevant safety data sheet;

- the level, type and duration of exposure;

- the circumstances of the work, including the amount of the substance involved;

- activities, such as maintenance, where there is the potential for a high level of exposure;

- any relevant occupational exposure standard, maximum exposure limit or similar occupational exposure limit;

- the effects of preventive and control measures which have been or will be taken in accordance with Regulation 7;

- the results of relevant health surveillance;

- the results of monitoring of exposure in accordance with Regulation 10;

- in circumstances where the work will involve exposure to more than one substance hazardous to health, the risk presented by exposure to such substances in combination;

- the approved classification of any biological agent; and

- such additional information as the employer may need in order to complete the risk assessment.

SUMMARY OF THE COSHH ASSESSMENT PROCESS

1. Are hazardous substances likely to be present in the workplace?

NO – No further action required

YES – Assessment required

2. Gather information about the substances, the work and working practices

- Decide who will carry out the assessment
- What substances are present or are likely to be present?
- Identify the hazards
- Find out who could be exposed

3. Evaluate the risks to health

EITHER to individual employees OR on a group basis

FIND OUT:

- The chance of exposure occurring
- What level of exposure could happen
- How long the exposure goes on for
- How often the exposure is likely to occur

CONCLUDE:

EITHER existing/potential exposure poses no significant risk OR exposures poses significant risk

---

4. **Decide what needs to be done in terms of:**
   - Controlling or preventing exposure
   - Maintaining controls
   - Using controls
   - Monitoring exposure
   - Health surveillance
   - Information, instruction and training

5. **Record the assessment**
   - Decide if it is necessary to record the assessment
   - If it is necessary, decide
     a) what and how much to record, and
     b) presentation and format

6. **Review the assessment**
   - Decide when review is needed
   - Decide what needs to be reviewed

Source: HSE

Fig 7: The COSHH assessment process

See:

- *Accident and ill health costs*
- *Accident and ill health data*
- *Accident reporting, recording and investigation*
- *Emergency procedures*
- *Health surveillance and health protection*
- *Information for employees*
- *Information, instruction and training*
- *Method statements*
- *Permit to work systems*
- *Personal protective equipment*
- *Risk assessment*
- *Ventilation in the workplace*

Health surveillance and health protection

Health surveillance is the regular review of the health of employees exposed to various forms of health risk, for instance from hazardous substances, manual handling operations or as a result of working on specific processes.

Whilst there is a general duty on an employer under section 2(1) of the HSWA 'to ensure, so far as is reasonably practicable, the health, safety and welfare at work of all his employees', more specific duties to provide same can be found in Regulations made under the Act, such as the COSHH Regulations (see *Hazardous substances*) and the MHSWR.

The ACOP to the MHSWR outlines the objectives of health surveillance, thus:

> 'The primary benefit, and therefore the objective, of health surveil-lance should be to detect adverse health effects at an early stage, thereby enabling further harm to be prevented.'

In addition the results of health surveillance can provide a means of:

a)   checking the effectiveness of control measures;

b)   providing feedback on the accuracy of risk assessment;

c)   identifying and protecting individuals at increased risk.

Once it is decided that health surveillance is appropriate, such health surveil-lance should be maintained during the employee's employment unless the risk to which the worker is exposed and associated health effects are short term. The minimum requirement for health surveillance is the keeping of an individual health record. Where it is appropriate, health surveillance may also involve one or more health surveillance procedures depending upon their suitability in the circumstances. Such procedures can include:

a) inspection of readily detectable conditions by a responsible person acting within the limits of their training and experience;

b) enquiries about symptoms, inspection and examination by a qualified person such as an occupational health nurse;

c) medical surveillance, which may include clinical examination and measurements of physiological or psychological effects by an appropriately qualified practitioner;

d) biological effect monitoring i.e. the measurements and assessment of early biological effects such as diminished lung function in exposed workers;

e) biological monitoring i.e. the measurement and assessment of workplace agents or their metabolites either in tissues, secreta, excreta, expired air or any combination of these in exposed workers.

Aspects of health surveillance

Health surveillance is a very broad area and must be viewed as part of an overall occupational health strategy aimed at protecting the health of people at work. Much will depend upon the risks to which people are exposed. What is important is that the form of health surveillance undertaken should be appropriate to these risks.

Health surveillance should be carried out by suitably qualified persons, such as a doctor with, preferably, a specialist qualification in occupational medicine (occupational physician) or an occupational health nurse. It may involve the assessment of hazardous substances or their by-products in the body (by the examination of urine or blood) or of body functions (e.g. blood pressure, lung function). In some cases, clinical examinations or tests may be necessary. Where medical examinations and inspections are called for, employers must provide suitable facilities on site.

Health protection

An appropriate strategy to protect people at work from health risks should incorporate the following elements.

Pre-employment health screening

This form of surveillance, carried out by an occupational health nurse, can include not only an assessment of general fitness for the job but also specific aspects of that job, such as vision screening of drivers and VDU operators, initial audiometry for people who may be exposed to noise and the assessment of individual disability levels where manual handling operations are involved.

Primary and secondary monitoring

Primary monitoring is concerned largely with the clinical observation of sick people who may seek treatment or advice on their conditions. Such observation will identify new risks which were previously not considered.

Secondary monitoring, on the other hand, is directed at controlling the hazards to health which have already been recognized. Audiometry is a classic form of secondary monitoring whereby the hearing levels of operators are tested on, say, a six monthly or annual basis to assess whether there has been a further deterioration in hearing due to exposure to noise. On a more general basis, the annual health screening of food handlers by an occupational health nurse is an important form of secondary monitoring.

Supervision of vulnerable groups

Certain groups, such as young persons, the aged, the disabled and pregnant women may be more vulnerable to health risks than others. Special attention must be given to these persons in terms of health counselling, assistance with rehabilitation and reorganization of their jobs to removal harmful factors.

Avoiding potential risks

This can involve an examination of the current work layouts and arrangements, taking into account ergonomic aspects of the job and the potential for fatigue. The effects of shift working, long periods of work and the physical and mental effects of repetitive tasks would be taken into account in the assessment of health risks. On this basis shift workers and those working long shifts could well be a subject for health surveillance.

Health records

Under the COSHH Regulations, employers must ensure that a health record, containing particulars approved by the HSE, in respect of each of his employees who have been or may have been exposed to substances hazardous to health, is made and maintained. That record, or a copy thereof, must be kept available in a suitable form for at least 40 years from the date of the last entry made in it.

However, apart from the duty to maintain health records under the COSHH Regulations, there is clearly a case for maintaining health records of all employees. Not only is it possible for the occupational health practitioner to obtain useful information on unidentified health risks from accumulated records, but a health record could well be important evidence where an individual may be taking a civil action for negligence against the organization many years later, or where the enforcement agency may be taking action under health and safety legislation.

The following records on individual employees may need to be maintained:

a) pre-employment and subsequent health questionnaires submitted by employees;

b) details of pre-employment and subsequent health examinations and screening tests undertaken by an occupational health nurse;

c) relevant medical and occupational history, smoking habits, disabilities and handicaps;

d) injuries resulting from occupational and non-occupational accidents;

e) illness occurring at work or on the way to or from work;

f) history of sickness absence;

g) details of occupational diseases and conditions diagnosed;

h) care and treatment provided;

i) advice given, recommendations and work limitations imposed;

j) referrals made to other medical specialists or agencies;

k) correspondence relating to the health of individual employees;

l) dispersal of cases following emergencies and treatment; and

m) details of communication between occupational health practitioners and others, including written reports.

The confidentiality of health records must be maintained at all times.

Forms of health surveillance

Health surveillance is, fundamentally, the regular review of the health of persons exposed to hazardous substances or working in specified processes. It should be carried out by a suitably qualified person, such as an occupational physician or an occupational health nurse.

It may involve the assessment of hazardous substances or their by-products in the body by the examination of urine or blood or the assessment of body functions, such as blood pressure, lung function. In some cases, clinical tests or examinations may be necessary.

Where medical examinations and inspections are required by law, employers must provide suitable facilities on site.

Where health surveillance is required, records must be kept listing the personal details of the employee, e.g. name, sex, age and previous and current occupations which involved exposure to hazardous substances. The records, or copies of same, should be kept for at least 30 years after the date of the last entry.

The purpose of health surveillance

Objectives

The objectives of health surveillance, wherever employees may be exposed to substances hazardous to health in the course of their work, are:

a) the protection of the health of individuals by detecting adverse changes, attributed to exposure to substances hazardous to health, at the earliest possible stage;

b) to help in assessing the effectiveness of control measures;

c) the collection, maintenance and use of data for the detection and evaluation of hazards to health; and

d) to assess the immunological status of employees doing specific work with micro-organisms hazardous to health.

Outcome

The results of any health surveillance procedure should lead to some form of action which will be to the benefit of employees.

Health surveillance under the COSHH Regulations

Biological monitoring

This could entail monitoring to detect, for instance, 2,5-hexane dione in urine (for hexane exposure) or carboxyhaemoglobin in the blood of workers exposed to methylene chloride.

Biological effect monitoring

One example is the presence of cholinesterase in the blood of workers exposed to certain organo-phosphorous pesticides.

Medical surveillance

This could include, for example, the provision of lung function tests for workers exposed to substances known to cause asthma and chest X-rays of workers exposed to respirable dusts, e.g. quartz.

Enquiries, inspection or examination by a suitably qualified person

Typical examples include an occupational health nurse administering a questionnaire covering the symptoms of asthma or rhinitis and visual examination of the hands and arms of employees for evidence of dermatitis.

Inspection by a responsible person

In certain cases, it may be common practice for a manager or supervisor to undertake visual examinations of hands and arms of employees for early evidence of chrome ulceration.

To ensure effective health surveillance, it is essential that occupational health practitioners are aware of the hazardous nature of substances, the control methods in operation, air monitoring carried out and personal protective equipment being used by employees.

Record keeping

A record keeping system established in connection with the COSHH Regulations should incorporate the following:

Information on hazardous substances

- Substances (safety data sheets)
- Processes
- Potential emission situations

Assessments

- Details of health risk assessment in specific areas
- Results of air monitoring surveys

Prevention and control measures

- Testing and planned maintenance procedures
- Elimination potential

- Substitution potential

- Storage and distribution arrangements

- Totally enclosed processes

- Local exhaust ventilation systems

Personal protective equipment
- Selection, testing and maintenance details

- Respiratory protective equipment maintenance

Individual personal health file
- Health assessment/screening details

- Information, instruction and training received

- Issue of personal protective equipment

- Details of acute exposure situations

See:

- *Biological agents*

- *Hazardous substances*

- *Health risk assessment*

- *Lead at work*

- *New or expectant mothers*

- *Occupational diseases and conditions*

- *Occupational exposure limits*

- *Occupational hygiene*

- *Toxicology*

- *Ventilation in the workplace*

Home working

Many employees work at home with little or no direct contact with their employer. The scale of work activities undertaken by home workers is extensive, such as:

a) the packaging of items, such as screws, for national store chains;

b) assembly of goods;

c) finishing and packing of goods;

d) work with computers;

e) telephone contact work, such as telesales operations; and

f) ironing and repairing clothing.

In the case of those involved in assembly work, components may be delivered, and finished items collected, on a weekly basis. Other home workers may receive information on their future work output requirements by letter or e-mail.

The hazards arising from home working activities

The hazards to home workers are extensive. These may include electrical hazards arising from badly maintained electrical equipment, such as soldering equipment, display screen equipment and hand irons, manual handling hazards, fire hazards, chemical hazards and the potential for contracting upper limb disorders. It is common for family members to assist with the work and, in some cases, children may be illegally involved in the home working activities as a means of meeting time deadlines and increasing income by the home worker.

The duties of employers

Employers have a general duty of care at common law to ensure that work activities undertaken by employees are safe and without risks to health and that employees are adequately trained to undertake the work. Under criminal law, employers have duties under the HSWA and certain regulations towards home workers comparable with the duties owed to employees working at a specific workplace.

Whilst a home worker's house may not be under the direct control of an employer, the general and specific duties of employers towards employees apply to this type of work.

Employers, therefore, must have some form of procedure for safety monitoring of home workers' work activities with particular reference to their working environment, the tasks undertaken, equipment, articles and substances used, and structural features of the room or area where the work is undertaken. Home workers should also receive appropriate information, instruction, training and supervision. In the latter case, supervision may take the form of regular visits by a home workers' co-ordinator or supervisor to ensure written safety procedures are being observed.

In particular, the employer should prepare and put into practice a statement of policy with respect to home working as part of the organization's Statement of Health and Safety Policy. Such a statement should incorporate the employer's duties towards home workers and the organization and arrangements for ensuring these duties are put into practice.

Work area inspections and risk assessment

Before employing people to undertake work at home, employers should ensure that an inspection of the home work area is undertaken, with particular reference to environmental working conditions, the safety of work equipment, including that owned by the home worker, fire safety, the storage of hazardous substances and the extent of manual handling required. Where appropriate, risk assessment should be undertaken with a view to identifying the significant hazards and the preventive and protective measures necessary.

It may be necessary for the employer to designate specific areas where the work must be undertaken.

Many home workers use display screen equipment as a significant part of their work. Under the Health and Safety (Display Screen Equipment) Regulations an employer must undertake a workstation risk analysis in the case of defined display screen equipment 'users', that is, 'employees who habitually use display screen equipment as a significant part of their normal work'. On this basis, workstations may need to be modified to meet the requirements of these regulations.

Similar provisions apply in the case of home workers involved in manual handling operations on a regular basis, where it would be necessary for a manual handling risk assessment to be undertaken by the employer with a view to preventing or controlling risks arising from this work.

See:

- Accident reporting, recording and investigation
- Display screen equipment
- Health and Safety at Work etc Act 1974
- Manual handling operations
- Health surveillance and health protection
- Information, instruction and training
- Risk assessment
- Safety monitoring systems

Human error

The HSE publication *Reducing Error and Influencing Behaviour* [HS(G)48] outlines a number of factors that can contribute to human error which can be a significant causative feature of accidents at work. These include:

Factors contributing to human error

Inadequate information

People do not make errors merely because they are careless or inattentive. Often they have understandable (albeit incorrect) reasons for acting in the way they did. One common reason is ignorance of the production processes in which they are involved and of the potential consequences of their actions.

Lack of understanding

This often arises as a result of a failure to communicate accurately and fully the stages of a process that an item has been through. As a result, people make presumptions that certain actions have been taken when this is not the case.

Inadequate design

Designers of plant, processes or systems of work must always take into account human fallibility and never presume that those who operate or maintain plant or systems have a full and continuous appreciation of their essential features. Indeed, failure to consider such matters is, itself, an aspect of human error.

Where it cannot be eliminated, error must be made evident or difficult. Compliance with safety precautions must be made easy. Adequate information as to hazards must be provided. Systems should 'fail safe', that is, refuse to produce unsafe modes of operation.

Lapses of attention

The individual's intentions and objectives are correct and the proper course of action is selected, but a slip occurs in performing it. This may be due to competing demands for (limited) attention. Paradoxically, highly skilled performers may be more likely to make a slip because they depend upon a finely tuned allocation of their attention to avoid having to think carefully about every minor detail.

Mistaken actions

This is the classic situation of doing the wrong thing under the impression that it is right. For example, the individual knows what needs to be done, but chooses an inappropriate method to achieve it.

Misperceptions

Misperceptions tend to occur when an individual's limited capacity to give attention to competing information under stress produces 'tunnel vision' or when a preconceived diagnosis blocks out sources of inconsistent information. There is a strong tendency to assume that an established pattern holds good so long as most of the indications are to that effect, even if there is an unexpected indication to the contrary.

Mistaken priorities

An organization's objectives, particularly the relative priorities of different goals, may not be clearly conveyed to, or understood by, individuals. A crucial area of potential conflict is between safety and other objectives, such as output or the saving of cost or time. Misperceptions may then be partly intentional as certain events are ignored in the pursuit of competing objectives. When top management's goals are not clear, individuals at any level in the organization may superimpose their own.

Wilfulness

Wilfully disregarding safety rules is rarely a primary cause of accidents. Sometimes, however, there is only a fine dividing line between mistaken priorities and wilfulness. Managers need to be alert to the influences that, in combination, persuade staff to take (and condone others taking) short cuts through the safety rules and procedures because, mistakenly, the perceived benefits outweigh the risks, and they have perhaps got away with it in the past.

Elimination of human error

For the potential for human error to be eliminated or substantially reduced, all the above factors need consideration in the design and implementation of safe systems of work, processing operations, work routines and activities.

Training and supervision routines should take account of these factors and the various features of human reliability.

> **See:**
>
> - *Ergonomics*
> - *Human factors and safety*
> - *Risk assessment*

Human factors and safety

Current health and safety legislation, in particular, the MHSWR, requires a human factors-related approach to occupational health and safety. Employers must consider human capability from a health and safety viewpoint when entrusting tasks to their employees. These factors may need to be covered when undertaking a suitable and sufficient assessment of risk.

'Human capability' implies having the capacity for certain actions. 'Capacity' implies both mental and physical capacity, for instance, the mental capacity to understand why a task should be undertaken in a particular way, and physical capacity, in terms of the actual physical strength and fitness to undertake the task in question.

Human factors, in its application to occupational health and safety, have been defined as:

> 'a range of issues including the perceptual, physical and mental capabilities of people and the interactions of individuals with their jobs and working environments, the influence of equipment and system design on human performance and those organizational characteristics which influence safety-related behaviour at work'.

Fundamentally, employees are influenced by a range of factors at work.

Areas of influence on people at work

Broadly there are three areas of influence on people at work, namely the organization, the job and personal factors. These areas are directly affected by:

a) the system for communication within the organization; and

b) the training systems and procedures in operation;

all of which are directed at preventing human error.

These factors are considered below.

The organization

Those organizational characteristics which influence safety-related behaviour include:

*   the need to promote a positive climate in which health and safety is seen by both management and employees as being fundamental to the organization's day to day operations i.e. they must create a positive safety culture;

*   the need to ensure that policies and systems which are devised for the control of risk from the organization's operations take proper account of human capabilities and fallibilities;

*   commitment to the achievement of progressively higher standards which is shown at the top of the organization and cascaded through successive levels of same;

*   demonstration by senior management of their active involvement, thereby galvanizing managers throughout the organization into action; and

*   leadership, whereby an environment is created which encourages safe behaviour.

The job

Successful management of human factors and the control of risk involves the development of systems of work designed to take account of human capabilities and fallibilities. Using techniques like job safety analysis, jobs should be designed in accordance with ergonomic principles so as to take into account limitations in human performance.

Major considerations in job design include:

- identification and comprehensive analysis of critical tasks expected of individuals and appraisal of likely errors;

- evaluation of required operator decision-making and the optimum balance between the human and automatic contributions to safety actions;

- application of ergonomic principles to the design of man-machine interfaces, including displays of plant and process information, control devices and panel layouts;

- design and presentation of procedures and operating instructions;

- organization and control of the working environment, including workspace, access for maintenance, noise, lighting and thermal conditions;

- provision of correct tools and equipment;

- scheduling of work patterns, including shift organization, control of fatigue and stress, and arrangements for emergency operations; and

- efficient communications, both immediate and over periods of time.

Personal factors

This aspect is concerned with how personal factors such as attitude, motivation, training, human error and the perceptual, physical and mental capabilities of people can interact with health and safety issues.

Attitudes are directly connected with an individual's self-image, the influence of groups and the need to comply with group norms or standards and, to some extent, opinions, including superstitions, like 'All accidents are Acts of God'.

Changing attitudes is difficult. They may be formed through past experience, the level of intelligence of the individual, specific motivation, financial gain and skills available to an individual. There is no doubt that management example is the strongest of all motivators to bring about attitude change.

Important factors in motivating people to work safely include joint consultation in planning the work organization, the use of working parties or committees to define objectives, attitudes currently held, the system for communication within the organization and the quality of leadership at all levels. Financially-related motivation schemes, such as safety bonuses, do not necessarily change attitudes, people frequently reverting to normal behaviour when the bonus scheme finishes.

See:

- *Consultation on health and safety*
- *Employee handbooks*
- *Human error*
- *Information for employees*
- *Information, instruction and training*
- *Stress at work*
- *Young persons*

Information for employees

The employer has a duty to provide particular information to employees.

Health and Safety (Information for Employees) Regulations 1999

- These Regulations require information relating to health, safety and welfare to be furnished to employees by means of posters or leaflets in the form approved and published for the purposes of the Regulations by the HSE.

- The Regulations also require the name and address of the enforcing authority and the address of the Employment Medical Advisory Service to be written in the appropriate space on the poster. Where the leaflet is given to employees, the same information should be specified in a written notice accompanying it.

- The Regulations provide for the issue of Certificates of Exemption by the HSE, provide for a defence for a contravention of the regulations and repeal, revoke and modify various enactments relating to the provision of information to employees.

- The Regulations do not apply to the Master and crew of a sea-going ship.

Modification to the regulations

The Health and Safety Information for Employees (Modifications and Repeals) Regulations 1995 amended the 1989 version of the Regulations, allowing the HSE to approve, as an alternative to the basic 'Health and Safety Law' poster, a particular form of poster or leaflet for use in relation to a particular employment or class of employment.

Information, instruction and training

In order to maintain a safe and healthy workplace, it is essential that employees and other persons, such as the employees of contractors, visitors and temporary workers, are adequately informed, firstly of the hazards that could arise and, secondly, the action they may need to take to protect themselves from these hazards.

The provision of information, instruction and training

Most modern health and safety legislation requires employers to provide their employees and other persons at work with information, instruction and training on a wide range of issues.

The duty to inform, instruct and train

The terms 'information', 'instruction' and 'training' are not defined in law. However, the giving of information implies the imparting of factual knowledge by one person to another. Instruction, on the other hand, involves actually telling people what to do and may incorporate an element of supervision to ensure they do it correctly. 'Training' is defined by the Department of Employment as 'the systematic development of attitude, knowledge and skill patterns required by an individual to perform adequately a given task or job'.'

The duties on the part of employers and others to provide information, instruction and training to employees and other persons are incorporated in the HSWA and regulations made under the HSWA. This duty is qualified by the term 'so far as is reasonably practicable'. However, under the MHSWR and other more recent legislation, this duty is absolute.

Comprehensible and relevant information

Employers must provide specific information, which is both comprehensible and relevant, to the employees concerned. What is both 'comprehensible' and 'relevant' to employees must be decided by the employer. It is inappropriate, for instance, for an employer to simply provide all employees who may be exposed to a hazardous substance with a copy of the supplier's safety data sheet. The hazards and precautions necessary in the use of the substance must be explained to them and written information must be in a style which is comprehensible to them and relevant to their operations.

Under the MHSWR:

- Information must further be provided on the procedures to be followed in an emergency and on those persons designated as 'competent persons' to oversee any emergency evacuation of the workplace.

- In shared workplaces, individual employers must exchange information on risks arising from their work and employees must be informed accordingly.

- Every employer shall provide his employees with comprehensible and relevant information on:

    a) the risks to their health and safety identified by the risk assessment;

    b) the preventive and protective measures;

    c) the procedures referred to in Regulation 7(1)(a) (emergency procedures);

    d) the identity of those people nominated by them in accordance with Regulation 7(1)(b) (competent persons for the purpose of emergencies); and

    e) the risks notified to then in accordance with Regulation 9(1)(c) (shared workplaces). (Regulation 8)

Risk assessments and training needs

One of the principal outcomes of a risk assessment carried out under the MHSWR is the need for the training of managers, supervisors and employees generally in the preventive and protective measures specified in that risk assessment. This may include basic skills training, e.g. in the correct use of PPE and personal hygiene procedures when using hazardous substances, specific on-the-job training, e.g. in the use of certain items of equipment, and training in emergency procedures, including evacuation of the workplace. Managers and supervisors may also need to be trained to ensure they understand their individual duties indicated in the organization's Statement of Health and Safety Policy.

The need for regular refresher training to maintain competence in safety procedures must also be considered.

See:

- *Accidents and accident prevention*
- *Hazardous substances*
- *Health and Safety at Work etc Act 1974*
- *Human factors and safety*
- *Information for employees*
- *Information sources*
- *Personal protective equipment*
- *Radiation and radiological protection*
- *Risk assessment*
- *Safety propaganda*

Information sources

A wide range of information is available on health and safety work. This includes primary sources, such as Acts of Parliament and Regulations, and secondary sources, such as product information, British Standards and text books.

All modern health and safety legislation requires employers to provide employees and other persons with information on hazards at work and the precautions necessary on the part of such persons.

Primary sources

EU directives

These are the Community instrument of legislation. Directives are legally binding on the governments of all Member States who must introduce national legislation, or use administrative procedures where applicable, to implement its requirements.

Acts of parliament (statutes)

Acts of Parliament can be innovatory, i.e. introducing new legislation, or consolidating, i.e. reinforcing, with modifications, existing law. Statutes empower the Minister or Secretary of State to make Regulations (delegated or subordinate legislation). Typical examples are the HSWA 1974 and the Environmental Protection Act 1990.

Regulations (statutory instruments)

Regulations are more detailed than the parent Act, which lays down the framework and objectives of the system. Specific details are incorporated in Regulations made under the Act e.g. the Control of Substances Hazardous to Health (COSHH) Regulations which were passed pursuant to the HSWA. Regulations are made by the appropriate Minister or Secretary of State whose powers to do so are identified in the parent Act.

Approved codes of practice

The HSC is empowered to approve and issue Codes of Practice for the purpose of providing guidance on health and safety duties and other matters laid down in Statute or Regulations. A Code of Practice can be drawn up by the HSC or the HSE. In every case, however, the relevant government department, or other body, must be consulted beforehand and approval of the Secretary of State must be obtained. Any Code of Practice approved in this way is an Approved Code of Practice (ACOP).

An ACOP enjoys a special status under the HSWA. Although failure to comply with any provision of the code is not in itself an offence, that failure may be taken by a court, in criminal proceedings, as proof that a person has contravened the legal requirement to which the provision relates. In such a case it will be open to that person to satisfy a court that he or she has complied with the requirement in some other way.

Examples of ACOPs are those issued with the Control of Substances Hazardous to Health (COSHH) Regulations entitled Control of Substances Hazardous to Health, Control of Carcinogenic Substances and Control of Substances Hazardous to Health in Fumigation Operations.

Case law (common law)

Case law is an important source of information. It is derived from common law because, traditionally, judges have formulated rules and principles of law as the cases occur for decision before the Courts.

What is important in a case is the ratio decidendi (the reason for the decision). This is binding on courts of equal rank who may be deciding the same point of law. Ratio decidendi is the application of such an established principle to the facts of a given case, for instance, negligence consists of omitting to do what a "reasonable man" would do in order to avoid causing injury to others.

Case law is found in law reports, for example, the All England Law Reports, the Industrial Cases Reports, the current *Law Year Book* and in professional journals, e.g. *Law Society Gazette, Solicitors Journal*. In addition, many newspapers carry daily law reports e.g. *The Times, Financial Times, Daily Telegraph* and *Independent*.

The supreme law court is the European Court of Justice whose reports are recorded in *The Times*.

Secondary sources

Many non-legal sources of information are available. These include:

HSE series of guidance notes

Guidance Notes issued by the HSE have no legal status. They are issued on a purely advisory basis to provide guidance on good health and safety practices, specific hazards, etc. There are five series of Guidance Notes: General, Chemical Safety, Plant and Machinery, Medical and Environmental Hygiene.

British standards

These are produced by the British Standards Institute. They provide sound guidance on numerous issues and are frequently referred to by enforcement officers as the correct way of complying with a legal duty.

British Standard EN ISO 12100 *Safety of Machinery*, for example, is commonly quoted in conjunction with the duties of employers under the Provision and Use of Work Equipment Regulations to provide and maintain safe work equipment.

Manufacturers' information and instructions

Under Section 6 of the HSWA (as amended by the Consumer Protection Act 1987) manufacturers, designers, importers and installers of 'articles and substances used at work' have a duty to provide information relating to the safe use, storage, etc of their products. Such information may include operating instructions for machinery and plant and safety data sheets in respect of dangerous substances. Information provided should be sufficiently comprehensive and understandable to enable a judgement to be made on their safe use at work.

The ACOP to the Chemicals (Hazard Information and Packaging for Supply) Regulations specifies a series of headings which must be incorporated in a safety data sheet for substances dangerous for supply.

Safety organizations

Safety organizations, such as the Royal Society for the Prevention of Accidents (RoSPA) and the British Safety Council, provide information in the form of magazines, booklets and videos on a wide range of health and safety-related topics.

Professional institutions and trade associations

Many professional institutions, such as the Institution of Occupational Safety and Health (IOSH), the Chartered Institute of Environmental Health (CIEH) and the British Occupational Hygiene Society (BOHS), provide information, both verbally and in written form. Similarly, a wide range of trade associations provide this information to members.

Insurance companies

Most insurance companies provide an information service to clients on a wide range of health and safety-related matters.

Department of social security

This government department publishes annual statistics on claims for industrial injuries benefit and other matters.

Published information

This takes the form of text books, magazines, law reports, updating services, microfiche systems, films and videos on general and specific topics.

Internal sources of information

There are many sources of information available within organizations. These include:

Existing written information

This may take the form of Statements of Health and Safety Policy, internal Health and Safety Codes of Practice, specific internal policies e.g. on the use and storage of dangerous substances, current agreements with trade unions, contractors' rules and regulations, methods, operating instructions, risk assessments etc.

Such documentation could be quoted in a court of law as an indication of the organization's intention to regulate activities in order to ensure legal compliance. Evidence of the use of such information in staff training is essential here.

Work study techniques

Included here are the results of activity sampling, surveys, method study, work measurement and process flows.

Job descriptions

A job description should incorporate health and safety responsibilities and accountabilities. It should take account of the physical and mental requirements and limitations of certain jobs and any specific risks associated with the job.

Accident and ill health statistics

Statistical information on past accidents and sickness may identify unsatisfactory trends in operating procedures which can be eliminated at the design stage of safe systems of work.

Job analysis and job safety analysis

Information produced by the analysis of jobs, such as the mental and physical requirements of a job, manual operations involved, skills required, influences on behaviour, hazards specific to the job, and learning methods necessary to impart job knowledge must be taken into account.

Job safety analysis, a development of job analysis, will provide the above information prior to the development of safe systems of work.

Direct observation

This is the actual observation of work being carried out. It identifies inter-relationships between operators, hazards, dangerous practices and situations and potential risk situations. It is an important source of information in ascertaining whether, for instance, formally designed safe systems of work are being operated or safety practices, imparted as part of former training activities, are being followed.

Personal experience

People have their own unique experience of specific tasks and the hazards which those tasks present.

The experiences of accident victims, frequently recorded in accident reports, are an important source of information. Feedback from accidents is crucial in order to prevent repetition of these accidents.

Incident recall

This is a technique used in a damage control programme to gain information about near-miss accidents.

Product complaints

A record of all product complaints and action taken should be maintained. Such information provides useful feedback in the modification of products and in the design of new products. Product complaints may also result in action by the enforcement authorities under section 6 of the HSWA and/or civil proceedings in the event of injury, damage or loss sustained as a result of a defective product or defect in a product.

See:

- *Accident and ill health data*

- *Approved codes of practice and HSE guidance notes*

- *Documentation requirements*

- *Information for employees*

- *Information, instruction and training*

- *Insurance*

- *Job safety analysis*

- *Product liability*

- *Safety data (hazardous substances)*

Insurance

Employers Liability (Compulsory Insurance) Regulations 1999

These Regulations consolidate with amendments former Regulations made under the 1969 Act and supplement the requirements of the Act relating to compulsory insurance of risks relating to employees.

Prohibited conditions

Under Regulation 2 certain conditions are prohibited in policies of insurance, namely any condition which provides (in whatever terms) that no liability (either generally or in respect of a particular claim) shall arise under the policy, or that any liability so arising shall cease, if:

- some specified thing is done or omitted to be done after the happening of the event giving rise to a claim under the policy;

- the policy holder does not take reasonable care to protect his employees against the risk of bodily injury or disease in the course of their employment;

- the policy holder fails to comply with the requirements of any enactment for the protection of employees against the risk of bodily injury or disease in the course of their employment; or

- the policy holder does not keep specified records or fails to provide the insurer with or make available to him information from such records.

Limit of the sum to be insured

Regulation 3 sets the limit of the sum to be insured at not less than £5,000,000.

Obligation on insurers

Regulation 4 and Schedule 1 place obligations on authorized insurers as to the issue of certificates, including the form of the certificates.

Obligation on employers

Certificates must be kept by insurers. They must be displayed at each place of business where an employer employs employees of the class or description to which the certificate relates (Regulation 5).

Where an employer is required to produce a certificate of insurance by form of a written notice from an inspector, he must produce same or send it to any person specified in the notice (Regulation 6).

An employer shall, during the currency of an insurance, permit the policy of insurance, or a copy of it, to be inspected:

- at such reasonable time as the inspector may require; and
- at such place of business of the employer (which, in the case of an employer who is a company, may include its registered office) as the inspector may require.

Certificate of employer's liability insurance

Schedule 1 states the form to be taken by a Certificate of Employer's Liability Insurance thus:

Policy Number:

- Name of policy holder
- Date of commencement of insurance policy
- Date of expiry of insurance policy

We hereby certify that subject to paragraph 2:

1. The Policy to which this certificate relates satisfies the relevant law applicable in Great Britain; and

2. a) the minimum amount of cover provided by this policy is no less than £5,000,000; or

    b) the cover provided under this policy relates to claims in excess of £X but not exceeding £Y.

Signed on behalf of:

_____ (Authorized Insurer)

Signature _____

J

Job safety analysis

Job safety analysis evolved from job or task analysis, and is defined as:

> 'the identification of all the accident prevention measures appropriate to a particular job or area of work activity and the behavioural factors which most significantly influence whether or not these measures are taken'.

Job/task analysis

The identification and specification of the skill and knowledge contents of jobs.

Job/task training analysis

The identification and specification of what has to be taught and learned for individual jobs.

Job safety analysis

The approach is both diagnostic and descriptive. It may be job-based or activity-based.

- **Job-based**: Machinery operators; fork lift truck drivers
- **Activity-based**: Manual handling operations; roof work; cleaning activities.

Job safety analysis evolved from:

a) task analysis; and

b) method study and work measurement (SREDIM).

The latter incorporates the SREDIM principle, namely:

SELECT   – the work to be studied

RECORD   – the method of doing the work

EXAMINE – the total operating system

DEVELOP – the optimum methods for doing the work

INSTALL   – the method into the company's operations

MAINTAIN – the defined and measured method

Applying the SREDIM principle to job safety analysis, the procedure is as follows:

- Select the job to be analysed.

- Break the job down into component parts in an orderly and chronological sequence job.

- Critically observe and examine each component part of the job to determine the risk of accident.

- Develop control measures to eliminate or reduce the risk of accident.

- Formulate written safe systems of work and job safety instructions.

- Review safe systems of work and job safe practices at regular intervals to ensure utilization.

Job safety instructions

These are used as a means of communicating the safe system of work to the operator. They can be produced as:

a) a general manual covering all jobs;

b) specific cards attached to machines or displayed in the work area.

Criteria for selection of jobs for analysis

- Past accident and loss experience
- Maximum potential loss
- Probability of accident recurrences
- Legal requirements
- Relative newness of the job
- Number of employees at risk

A Job Safety Analysis record should be maintained for each job analysed.

Stages of job safety analysis

Job safety analysis usually takes place in two specific stages, each of which has different information requirements.

Initial job safety analysis

The following factors are considered:

Job title	Department/Section
Job operations	Machinery/equipment used
Materials used	Protection needed
Hazards	Degree of risk
Work organization	Specific tasks

Total job safety analysis

The following factors are considered:

Operations	Hazards
Skills required	External influences on behaviour
Learning methods	

See:

- *Permit to Work systems*
- *Safety management systems*

L

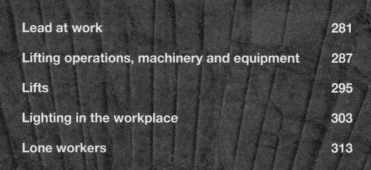

Lead at work

Exposure to lead

Lead poisoning is, perhaps, the oldest known occupational disease being first recorded in Roman times.

Lead can enter the body as a result of inhalation of lead fume or dust, by ingestion of contaminated food or through pervasion of the unbroken skin in the form of organic compounds such as tetra-ethyl lead.

Lead poisoning can result from work in a range of processes, such as lead smelting, melting and burning, the glazing of pottery, the manufacture of lead accumulators, plumbing and soldering activities and in the manufacture of rubber. Lead poisoning occurs in two distinct forms, namely by inorganic lead and organic lead, the latter occurring as tetra-ethyl lead and tetra-methyl lead. In acute cases, where there has been exposure to lead fume, the initial symptoms are a sweetish taste in the mouth, with anorexia, nausea, vomiting and headache. Acute poisoning is often fatal. In severe cases, there is a marked effect on the central nervous system shown by restlessness, excitement, muscular twitchings accompanied by insomnia, delusions, hallucinations and even violent and acute mania.

In more chronic cases, there is evidence of a blue line around the gums accompanied by headache, pallor, anaemia, palsy and encephalopathy, a form of mental disorder characterized by mental dullness, inability to concentrate, faulty memory, tremors, deafness, convulsion and coma. The majority of lead poisoning cases are associated with inhalation of fume containing lead arising from heating of the metal above a temperature of 500°C.

Control of Lead at Work Regulations 2002

These regulations define 'lead' as meaning lead (including lead alkyls, lead alloys, any compounds of lead and lead as a constituent of any substance or material) which is liable to be inhaled, ingested or otherwise absorbed by persons except where it is given off from the exhaust system of a vehicle on a road within the meaning of Section 192 of the Road Traffic Act 1998.

The Regulations are comprehensive and impose requirements for the protection of employees who might be exposed to lead at work and of other persons who might be affected by such work. They also impose certain duties on employees concerning their own protection from such exposure.

The Regulations specify an occupational exposure limit for lead thus:

- lead other than lead alkyls, a concentration of lead in the atmosphere to which an employee is exposed of $0.15mg/m^3$; and

- lead alkyls, a concentration of lead contained in lead alkyls in the atmosphere to which an employee is exposed of $0.10mg/m^3$,

  assessed:

  i) by reference to the content of the element lead in the concentration; and

  ii) in relation to an eight hour time-weighted average reference period when calculated by a method approved by the HSC.

These regulations further:

- specify action levels for lead in respect of women of reproductive capacity, young persons and other employees;

- specify suspension levels in terms of:
  - blood-lead concentrations; and
  - urinary lead concentrations; and

- prohibit:
    - the use of a glaze by an employee other than a leadless glaze or a low solubility glaze in the manufacture of pottery; and
    - the employment of young persons and women of reproductive capacity in certain activities specified in Schedule 1.

- Employers shall not carry out work which is liable to expose any employees to lead unless they have:
    - made a suitable and sufficient assessment of the risk created by that work to the health of those employees and the steps that need to be taken to meet the requirements of the regulations; and
    - implemented the steps referred to above.

Risk assessment

The risk assessment shall include consideration of:

- the hazardous properties of the lead;
- information on health effects provided by the supplier, including information contained in any relevant safety data sheet;
- the level, type and duration of exposure;
- the circumstances of the work, including the amount of lead involved;;
- activities, such as maintenance, where there is the potential for high level of exposure;
- any relevant occupational exposure limit, action level and suspension level;
- the effect of preventive and control measures which have been, or will be taken, in accordance with Regulation 6;
- the results of relevant medical surveillance;
- the results of monitoring exposure in accordance with Regulation 9;

- in circumstances where the work will involve exposure to lead and another substance hazardous to health, the risk presented by exposure to those substances in combination;

- whether the exposure of any employee to lead is liable to be significant; and

- such additional information as the employer may need in order to complete the risk assessment.

Any risk assessment must be reviewed regularly and the significant findings of the risk assessment, together with the steps taken to meet the requirements of Regulation 6, recorded.

Prevention or control of exposure

There is a general duty on employers to either prevent exposure to lead or, where this is not reasonably practicable, to adequately control this exposure.

Substitution shall by preference be undertaken whereby the employer shall avoid, so far as is reasonably practicable, the use of lead at the workplace by replacing it with a substance or process which, under the conditions of its use, either eliminates or reduces the risk to the health of employees.

A hierarchy of protection measures is laid down including:

- the design and use of appropriate work processes, systems and engineering controls and the provision and use of suitable and work equipment and materials;

- the control of exposure at source; and

- where adequate control of exposure cannot be achieved by other means, the provision of suitable PPE in addition to the above measures.

Employers must ensure, so far as is reasonably practicable, that employees do not eat, drink or smoke in any place which is, or which is liable to be, contaminated by lead. Employees have an absolute duty not to eat, drink or smoke in any area contaminated by lead.

Any control measure must be maintained in an efficient state, in efficient working order, in good repair and in a clean condition. Where engineering controls are concerned, the employer must ensure they are examined and tested. Similar provisions apply in the case of respiratory protective equipment. PPE, including protective clothing, must be properly stored, checked at suitable intervals and repaired or replaced when defective.

Where the risk assessment indicates that employees may be liable to receive significant exposure to lead, air monitoring must be undertaken by the employer.

Every employer must ensure that each of his employees who is, or is liable to be, exposed to lead is under suitable medical surveillance, which may include biological monitoring, by a relevant doctor.

An adequate health record of each employee must be made and maintained and that record kept available in suitable form for at least 40 years.

Employees must be provided with suitable and sufficient information, instruction and training, with particular respect to:

- details of the form of lead to which the employee is liable to be exposed;
- the significant findings of the risk assessment;
- the appropriate precautions and action to be taken by the employee;
- the results of any air monitoring undertaken; and
- the collective results of any medical surveillance undertaken.

Specific emergency procedures and arrangements must be provided including appropriate first aid facilities and undertaking relevant safety drills, information on emergency arrangements must be available and suitable warning and other communication systems established to enable an appropriate response to be made immediately an accident, incident or emergency arises.

Schedule 1 outlines activities in which the employment of young persons and women of reproductive capacity is prohibited.

See:

- *Hazardous substances*
- *Health surveillance and health protection*
- *Occupational diseases and conditions*

Lifting operations, machinery and equipment

Lifting operations using a wide range of lifting equipment have been a contributory factor in fatal and major injury accidents in many sectors of industry.

Lifting Operations and Lifting Equipment Regulations (LOLER) 1998

LOLER applies over and above the general requirements of the Provision and Use of Work Equipment Regulations 1998 in dealing with specific hazards and risks associated with lifting equipment and lifting operations. The Regulations are supported by an ACOP and HSE Guidance *Safe Use of Lifting Equipment*.

Under LOLER there is an absolute duty on employers and others to undertake lifting operations safely.

Important definitions

Accessory for lifting means lifting equipment for attaching loads to machinery for lifting.

Examination scheme means a suitable scheme drawn up by a competent person for such thorough examinations of lifting equipment at such intervals as may be appropriate for the purpose described in Regulation 9(3).

Lifting equipment means work equipment for lifting or lowering loads and includes its attachments used for anchoring, fixing or supporting it.

Lifting operation means an operation concerned with the lifting or lowering of a load. (Regulation 8).

Load includes a person.

Thorough examination in relation to a thorough examination under paragraph 1, 2 or 3 of Regulation 9:

a) means a thorough examination by a competent person;

b) where it is appropriate to carry out testing for the purpose described in the paragraph, includes such testing by a competent person as is appropriate for the purpose.

Work equipment means any machinery, appliance, apparatus, tool or installation for use at work (whether exclusively or not).

Specific requirements of the regulations

Every employer shall ensure that:

a) lifting equipment is of adequate strength and stability for each load, having regard in particular to the stress induced at its mounting or fixed point;

b) every part of a load and anything attached to it and used in lifting it is of adequate strength.

Every employer shall ensure that lifting equipment for lifting persons:

a) subject to sub-paragraph (b), is such as to prevent a person using it being crushed, trapped or struck or falling from the carrier;

b) is such as to prevent so far as is reasonably practicable a person using it, while carrying out activities from the carrier, being crushed, trapped or struck or falling from the carrier;

c) subject to paragraph 2, has suitable devices to prevent the risk of a carrier falling;

d) is such that a person trapped in any carrier is not thereby exposed to danger and can be freed.

Every employer shall ensure that if the risk described in paragraph 1(c) cannot be prevented for reasons inherent in the site and height differences:

a) the carrier has an enhanced safety coefficient suspension rope or chain; and

b) the rope or chain is inspected by a competent person every working day.

Every employer shall ensure that lifting equipment is positioned or installed in such a way as to reduce to as low as is reasonably practicable the risk:

a) of the lifting equipment or a load striking a person; or

b) from a load:

    i) drifting;

    ii) falling freely; or

    iii) being released unintentionally,

    and it is otherwise safe.

Every employer shall ensure that there are suitable devices to prevent a person from falling down a shaft or hoistway.

Every employer shall ensure that:

a) subject to sub-paragraph (b), the machinery and accessories for lifting loads are clearly marked to indicate their safe working loads (SWLs);

b) where the SWL of machinery for lifting depends upon its configuration:

    i) the machinery is clearly marked to indicate its SWL for each configuration; or

    ii) information which clearly indicates its SWL for each configuration is kept with the machinery;

c) accessories for lifting are clearly marked in such a way that it is possible to identify the characteristics necessary for their safe use;

d) lifting equipment which is designed for lifting persons is appropriately and clearly marked to this effect; and

e) lifting equipment which is not designed for lifting persons but which might be so used in error is appropriately and clearly marked to the effect that it is not designed for lifting persons.

Every employer shall ensure that every lifting operation involving lifting equipment is:

a) properly planned by a competent person;

b) appropriately supervised; and

c) carried out in a safe manner.

Every employer shall ensure that before lifting equipment is put into service for the first time by him it is thoroughly examined by him for any defect unless either:

a) the lifting equipment has not been used before; and

b) in the case of lifting equipment for which an EC declaration of conformity could or (in the case of a declaration under the Lifts Regulations 1997) should have been drawn up, the employer has received such declaration made not more than 12 months before the lifting equipment is put into service;

or, if obtained from the undertaking of another person, it is accompanied by physical evidence referred to in paragraph 4.

Every employer shall ensure that, where the safety of lifting equipment depends upon the installation conditions, it is thoroughly examined:

a) after installation and before being put into service for the first time; and

b) after assembly and before being put into service at a new site or in a new location, to ensure that it has been installed correctly and is safe to operate.

Subject to paragraph 6, every employer shall ensure that lifting equipment which is exposed to conditions causing deterioration which is liable to result in dangerous situations is:

a) thoroughly examined:

   i) in case of lifting equipment for lifting persons or an accessory for lifting, at least every six months;

   ii) in the case of other lifting equipment, at least every 12 months; or

   iii) in either case, in accordance with an examination scheme; and

   iv) each time that exceptional circumstances which are liable to jeopardize the safety of the lifting equipment have occurred; and

b) if appropriate for the purpose, is inspected by a competent person at suitable intervals between thorough examinations.

Every employer shall ensure that no lifting equipment:

a) leaves his undertaking; or

b) if obtained from the undertaking of another person, is used in his undertaking, unless it is accompanied by physical evidence that the last thorough examination required to be carried out under this regulation has been carried out.

A person making a thorough examination for an employer shall:

a) notify the employer forthwith of any defect in the lifting equipment which in his opinion is, or could become, a danger to persons;

b) as soon as is practicable make a report of the thorough examination in writing authenticated by him or on his behalf by signature or equally secure means and containing the information specified in Schedule 1 to:

   i) the employer; and

   ii) any person from whom the lifting equipment has been hired or leased:

c) where there is in his opinion a defect in the lifting equipment involving an existing or imminent risk of serious personal injury send a copy of the report as soon as is practicable to the relevant enforcing authority.

A person making an inspection for an employer under Regulation 9 shall:

a) notify the employer forthwith of any defect in the lifting equipment which in his opinion is, or could become, a danger to persons;

b) as soon as is practicable make a record of his inspection in writing.

Every employer who has been notified shall ensure that the lifting equipment is not used:

a) before the defect is rectified; or

b) in a case to which sub-paragraph (c) of paragraph 8 of Schedule 1 applies, after a time specified under that sub-paragraph and before the defect is rectified.

In this regulation relevant enforcing authority means:

a) where the defective lifting equipment has been hired or leased by the employer, the HSE; and

b) otherwise, the enforcing authority for the premises in which the defective lifting equipment was thoroughly examined.

Where an employer obtaining lifting equipment to which these regulations apply receives an EC declaration of conformity relating to it, he shall keep the declaration for so long as he operates the lifting equipment.

The employer shall ensure that the information contained in:

a) every report made to him under Regulation 10(1)(b) is kept available for inspection:

i) in the case of a thorough examination under paragraph 1 of Regulation 9 of lifting equipment other than an accessory for lifting, until he ceases to use the lifting equipment;

ii) in the case of a thorough examination under paragraph 1 of Regulation 9 of an accessory for lifting, for 2 years after the report is made;

iii) in the case of a thorough examination under paragraph 2 of Regulation 9, until he ceases to use the lifting equipment at the place it was installed or assembled;

iv) in the case of a thorough examination under paragraph 3 of Regulation 9, until the next report is made under that paragraph or the expiration of two years, whichever is later;

b) every record made under Regulation 10(2) is kept available until the next such record is made.

Safe use of hoists and cranes, lifting appliances and lifting gear

The following matters need consideration to ensure the safe use of lifting appliances and lifting gear.

- Packing or other means must be used to prevent the edges of a load coming into contact with slings, ropes or chains, if this would cause danger.

- The angle between the legs of multiple slings must not be so great that the safe working load (SWL) is exceeded.

- Every part of a load must be securely suspended and supported and secured to prevent displacement or slipping.

- Slings must be attached securely to the appliance and in a way not likely to damage the slings of any lifting gear.

- The hoisting mechanism of a crane must be used only for vertical raising or lowering, unless it can be used otherwise without imposing undue stress or endangering stability, and if so used under the supervision of a competent person.

- The SWL not to be exceeded.

- The radius of the load must not exceed the maximum working radius of the jib.

- Where a load is equal to, or nearly equal to the SWL, lifting must be halted for a moment after the load has been raised for a short distance.

- All practicable measures must be taken to prevent a load coming into contact, and displacing, any other object.

- No load must be left suspended unless a competent person is actually in charge of the lifting appliance.

- Loads being lowered on to a scaffold must be deposited without causing any violent shock to the scaffold.

- No crane must be used for raising or lowering unless it is either securely anchored or adequately weighted with ballast properly placed and secured. (Rails on which cranes are mounted must not be used as anchorages.)

- Only trained and competent persons must operate lifting machines.

- No person under 18 years should operate any lifting appliance driven by mechanical power, or give signals to the driver of a power-operated lifting appliance.

See:

- *Chains, ropes and lifting tackle*
- *Machinery and work equipment*

Lifts

Safety requirements for lifts are principally incorporated in Schedule 1 to the Lifts Regulations 1997 which implements Annex 1 to the Lifts Directive thus:

- **Essential Health and Safety Requirements**

- **Relating to the Design and Construction of Lifts and Safety Components**

Preliminary remarks

1. Obligations under the Essential Health and Safety Requirements (EHSRs) apply only where the lift or safety component is subject to the hazard in question when used as intended by the installer of the lift or the manufacturer of the safety components.

2. The EHSRs contained in the Directive are imperatives. However, given the present state of the art, the objectives which they lay down may not be attainable. In such cases, and to the greatest extent possible, the lift or safety components must be designed and built in such a way as to approximate to those objectives.

3. The safety component manufacturer and the installer of the lift are under an obligation to assess the hazards in order to identify all those which apply to their products; they must then design and construct them taking account of the assessment.

4. In accordance with Article 14, the essential requirements laid down in Directive 89/106/EEC not included in this Directive, apply to lifts.

1. General

1.1 Application of Directive 89/392/EEC as amended by Directives 91/368/EEC, 93/44/EEC and 93/68/EEC

Where the relevant hazard exists and is not dealt with in this Annex, the EHSRs of Annex 1 to the Directive 89/392/EEC apply. The essential requirement of Section 1.1.2 of Annex 1 to Directive 89/392/EEC must apply in any event.

1.2 Car

The car must be designed and constructed to offer the space and strength corresponding to the maximum number of persons and the rated load of the lift set by the installer.

In the case of lifts intended for the transport of persons, and where its dimensions permit, the car must be designed and constructed in such a way that its structural features do not obstruct or impede access and use by disabled persons and so as to allow any appropriate adjustments intended to facilitate its use by them.

1.3 Means of suspension and means of support

The means of suspension and/or support of the car, its attachments and any terminal parts thereof must be selected and designed so as to ensure an adequate level of overall safety and to minimize the risk of the car falling, taking into account the conditions of use, the materials used and the conditions of manufacture.

Where ropes or chains are used to suspend the car, there must be at least two independent cables or chains, each with its own anchorage system. Such ropes and chains must have no joins or splices except where necessary for fixing or forming a loop.

1.4 Control of loading (including overspeed)

1.4.1 Lifts must be so designed, constructed and installed as to prevent normal starting if the rated load is exceeded.

1.4.2 Lifts must be equipped with an overspeed limitation device.

These requirements do not apply to lifts in which the design of the drive system prevents overspeed.

1.4.3 Fast lifts must be equipped with a speed-monitoring and speed-limiting device.

1.4.4 Lifts driven by friction pulleys must be so designed as to ensure stability of the traction cables on the pulley.

1.5 Machinery

1.5.1 All passenger lifts must have their own individual lift machinery. This requirement does not apply to lifts in which the counter-weights are replaced by a second car.

1.5.2 The installer of the lift must ensure that the lift machinery and the associated devices of a lift are not accessible except for maintenance and in emergencies.

1.6 Controls

1.6.1 The controls of lifts intended for use by unaccompanied disabled persons must be designed and located accordingly.

1.6.2 The function of the controls must be clearly indicated.

1.6.3 The call circuits of a group of lifts may be shared or interconnected.

1.6.4 Electrical equipment must be so installed and connected that:

- there can be no possible confusion with circuits which do not have any direct connection with the lift;
- the power supply can be switched while on load;
- movements of the lift are dependent on electrical safety devices in a separate electrical safety circuit;
- a fault in the electrical installation does not give rise to a dangerous situation.

2. Hazards to persons outside the car

2.1   The lift must be designed and constructed to ensure that the space in which the car travels is inaccessible except for maintenance and emergencies. Before a person enters that space, normal use of the lift must be made impossible.

2.2   The lift must be designed and constructed to prevent the risk of crushing when the car is in one of its extreme positions. The objective will be achieved by means of free space or refuge beyond the extreme positions.

However, in specific cases, in affording Member States the possibility of giving prior approval, particularly in existing buildings, where this solution is impossible to fulfil, other appropriate means may be provided to avoid this risk.

2.3   The landings at the entrance and exit of the car must be equipped with landing doors of adequate mechanical resistance for the conditions of use envisaged.

During normal operation an interlocking device must prevent:

- starting movement of the car, whether or not deliberately activated, unless all landing doors are shut and locked;
- the opening of a landing door when the car is still moving and outside a prescribed landing zone.

However, all landing movements with the doors open shall be allowed in specified zones on condition that the levelling speed is controlled.

3. Hazards to persons in the car

3.1   Lift cars must be completely enclosed by full-length walls, fitted floors and ceilings included, with the exception of ventilation apertures, and with full-length doors. These doors must be so designed and installed that the car cannot move, except for the landing movements referred to in the third sub-paragraph of

Section 2.3, unless the doors are closed, and comes to a halt if the doors are opened.

The doors of the car must remain closed and interlocked if the lift stops between two levels where there is a risk of a fall between the car and the shaft or if there is no shaft.

3.2 In the event of a power cut or failure of components, the lift must have devices to prevent free fall or uncontrolled upward movements of the car.

The device preventing the free fall of the car must be independent of the means of suspension of the car.

This device must be able to stop the car at its rated load and at the maximum speed anticipated by the installer of the lift. Any stop occasioned by this device must not cause deceleration harmful to the occupants whatever the load conditions.

3.3 Buffers must be installed between the bottom of the shaft and the floor of the car.

In this case the free space referred to in Section 2.2 must be measured with the buffers totally compressed.

The requirement does not apply to lifts in which the car cannot enter the free space referred to in Section 2.2 by reason of the design of the drive system.

3.4 Lifts must be so designed and constructed as to make it impossible for them to be set in motion if the device provided for in Section 3.2 is not in an operational position.

4. Other hazards

4.1 The landing doors and car doors or the two doors together, where motorized, must be fitted with a device to prevent the risk of crushing when they are moving.

4.2 Landing doors, where they have to contribute to the protection of the building against fire, including those with glass parts, must be suitably resistant to fire in terms of their integrity and their properties with regard to insulation (containment of flames) and transmission of heat (thermal radiation).

4.3 Counterweights must be installed so as to avoid any risk of colliding with, or falling on to, the car.

4.4 Lifts must be equipped with means enabling people trapped in the car to be released and evacuated.

4.5 Cars must be fitted with two-way means of communication allowing permanent contact with a rescue service.

4.6 Lifts must be so designed and constructed that, in the event of the temperature in the lift machine room exceeding the maximum set by the installer, they can complete movements in progress but refuse new commands.

4.7 Cars must be designed and constructed to ensure sufficient ventilation for passengers, even in the event of prolonged stoppage.

4.8 The car should be adequately lit whenever in use or whenever a door is opened; there must also be emergency lighting.

4.9 The means of communication referred to in Section 4.5 and the emergency lighting referred to in Section 4.8 must be designed and constructed so as to function even without the normal power supply. Their period of operation should be long enough to allow normal operation of the rescue procedure.

4.10 The control circuits of lifts which may be used in the event of fire must be designed and manufactured so that lifts may be prevented from stopping at certain levels and allow for priority control of the lift by rescue teams.

5. Marking

5.1 In addition to the minimum particulars required for any machine pursuant to Section 1.7.3 of Annex 1 to Directive 89/392/EEC, each car must bear an easily visible plate clearly showing the rated load in kilograms and the maximum number of passengers which may be carried.

5.2   If the lift is so designed to allow people trapped in the car to escape without outside help, the relevant instructions must be clear and visible in the car.

6. Instructions for use

6.1   The safety components referred to in Annex IV must be accompanied by an instruction manual drawn up in an official language of the Member State of the lift installer or another Community language acceptable to him, so that:

- assembly,

- connection,

- adjustment, and

- maintenance,

can be carried out effectively and without danger.

6.2   Each lift must be accompanied by documentation drawn up in the official language(s) of the Community, which may be determined in accordance with the Treaty by the Member State in which the lift is installed. The documentation shall contain at least:

- an instruction manual containing the plans and diagrams necessary for normal use and relating to maintenance, inspection, repair periodic checks and the rescue operations referred to in Section 4.4;

- a log book in which repairs and, where appropriate, checks can be noted.

Lighting in the workplace

Health and safety legislation has always placed an absolute or strict duty on employers to ensure that all parts of a workplace, both internally and externally, are adequately illuminated. This has entailed the provision of both ambient or background lighting to maintain safe working areas and specific lighting at machinery and workstations where a higher level of lighting may be required because of the hazards arising from work activities.

The duty to provide and maintain light

The WHSWR impose an absolute duty on an employer to ensure that every workplace has both 'suitable' and 'sufficient' lighting.

- Lighting shall, so far as is reasonably practicable, be by natural light.

- Suitable and sufficient emergency lighting shall further be provided in any room in circumstances in which persons at work are specially exposed to danger in the event of failure of artificial lighting.

- Lighting must be 'suitable' in terms of freedom from various forms of glare. It must also be adequately distributed and maintained. 'Sufficient' lighting, on the other hand, is considered to be the amount of light necessary to generally ensure safe working and to enable people to undertake specific tasks without suffering visual fatigue or eyestrain.

- The ACOP on this matter must be read in conjunction with these general duties under the regulations. HSE Guidance is also available on the subject.

- These regulations further place an absolute duty on employers in terms of maintenance of lighting arrangements. In this case, there is an absolute duty on the employer to ensure the workplace, equipment, systems and devices are maintained (including cleaned as appropriate) in an efficient state, in efficient working order and in good repair. Moreover, where appropriate, devices and systems to which this regulation applies must be subject to a suitable system of maintenance.

- The Provision and Use of Work Equipment Regulations 1998 also impose an absolute duty on employers to ensure that suitable and sufficient lighting, which takes account of the operations to be carried out, is provided at any place where a person uses work equipment.

All these requirements must be taken into account in any risk assessment process undertaken by the employer.

Assessing workplace lighting

Any assessment of lighting in the workplace should take account of the following aspects:

- the adequacy of natural and artificial lighting, particularly where work equipment is in use;

- procedures for measuring levels of illumination;

- the presence of glare in its various forms;

- the efficiency of light distribution;

- lighting maintenance and cleaning arrangements; and

- emergency lighting arrangements.

HSC approved code of practice (ACOP)

The ACOP makes the following points about lighting in the workplace.

- Lighting should be sufficient to enable people to work, use facilities and move from place to place safely and without experiencing eye-strain. Stairs should be well-lit in such a way that shadows are not cast over the main part of the treads. Where necessary, local lighting should be provided at individual workstations, and at places of particular risk such as pedestrian crossing points on vehicular traffic routes. Outdoor traffic routes used by pedestrians should be adequately lit after dark.

- Dazzling lights and annoying glare should be avoided. Lights and light fittings should be of a type, and so positioned, that they do not cause a hazard (including electrical, fire, radiation or collision hazards). Light switches should be positioned so that they may be found and used easily and without risk.

- Lights should not be allowed to become obscured, for example by stacked goods, in such a way that the level of light becomes insufficient. Lights should be replaced, repaired or cleaned, as necessary, before the level of lighting becomes insufficient. Fittings or lights should be replaced immediately if they become dangerous, electrically or otherwise.

- Windows and skylights should where possible be cleaned regularly and kept free from unnecessary obstructions to admit maximum daylight. Where this would result in excessive heat or glare at a workstation, however, the workstation should be repositioned or the window or skylight should be shaded.

- The normal precautions required by these and other regulations, for example on the prevention of falls and fencing of dangerous parts of machinery, mean that workers are not in most cases 'specially exposed' to risk if normal lighting fails. Emergency lighting is not therefore essential in most cases. Emergency lighting should, however, be provided in workrooms where sudden loss of light would present a serious risk, for example if process plant needs to be shut down under manual control or if a potentially hazardous process needs to be made safe, and this cannot be done safely without lighting.

- Emergency lighting should be powered by a source independent from that of normal lighting. It should be immediately effective in the event of failure of the normal lighting, without need for action by anyone. It should provide sufficient light to enable persons at work to take any action necessary to ensure their, and others', health and safety.

The quantity of light

The current criteria for deciding what is sufficient lighting are the recommended average and minimum measured illuminance published in HSE Guidance Note HS(G)38: *Lighting at Work*.

Light flow or 'illuminance' is the quantity of light emitted from a light source, such as a fluorescent strip or a bulb. Lighting is measured quantitatively in Lux. Average and minimum measured illuminances (in Lux) are based on both the general activity undertaken and the type of work location and/or work carried out. No maximum illuminance level is specified. See Tables 5 and 6 below.

General activity	Typical locations/ types of work	Average illuminance Lux (Lx)	Minimum measured illuminance Lux (Lx)
Movement of people, machines and vehicles	Lorry parks, corridors, circulation routes	20	5
Movement of people, machines and vehicles in hazardous areas; rough work not requiring any perception of detail (1)	Construction site clearance, excavation and soil work, docks, loading bays, bottling and canning plants	50	20

General activity	Typical locations/ types of work	Average illuminance Lux (Lx)	Minimum measured illuminance Lux (Lx)
Work requiring limited perception of detail (2)	Kitchens, factories assembling large components, potteries	100	50
Work requiring perception of detail (2)	Offices, sheet metal work, bookbinding	200	100
Work requiring perception of fine detail (2)	Drawing offices, factories assembling electronic components, textile production	500	200

Table 5: Average illuminances and minimum measured illuminances for different types of work

Notes

1. Only safety has been considered, because no perception of detail is needed and visual fatigue is unlikely. However, where it is necessary to see detail, to recognize a hazard or where error in performing the task could put someone else at risk, for safety purposes as well as to avoid visual fatigue, the figure should be increased to that for work requiring the perception of detail.

2. The purpose is to avoid visual fatigue; the illuminances will be adequate for safety purposes.

Situations to which recommendation applies	Typical location	Maximum ratio of illuminances	
		Working area	Adjacent area
Where each task is individually lit and the area around the task is lit to a lower illuminance	Local lighting in an office	5	1
Where two working areas are adjacent, but one is lit to a lower illuminance than the other	Localized lighting in a works store	5	1
Where two working areas are lit to different illuminances and are separated by a barrier but there is frequent movement between them	A storage area inside a factory and a loading bay outside	10	1

Table 6: Maximum ratios of illuminance for adjacent areas

Lighting of the work area and adjacent areas is important. Large differences between them may cause visual discomfort or even affect safety in places where there is frequent movement of traffic. This problem arises most often where local or localized lighting in an interior exposes a person to a range of illuminances for a long time, or where there is movement between interior and exterior working areas exposing a person to sudden changes of illuminance.

To guard against danger and discomfort the recommendations in the Table should be followed.

Recommended lighting levels

The Chartered Institution of Building Services Engineers (CIBSE) recommend the following lighting levels (measurements in Lux):

1.	**Commercial offices**	
	General offices	500
	Computer workstations	300 – 500
	Conference rooms, executive offices	500
	Computer and data preparation rooms	500
	Filing rooms	300
2.	**Banks and building societies**	
	Counter, office area	500
	Public area	300
3.	**Hotels**	
	Entrance halls	100
	Reception, cashier's and porter's desks	300
	Bars, coffee bars, dining rooms, grill rooms, restaurants, lounges	50 – 200
	Cloakrooms, baggage rooms	100
	Bedrooms	50 – 100
	Bathrooms	150
4.	**Retailing**	
	Small retail outlets	500
	Grocery/vegetable stores	500
	Hypermarkets/superstores	1000
	Showrooms	500 – 750
	Covered arcades and malls	50 – 300

Table 7: Recommended lighting levels

The quality of lighting

Average illuminance and minimum measured illuminance relate to the quantity of light for a particular task. For lighting to be suitable, it is necessary to consider the qualitative aspects of lighting and the design of lighting.

The following aspects are significant in the design of lighting for workstations and installations.

Glare

This is the effect of light which causes impaired vision or discomfort, and is experienced when parts of the visual field are excessively bright compared with the general surroundings. Glare, in its various forms, can be a contributory factor in accidents.

Glare is experienced in three forms:

a) disability glare – the visually disabling effect caused by bright bare lamps directly in the line of sight;

b) discomfort glare – the visual discomfort caused mainly by too much contrast of brightness between an object and its background; and

c) reflected glare – where the reflection of bright light sources on wet or shiny work surfaces, such as plated metal or glass, can almost conceal the detail in or behind the surface which is glinting.

Distribution

The way in which light is distributed or spread is an important feature of lighting design. The British Zonal Method classifies luminaires (light fittings) according to the way in which they distribute light from BZ1 (all light down in a narrow column) to BZ10 (light in all directions).

This is particularly important where it may be necessary to illuminate danger areas and hazards arising from machinery.

Colour rendition

This refers to the appearance of an object under a given light source compared with its colour under a reference illuminant e.g. natural light. Colour rendition enables correct perception of the colour. Incorrect perception of colour by an individual can be a contributory factor in incidents involving, for instance, electricity supply e.g. incorrect wiring of a fitting.

Diffusion

This is the projection of light in many directions with no directional predominance. Diffused lighting, in many cases, will reduce or soften the output from a particular source and so limit the amount of glare that may be encountered from bare fittings. To be effective, diffusers must be cleaned on a regular basis.

Lighting maintenance

There is an absolute duty on employers to maintain the workplace, equipment, systems and devices 'in an efficient state, in efficient working order and in good repair'. This includes lighting systems and fittings.

A planned preventative maintenance programme, including the keeping of records of assessment and maintenance, is necessary to ensure compliance with this general duty. On this basis, lighting maintenance should feature in an organization's planned preventative maintenance programme. This should include regular cleaning and replacement of lamps, maintenance of systems and fittings, together with regular assessment of illuminance using a standard photometer (light meter) in order to ensure these illuminances are maintained.

Emergency lighting arrangements

Emergency lighting may be necessary in any part of a workplace where danger can arise from a failure of the lighting system. In the event of the artificial lighting system failing, the emergency lighting arrangements should come into operation. This takes two forms:

    a)   standby lighting – which enables essential work to continue; and

    b)   escape lighting – which enables a building to be evacuated safely.

Current fire safety legislation requires the lighting of escape routes.

Standby lighting

Much will depend upon the nature of the work undertaken and the risks arising from same. It may be between 5% and 100% of the illuminance level currently provided.

Escape lighting

The general recommendation is that escape lighting should reach the necessary illuminance level within five seconds of the failure of the principal lighting system, although if the occupants are familiar with the layout of the premises this may be increased to 15 seconds.

Escape lighting may take the form of battery-powered installations designed to operate for between one and three hours according to the size of the premises and problems arising from evacuation. Other systems powered by generators will operate for as long as the generator functions and should at least match the operating times of battery-powered installations.

> **See:**
>
> • *Display screen equipment*

Lone workers

What is a lone worker?

A 'lone worker' or 'solitary worker' is defined as anyone who works alone out of contact with other persons. A housing officer, clerk of works and project staff may, for example, be classified as lone workers even though they may be in contact with other people, such as customers, sub-contractors or suppliers.

General duties of employers

Whilst there is no specific legal prohibition on lone working, the employer must, under the MHSWR, plan, organize, control, monitor and review the activities of lone workers to ensure that they are not subjected to any more significant risks than other employees who may work together.

There is also a general duty on employers, under the HSWA to ensure, so far as is reasonably practicable, a safe system of work, safe access to, and safe egress from, the workplace.

Lone working arrangements

In the design of systems of work involving lone working, the following factors should be considered:

- careful selection of operators who are fit, competent and reliable;

- the need to undertake a suitable and sufficient risk assessment of the lone working activity, which must be kept under review, together with regular monitoring of individual performance;

- the operators concerned must be provided with such information, instruction and training so that they are quite clear as to all the significant foreseeable risks which may arise and the measures they must take to ensure their own safety and the safety of other persons;

- a formally established safe system of work, such as a Permit to Work system, which incorporates detailed emergency procedures, must always be operated;

- suitable and sufficient communication must be maintained, such as a radio or telephone-based buddy system, central control or electronic monitoring incorporating non-body movement indication/panic alarm and radio/satellite location, appropriate to the environment in which operators may be working; and

- there must be adequate recognition of the more serious consequences for lone workers of fatigue and stress whilst travelling or undertaking their particular duties.

See:

- *Confined spaces*
- *Homeworking*
- *Permit to Work systems*
- *Risk assessment*
- *Work away from base*

M

Machinery and work equipment

Injuries associated with machinery and various forms of work equipment are common. Such injuries include amputations of limbs and parts of limbs, crushing injuries, entanglement of limbs, clothing and hair in moving parts of machinery, injuries associated with items being emitted from machines and various contact injuries, such as burns, where people come into contact with hot surfaces of machinery and plant.

Principles of machinery safety

Any accident prevention strategy must, therefore, be directed to reducing the objective danger from machinery through the use of well-designed machinery guarding systems and various forms of safety device aimed at preventing the operator or other persons from coming anywhere near the danger points or areas of a machine. This should be supported by the provision of information, instruction, training and supervision directed at increasing people's perception of risk.

Current legal requirements are incorporated in the HSWA and Provision and Use of Work Equipment Regulations 1998 (PUWER). HSE Guidance Notes, particularly those in the Plant and Machinery series of Guidance Notes, together with British Standard EN ISO 12100 *Safety of Machinery,* provide excellent guidance on this matter.

BS EN ISO 12100 defines a 'machine' as 'an apparatus for applying power having fixed and moving parts, each with definite functions'. Machines have:

a) **operational parts**, which perform the primary output function of the machine, for instance, the manufacture of a product or a component; and

b) **non-operational** or **functional parts**, which convey power or motion to the operational parts, for instance, drives to motors.

The functional parts comprise the prime mover and transmission machinery, defined as follows:

- **Prime mover** means any engine, motor or other appliance which provides mechanical energy derived from steam, water, wind, electricity, the combustion of fuel or other source.

- **Transmission machinery** means every shaft, wheel, pulley, drum, system of fast and loose pulleys, coupling, clutch, driving belt or other device by which the motion of a prime mover is transmitted to, or received by, any machine or appliance.

Work equipment risk assessment

This should take into account:

- design features of the equipment – the form and distribution of harm;

- the actual persons at risk – operator, supervisor, third parties – and general circumstances of operation; and

- specific hazardous features of the work equipment and events that could lead to injury

- together with the requirements of PUWER.

Machinery hazards

Many machines, including new machines, incorporate hazards in their basic design. These hazards can be classified as follows:

1. Traps

Traps can take a number of forms:

a) **reciprocating trap** – these may have an up and down motion e.g. presses; at the point where the injury occurs, the limb is stationary;

b) **shearing trap** – these have a guillotine effect; and

c) **in-running nips** – these are to be found on rollers, conveyors and gears.

2. Entanglement

This entails the risk of entanglement of hair, clothing and limbs in, for instance, revolving shafts, line shafts, chucks and drills.

3. Ejection

Ejection involves the emission or throwing off of particles from a machine e.g. abrasive wheels, disintegration of swarf on a lathe.

4. Contact

Contact with a machine at a particular point can cause injury e.g. heat, temperature extremes, sharp projections, as in plastic moulding machines, circular saws.

General circumstances involving operators and others

The tasks that people undertake can be a source of danger e.g. job loading and removal, tool changing, waste removal, operation of process, routine and emergency maintenance, gauging, breakdown situations and trying out. Another source of danger can be associated with unauthorized presence and/or use.

Specific events leading to injury

Events leading to machinery-related injuries vary considerably. Typical events include:

a) unexpected start-up or movement;

b) reaching into a feed device;

c) uncovenanted stroke by a machine; and

d) machine failure.

Safeguarding of machinery

BS EN ISO 12100 defines a 'safeguard' as 'a guard or device to protect persons from danger'. In the Standard, "danger" is defined thus: 'When applied to machinery in motion, it is a situation in which there is a reasonably foreseeable risk of injury from the mechanical hazards referred to in clause 6'. (See above)

It should be noted that the law defines machinery as 'dangerous' when 'it is a possible cause of injury to anybody acting in a way in which a human being may be reasonably expected to act in circumstances which may reasonably expected to occur'. (*Walker v Bletchley Flettons Ltd [1973] 1 AER 170*)

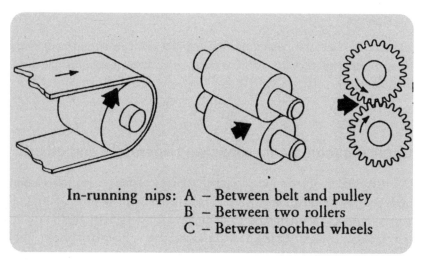

In-running nips: A – Between belt and pulley
B – Between two rollers
C – Between toothed wheels

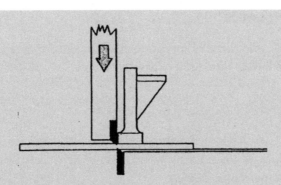

Shearing traps – A moving part traversing a fixed part.

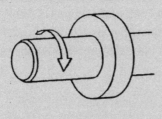

Entanglement risks

Nip

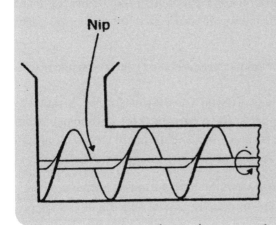

Machinery guards

Fundamentally, there are five specific forms of machinery guard. In many cases they are linked with a safety device.

Fixed guard

This is a guard which has no moving parts associated with it, or dependent on the mechanism of any machinery, and which, when in position, prevents access to a danger point or area.

This form of guard is designed to prevent all access to the dangerous parts and is principally used to cover non-operational parts. Many fixed guards are solid castings, sheet metal (minimum 18 SWG – 1.22 mm), perforated or expanded metal (minimum 17 SWG), 'Weldmesh' (minimum 14 SWG), safety glass panels or polycarbonate panels. Wood as a guard material is not recommended, except where there may be a risk of electric shock.

Interlocking guard

This is a guard which has a movable part so connected with the machinery controls that

a) the part(s) of the machinery causing danger cannot be set in motion until the guard is closed;

b) the power is switched off and the motion braked before the guard can be opened sufficiently to allow access to the dangerous parts; and

c) access to the danger point or area is denied while the danger exists.

It is also defined as a moving guard which, in the closed position, prevents all access to the dangerous parts. The control gear for starting up cannot be operated until the guard is fully closed, and the guard cannot be opened until the dangerous parts are at rest.

For a true interlock system, everything must be at rest before the guard or gate can be opened. Some interlocks control only the power supply, and others, the power supply and the movement. In order to achieve the same level of safety as with fixed guards, the reliability and maintenance of interlocking guards are significant.

Methods of interlocking include:

a) mechanical;

b) electro-mechanical;

c) pneumatic (compressed air);

d) hydraulic (electro) – use of hydraulic fluid to vary pressure;

e) key exchange (electrical); and

f) simple electrical.

Automatic guard

This is a guard which is associated with, and dependent upon, the mechanism of the machinery and operates so as to remove physically from the danger area any part of a person exposed to danger.

These guards incorporate a device so fitted in relation to the dangerous parts that the operator is automatically prevented from contacting same e.g. heavy power presses, press brakes, paper-cutting guillotines. The guard is independent of the operator.

The function of an automatic guard is to remove the operator from the dangerous parts of the machine by means of a moving barrier or arm. There is some degree of risk in that the operator can be injured by the moving barrier, and this type of guard is only suitable for large slow-moving barriers as on presses. These guards operate on a side to side, sweep away or push out motion.

Automatic guards have a number of disadvantages e.g.

a) risk of injury to the operator as a result of the sweep-away motion;

b) the linkages to the motion must be rigidly connected as they can become loose through constant use;

c) when the linkages become worn the guard is often racing the tools to maintain safe operation (and can lose!); and

d) they need extensive careful maintenance and frequent inspection.

Distance guard

This is a guard which does not completely enclose a danger point or area but which places it out of normal reach. This may incorporate a tunnel, fixed grill or rail positioned at sufficient distance so that access to the moving parts cannot be gained except by a deliberate unsafe act.

Adjustable guard

This is a guard incorporating an adjustable element which, once adjusted, remains in that position during a particular operation. Such a guard is the least reliable form of guard in that it requires the operator to adjust same prior to operation of the machine. Adjustable guards feature in woodworking machinery in particular e.g. circular saws and band saws. See Figure 9: Machinery guards.

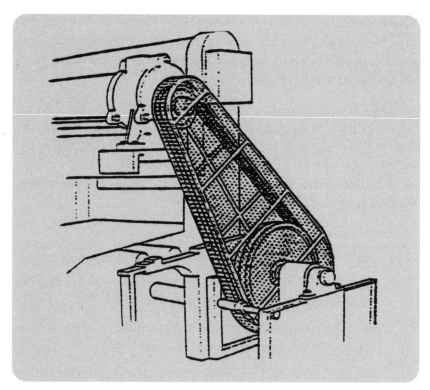

Fig 9: Machinery guards – fixed guard to transmission machinery

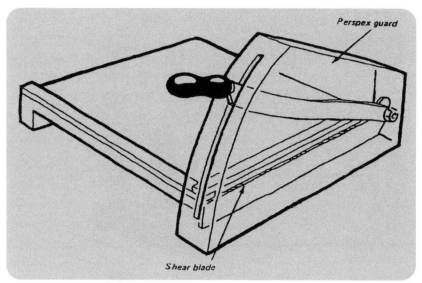

Fig 9: Machinery guards – fixed guard to hand-operated guillotine

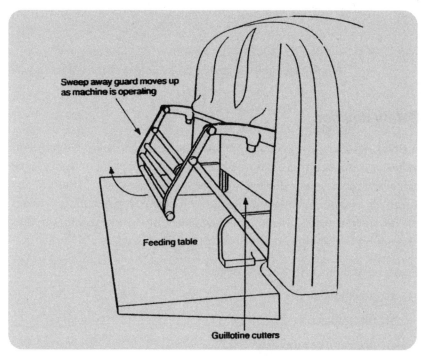

Fig 9: Machinery guards – fixed guard to power-operated guillotine

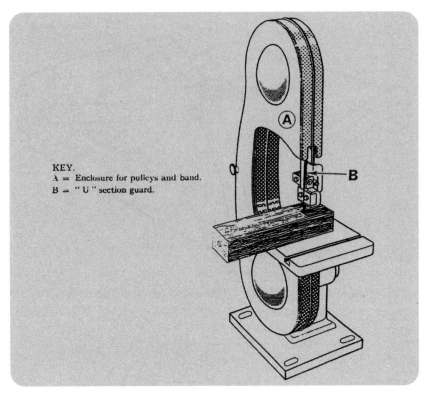

KEY.
A = Enclosure for pulleys and band.
B = " U " section guard.

Fig 9: Machinery guards – adjustable guard for a band saw

Safety devices

A safety device is a protective appliance, other than a guard, which eliminates or reduces danger before access to a danger point or area can be achieved. Most safety devices operate on a trip system whereby any approach by a person beyond the safe limit of working machinery causes the device to actuate and stop the machinery, or reverse its motion, thus preventing or minimizing injury at the danger point.

There are various forms of trip device:

    a)   mechanical;

    b)   photo-electric;

    c)   pressure sensitive mat;

    d)   ultrasonic device;

e) two-hand control device;

f) over-run device; and

g) mechanical restraint device.

The safety of hand tools

The abuse and misuse of hand tools frequently result in injuries, many of which are of a serious nature, e.g. amputations of fingers, blinding, severing of arteries as a result of deep cuts. They account for approximately 10% of all lost-time injuries.

As with other forms of work equipment, hand tools should be maintained in an efficient state, in efficient working order and in good repair. This implies the need for frequent inspection of hand tools to ensure their relative safety. Furthermore, the correct use of hand tools should be ensured through training and regular supervision of users. Hand tools used by contractors and their employees should also be subject to regular examination.

Hand tool inspections

A number of points should be considered when examining hand tools.

Chisels

'Mushroomed' chisel heads are a frequent cause of blinding and eye injuries and any mushrooming should be removed through grinding. Chisel heads should be kept free from dirt, oil and grease.

Hammers

The shaft should be in sound condition and soundly fixed to the head. Where the shaft is split, loose to the head, broken or damaged, it should be replaced. Chipped, rounded or badly worn hammer heads should not be used, and heads should be kept free of oil and grease.

Files

A file should never be used without a handle, and the handle should be in sound condition. Evidence of chips and other signs of damage indicate a file could be dangerous.

Spanners

Open-end spanners which are splayed or box spanners with splits should be discarded. Adjustable spanners and monkey wrenches should be examined regularly for evidence of free play and splaying of the jaws.

Screwdrivers

Handles and tips should be in sound condition and worn-ended screwdrivers should never be used. A screwdriver should never be used as a chisel and when using a screwdriver, the work should be clamped or secured, never held in the hand. Employees must be trained to use the correct size screwdriver at all times.

Provision and Use of Work Equipment Regulations 1998

The Regulations are supported by guidance prepared by the HSE and HSC. The majority of the requirements are of an absolute nature.

Important definitions

Inspection in relation to an inspection under paragraph 1 or 2 of Regulation 6:

a) means such visual or more rigorous inspection by a competent person as is appropriate for the purpose described in that paragraph;

b) where it is appropriate to carry out testing for the purpose, includes testing the nature and extent of which are appropriate for the purpose.

Thorough inspection in relation to a thorough examination under paragraph 1, 2, 3 or 4 of Regulation 32:

a) means a thorough examination by a competent person;

b) includes testing the nature and extent of which are appropriate for the purpose described in the paragraph.

'**Work equipment**' means any machinery, appliance, apparatus or tool or installation for use at work (whether exclusively or not).

'**Use**' in relation to work equipment means any activity involving work equipment and includes starting, stopping, programming, setting, transporting, repairing, modifying, maintaining, servicing and cleaning.

Principal requirements of the regulations

- Every employer shall ensure that work equipment is so constructed or adapted as to be suitable for the purpose for which it is used or provided.

- In selecting work equipment, every employer shall have regard to the working conditions and the risks to health and safety of persons which exist in the premises or undertaking in which that work equipment is to be used and any additional risk posed by the use of that work equipment.

- Every employer shall ensure that work equipment is used only for operations for which, and under conditions for which, it is suitable.

- 'Suitable' means suitable in any respect which it is reasonably foreseeable will affect the health or safety of any person.

- Every employer shall ensure that work equipment is maintained in an efficient state, in efficient working order and in good repair.

- Every employer shall ensure that where any machinery has a maintenance log, the log is kept up to date.

- Every employer shall ensure that, where the safety of work equipment depends on the installation conditions, it is inspected:
  a) after installation and before being put into service for the first time; or
  b) after assembly at a new site or in a new location, to ensure that it has been installed correctly and is safe to operate.

- Every employer shall ensure that work equipment exposed to conditions causing deterioration which is liable to result in dangerous situations is inspected:

  a) at suitable intervals; and

  b) each time that exceptional circumstances which are liable to jeopardize the safety of the work equipment have occurred, to ensure that health and safety conditions are maintained and that any deterioration can be detected and remedied in good time.

- Every employer shall ensure that the result of an inspection made under this Regulation is recorded and kept until the next inspection under this Regulation is recorded.

- Every employer shall ensure that no work equipment:

  a) leaves his undertaking; or

  b) is obtained from the undertaking of another person, is used in his undertaking, unless it is accompanied by physical evidence that the last inspection required to be carried out under this Regulation has been carried out.

- Where the use of work equipment is likely to involve a specific risk to health or safety, every employer shall ensure that

  a) the use of that work equipment is restricted to those persons given the task of using it; and

  b) repairs, modifications, maintenance or servicing of that work equipment is restricted to those persons who have been specifically designated to perform operations of that description (whether or not also authorized to perform other operations).

- The employer shall ensure that the persons designated for the purposes of paragraph 1(b) above have received adequate training related to any operations in respect of which they have been so designated.

- Every employer shall ensure that all persons who use work equipment have available to them adequate health and safety information and, where appropriate, written instructions pertaining to the use of that work equipment.

- Every employer shall ensure that any of his employees who supervises or manages the use of work equipment has available to him adequate health and safety information and, where appropriate, written instructions pertaining to the use of that work equipment.

- The information and instructions required shall include information and, where appropriate, written instructions on

  a) the conditions in which, and the methods by which, the work equipment may be used;

  b) foreseeable abnormal situations and the action to be taken if such a situation were to occur; and

  c) any conclusions to be drawn from experience in using the work equipment.

- Information and instruction shall be readily comprehensible to those concerned.

- Every employer shall ensure that all persons who use work equipment have received adequate training for the purposes of health and safety, including training in the methods which may be adopted when using the work equipment, any risks which such use may entail and the precautions to be taken.

- Every employer shall ensure that any of his employees who supervises or manages the use of work equipment has received adequate training for purposes of health and safety, including training in the methods which may be adopted when using the work equipment, any risks which such use may entail and precautions to be taken.

- Every employer shall ensure that any item of work equipment provided conforms at all times with any essential requirements, other than requirements which, at the time of its being first supplied or put into service in any place in which these Regulations apply, did not apply to work equipment of its type.

- In this regulation **essential requirements**, in relation to any item of work equipment, means requirements relating to the design and construction of work equipment of its type in any of the instruments listed in Schedule 1 (being instruments which give effect to Community directives concerning the safety of products).

- Every employer shall ensure that measures are taken in accordance with the paragraph below which are effective:

  a) to prevent access to any dangerous part of machinery to any rotating stock-bar; or

  b) to stop the movement of any dangerous part of machinery or rotating stock-bar before any part of a person enters a danger zone.

- The measures required by the above paragraph shall consist of:

  a) the provision of fixed guards enclosing every dangerous part or rotating stock-bar where and to the extent that it is practicable to do so, but where or to the extent that it is not, then

  b) the provision of other guards or protection devices where and to the extent that it is practicable to do so, but where or to the extent that it is not, then

  c) the provision of jigs, holders, push-sticks or similar protection appliances used in conjunction with the machinery where and to the extent that it is practicable to do so,

  and the provision of information, instruction, training and supervision as is necessary.

- All guards and protection devices shall -

  a) be suitable for the purpose for which they are provided;

  b) be of good construction, sound material and adequate strength;

  c) be maintained in an efficient state, in efficient working order and in good repair;

  d) not give rise to any increased risk to health or safety;

  e) not be easily bypassed or disabled;

  f) be situated at sufficient distance from the danger zone;

  g) not unduly restrict the view of the operating cycle of the machinery, where such a view is necessary;

  h) be so constructed or adapted that they allow operations necessary to fit or replace parts and for maintenance work, restricting access so that it is allowed only to the area where the work is to be carried out and, if possible, without having to dismantle the guard or protection device.

- Every employer shall take measures to ensure that the exposure of a person using work equipment to any risk to his health or safety from any hazard specified in the paragraph below is either prevented, or, where that is not reasonably practicable, adequately controlled.

- The measures required by the above paragraph shall

    a) be measures other than the provision of personal protective equipment or of information, instruction, training and supervision, so far as is reasonably practicable; and

    b) include, where appropriate, measures to minimize the effects of the hazard as well as to reduce the likelihood of the hazard occurring.

- The hazards referred to above are

    a) any article or substance falling or being ejected from work equipment;

    b) rupture or disintegration of parts of work equipment;

    c) work equipment catching fire or overheating;

    d) the unintended or premature discharge of any article or of any gas, dust, liquid, vapour or other substance which, in each case, is produced, used or stored in the work equipment;

    e) the unintended or premature explosion of the work equipment or any article or substance produced, used or stored in it.

- 'Adequate' means adequate having regard only to the nature of the hazard and the nature and degree of exposure to the risk.

- Every employer shall ensure that work equipment, parts of work equipment and any article or substance produced, used or stored in work equipment which, in each case, is at a high or very low temperature shall have protection where appropriate so as to prevent injury to any person by burn, scald or sear.

- Every employer shall ensure that, where appropriate, work equipment is provided with one or more controls for the purposes of:

  a) starting the work equipment (including re-starting after a stoppage for any reason); or

  b) controlling any change in the speed, pressure or other operating conditions of the work equipment where such conditions after the change result in risk to health and safety which is greater than, or of a different nature from, such risks before the change.

- Every employer shall ensure that where a control is required by paragraph 1, it shall not be possible to perform any operation mentioned above except by a deliberate action on such control.

- Every employer shall ensure that, where appropriate, work equipment is provided with one or more readily accessible controls the operation of which will bring the work equipment to a safe condition in a safe manner.

- Any control required by the above paragraph shall bring the work equipment to a complete stop where necessary for reasons of health and safety.

- Any control shall, if necessary for reasons of health and safety, switch off all sources of energy after stopping the functioning of the work equipment.

- Any control shall operate in priority to any control which starts or changes the operating conditions of the work equipment.

- Every employer shall ensure that, where appropriate, work equipment is provided with one or more emergency stop controls unless it is not necessary by reason of the nature of the hazards and the time taken for the work equipment to come to a complete stop as a result of the action of any control.

- Every employer shall ensure that all controls for work equipment shall be clearly visible and identifiable, including by appropriate marking where necessary.

- Except where necessary, the employer shall ensure that no control for work equipment is in a position where any person operating the control is exposed to risk to his health or safety.

- Every employer shall ensure where appropriate:

  a) that, so far as is reasonably practicable, the operator of any control is able to ensure from the position of that control that no person is in a place where he would be exposed to any risk to his health or safety as a result of the operation of that control, but where or to the extent that it is not reasonably practicable;

  b) that, so far as is reasonably practicable, systems of work are effective to ensure that, when work equipment is about to start, no person is in a place where he would be exposed to a risk to his health or safety as a result of the work equipment starting, but where neither of these is reasonably practicable;

  c) that an audible, visible or other suitable warning is given by virtue of Regulation 24 whenever work equipment is about to start.

- Every employer shall ensure, so far as is reasonably practicable, that all control systems of work equipment are:

  a) safe; and

  b) chosen to make due allowance for the failures, faults and constraints to be expected in the planned circumstances of use.

- A control system shall not be safe unless

  a) its operation does not create an increased risk to health or safety;

  b) it ensures, so far as is reasonably practicable, that any fault in, or damage to, any part of the control system or the loss of supply of any source of energy used by the work equipment cannot result in additional or increased risk to health or safety;

  c) it does not impede the operation of any control required by Regulation 15 or 16.

- Every employer shall ensure that where appropriate work equipment is provided with suitable means to isolate it from all its sources of energy.

- The means mentioned above shall not be suitable unless they are clearly identifiable and readily accessible.

- Every employer shall take appropriate measures to ensure that reconnection of any energy source to work equipment does not expose any person using the work equipment to any risk to his health or safety.

- Every employer shall ensure that work equipment or any part of work equipment is stabilized by clamping or otherwise where necessary for purposes of health or safety.

- Every employer shall ensure that suitable and sufficient lighting, which takes account of the operations to be carried out, is provided at any place where a person uses work equipment.

- Every employer shall take appropriate measures to ensure that work equipment is so constructed or adapted that, so far as is reasonably practicable, maintenance operations which involve a risk to health or safety can be carried out while the work equipment is shut down or, in other cases

    a) maintenance operations can be carried out without exposing the person carrying them out to a risk to his health or safety; or

    b) appropriate measures can be taken for the protection of any person carrying out maintenance operations which involve a risk to his health or safety.

- Every employer shall ensure that work equipment is marked in a clearly visible manner with any marking appropriate for reasons of health and safety.

- Every employer shall ensure that work equipment incorporates any warnings or warning devices which are appropriate for the reasons of health and safety.

- Warnings given by warning devices on work equipment shall not be appropriate unless they are unambiguous, easily perceived and easily understood.

- Every employer shall ensure that no employee is carried by mobile work equipment unless:

    a) it is suitable for carrying persons; and

    b) it incorporates features for reducing to as low as is reasonably practicable risks to their safety, including risks from wheels and tracks.

- Every employer shall ensure that, where there is a risk to an employee riding on mobile work equipment from its rolling over, it is minimized by:

    a) stabilizing the work equipment;

    b) a structure which ensures that the work equipment does no more than fall on its side;

    c) a structure giving sufficient clearance to anyone being carried if it overturns further than that; or

    d) a device giving comparable protection.

- Where there is a risk of anyone being carried by mobile work equipment being crushed by its rolling over, the employer shall ensure that it has a suitable restraining system for him.

- Every employer shall ensure that a fork-lift truck that carries an employee is adapted or equipped to reduce to as low as is reasonably practicable the risk to safety from its overturning.

- Every employer shall ensure that, where self-propelled work equipment may, while in motion, involve risk to the safety of persons:

    a) it has facilities for preventing it being started by anyone other than an unauthorized person;

    b) it has appropriate facilities for minimizing the consequences of a collision where there is more than one item of rail-mounted work equipment in motion at the same time;

    c) it has a device for braking and stopping;

    d) where safety constraints so require, emergency facilities operated by readily accessible controls or automatic systems are available for braking and stopping the work equipment in the event of failure of the main facility;

    e) where the driver's direct field of vision is inadequate to ensure safety, there are adequate devices for improving his vision so far as is reasonably practicable;

    f) if provided for use at night or in dark places:

        i) it is equipped with lighting appropriate to the work being carried out; and

ii) it is otherwise sufficiently safe for such use;

g) if it, or anything carried or towed by it, constitutes a fire hazard and is liable to endanger employees, it carries appropriate fire-fighting equipment unless such equipment is kept sufficiently close to it.

- Every employer shall ensure that where remote-controlled self-propelled work equipment involves a risk to safety while in motion:

   a) it stops automatically once it leaves its control range; and

   b) where the risk is of crushing or impact it incorporates features guard against such risk unless other appropriate devices are able to do so.

- Where the seizure of the drive shaft between mobile work equipment and its accessories or anything towed is likely to involve a risk to safety every employer shall:

   a) ensure that the work equipment has a means of preventing such seizure; or

   b) where such seizure cannot be avoided, take every possible measure to avoid an adverse effect on the safety of an employee.

- Every employer shall ensure that:

   a) where mobile work equipment has a shaft for the transmission of energy between it and other mobile work equipment; and

   b) the shaft could become soiled or damaged by contact with the ground while uncoupled, the work equipment has a system for safeguarding the shaft.

- Every employer shall ensure that a power press is not put into service for the first time after installation, or after assembly at a new site or in a new location unless:

   a) it has been thoroughly examined to ensure that it:

      i)   has been installed correctly; and

      ii) would be safe to operate; and

   b) any defect has been remedied.

- Every employer shall ensure that a guard, other than one to which paragraph 3 relates, or protection device is not put into service for the first time on a power press unless:

    a) it has been thoroughly examined when in position on that power press to ensure that it is effective for its purpose; and

    b) any defect has been remedied.

- Every employer shall ensure that a part of a closed tool which acts as a fixed guard is not used on a power press unless:

    a) it has been thoroughly examined when in position on any power press in the premises to ensure that it is effective for its purpose; and

    b) any defect has been remedied.

- For the purpose of ensuring that health and safety conditions are maintained, and that any deterioration can be detected and remedied in good time, every employer shall ensure that:

    a) every power press is thoroughly examined, and its guards and protection devices are thoroughly examined when in position on that power press:

        i) at least every 12 months, where it has fixed guards only; or

        ii) at least every six months, in other cases; and

        iii) each time that exceptional circumstances have occurred which are liable to jeopardize the safety of the power press or its guards or protection devices; and

    b) any defect is remedied before the power press is used again.

- Every employer shall ensure that a power press is not used after the setting, re-setting or adjustments of its tools, save in trying out its tools or save in die proving, unless:

    a) its every guard and protection device has been inspected and tested while in position on the power press by a person appointed in writing by the employer who is:

        i) competent; or

ii) undergoing training for that purpose and acting under the immediate supervision of a competent person;

and who has signed a certificate which complies with paragraph 3; or

b) the guards and protection devices have not been altered or disturbed in the course of the adjustment of its tools.

- Every employer shall ensure that a power press is not used after the expiration of the fourth hour of a working period unless its every guard and protection device has been inspected and tested while in position on the power press by a person appointed in writing by the employer who is:

a) competent; or

b) undergoing training for that purpose and acting under the immediate supervision of a competent person;

and who has signed a certificate that complies with paragraph 3.

- A certificate shall:

a) contain sufficient particulars to identify every guard and protection device inspected and tested and the power press on which it was positioned at the time of the inspection and test;

b) state the date and time of the inspection and test; and

c) state that every guard and protection device on the power press is in position and effective for its purpose.

- 'Working period', in relation to a power press, means:

a) the period in which the day's or night's work is done; or

b) in premises where a shift system is in operation, a shift.

- A person making a thorough examination for an employer shall:

a) notify the employer forthwith of any defect in a power press or its guard or protection device which in his opinion is, or could become, a danger to persons;

b) as soon as is practicable make a report of the thorough examination to the employer in writing authenticated by him or on his behalf by signature or equally secure means and containing the information specified in Schedule 3; and

c) where there is in his opinion a defect in a power press or its guard or protection device which is or could become a danger to persons send a copy of the report as soon as is practicable to the enforcing authority for the premises in which the power press is situated.

- A person making an inspection and test for an employer shall forthwith notify the employer of any defect in a guard or protection device which in his opinion is, or could become, a danger to persons and the reason for his opinion.

- Every employer shall ensure that the information in every report is kept available for inspection for two years after it is made.

- Every employer shall ensure that a certificate is kept available for inspection:

a) at or near the power press to which it relates until superseded by a later certificate; and

b) after that, until six months have passed since it was signed.

Second-hand, hired and leased work equipment

Second-hand equipment

In situations where existing work equipment is sold by one organization to another and brought into use by the second organization, it becomes 'new equipment' and must meet the requirements for such equipment, even though it is second-hand. This means that the purchasing organization will need to ascertain that the equipment meets the specific hardware provisions of regulations 11 to 24 of PUWER before putting it into use.

Hired and leased equipment

Such equipment is treated in the same way as second-hand equipment, namely that it is classed as 'new equipment' at the hire/lease stage. On this basis, organizations hiring or leasing an item of work equipment must ensure that it meets the requirements of regulations 11 to 24 of PUWER before putting it into use.

> **See:**
>
> - *Information, instruction and training*
> - *Lifting operations, machinery and equipment*
> - *Lifts*
> - *Lighting in the workplace*
> - *Mechanical handling*
> - *Mobile work equipment*
> - *Powered working platforms*
> - *Power presses*
> - *Pressure systems*
> - *Risk assessment*

Maintenance operations

Maintenance work is frequently undertaken at locations. This work may be undertaken by an organization's own employees or by contractors and could include, for instance, rewiring of premises, boiler servicing, repairs to roofs, plumbing work, maintenance of equipment, such as wheelchairs, redecoration and renovation work.

The principal hazards

The principal hazards associated with maintenance operations can be classified thus:

- **Mechanical** – trapping, entanglement, contact and ejection hazards associated with machinery and equipment.

- **Electrical** – the risk of electrocution, shock or burns.

- **Pressure** – unexpected pressure releases and/or explosions.

- **Physical** – health risks arising from exposure to extremes of temperature, noise, vibration, dust and fume.

- **Chemical** – health risks arising from exposure to gases, fogs, mists, fumes, etc.

- **Structural** – contact with obstructions, falls through floor openings.

- **Access** – work at heights or entry into confined spaces.

Precautions

A number of both general and specific precautions are necessary for these types of activity, in particular:

a) the operation of safe systems of work, in certain cases Permit to Work systems;

b) designation of competent persons for certain high risk operations, e.g. electrical installation and repairs to appliances;

c) the use of Method Statements, particularly where contractors may be involved in maintenance operations;

d) enforcement of the organization's Contractors' Regulations where contractors are involved;

e) designation of controlled areas, to which access is limited, where there may be a risk to clients and staff;

f) the provision of information, instruction and training to all persons (including contractors' employees) where they may be exposed to hazards;

g) the provision of signs, marking and labelling; and

h) the use of appropriate personal protective equipment, e.g. safety helmets, gloves.

Planned preventive maintenance programmes

Under the WHSWR, the workplace and equipment, devices and systems shall be maintained (including cleaned as appropriate) in an efficient state, in efficient working order and in good repair. Similar provisions apply in the case of work equipment under PUWER.

An important feature of health and safety management is, therefore, the operation of planned preventive maintenance programmes for the workplace, items of work equipment, systems and devices and, in some cases, for vehicles, in particular fork lift trucks.

Planned maintenance programmes incorporate written schedules which should cover the following features:

- the workplace structure, item of work equipment, structure, vehicle, etc to be maintained by reference to a plant, structural or vehicle maintenance register;

- the maintenance procedure, including specific methods of maintenance, the materials and equipment to be used and, for equipment, the criteria for testing following the maintenance operation;

- the frequency of maintenance, e.g. at the end of each production run, daily, weekly, every 1000 miles, etc.;

- identification of the person with specific responsibility for ensuring the written maintenance procedure has been correctly applied; and

- details of hazards and the specific precautions to be taken by maintenance staff.

Regular monitoring to ensure correct implementation of the programme should be undertaken by a senior manager, e.g. engineering director, chief engineer, with corrective action being taken where necessary.

See:

- *Electrical installations*
- *Portable electrical appliances*
- *Powered working platforms*
- *Welding and similar operations ('Hot work')*

Manual handling operations

More than a third of all work-related injuries result from manual handling activities. The vast majority of reported manual handling accidents result in over three day injury, most commonly a sprain or strain, often of the back.

Not only manual workers contribute to the handling injuries statistics, however. Those in sedentary occupations are similarly at risk, e.g. office workers, library staff, catering staff, hospital workers and people working in shops.

What comes out of the statistical information on manual handling injuries is the fact that four out of five people will suffer some form of back condition at some time in their lives, the majority of these conditions being associated with work activities.

Manual handling injuries and conditions

Injuries and conditions associated with manual handling can be both external and internal. External injuries include cuts, bruises, crush injuries and lacerations to fingers, forearms, ankles and feet. Generally, such injuries are not as serious as the internal forms of injury which include muscle and ligamental tears, hernias (ruptures), prolapsed intervertebral discs (slipped discs) and damage to knee, shoulder and elbow joints.

Muscle and ligamental strain

When muscles are utilized for manual handling purposes, they are subjected to varying degrees of stress. Carrying generally imposes a pronounced static strain of many groups of muscles, especially those of the arms and the trunk. As a result, fatigue very soon sets in, with pains in the back muscles, which perform static work only, occurring sooner than in the arm muscles, which perform essentially dynamic work.

Ligaments are fibrous bands occurring between two bones at a joint. They are flexible but inelastic, come into play only at the extremes of movement, and cannot be stretched when they are taut. Ligaments set the limits beyond which no movement is possible in a joint. A joint can be forced beyond its normal range only by tearing a ligament: this is a sprain. There are many causes of torn ligament, in particular, jerky handling movements which place stress on a joint, unco-ordinated team lifting, and dropping a load half-way through a lift, often caused by failing to assess the load prior to lifting.

Hernia (rupture)

A hernia is a protrusion of an organ from one compartment of the body into another, e.g. a loop of intestine into the groin or through the frontal abdominal wall. Both these forms of hernia can result from incorrect handling techniques and particularly from the adoption of bent back stances, which produce compression of the abdomen and lower intestines.

The most common form of hernia or 'rupture' associated with manual handling is the inguinal hernia. The weak point is the small gap in the abdominal muscles where the testis descends to the scrotum. Its vessels pass through the gap, which therefore cannot be sealed. Excessive straining, and even coughing, may cause a bulge at the gap and a loop of intestine or other abdominal structure easily slips into it. An inguinal hernia some-times causes little trouble, but it can, without warning, become strangulated, whereby the loop of intestine is pinched at the entrance to the hernia. Its contents are obstructed and fresh blood no longer reaches the area. Prompt attention is needed to preserve the patient's health, and even his life may be at risk if the condition does not receive swift attention. The defect, in most cases, must be repaired surgically.

Prolapsed or 'slipped' disc

The spine consists of a number of small interlocking bones or vertebrae. There are seven neck or cervical vertebrae, twelve thoracic vertebrae, five lumbar vertebrae, five sacral vertebrae and four caudal vertebrae. The sacral vertebrae are united, as are the caudal vertebrae, the others being capable of independent but co-ordinating articulating movement. Each vertebra is separated from the next by a pad of gristle-like material (intervertebral disc). These discs act as shock absorbers to protect the spine. A prolapsed or slipped disc occurs when one of these intervertebral discs is displaced from its normal position and is no longer performing its function properly. In other cases, there may be squashing or compression of a disc. This results in a painful condition, sometimes leading to partial paralysis, which may be caused when the back is bent while lifting, as a result of falling awkwardly, getting up out of a low chair or even through over-energetic dancing.

Rheumatism

This is a painful disorder of joints or muscles not directly due to infection or injury. This rather ill-defined group includes rheumatic fever, rheumatoid arthritis, osteoarthritis, gout and 'fibrositis', itself an ill-defined group of disorders in which muscular and/or joint pain are common factors. There is much evidence to support the fact that stress on the spine, muscles, joints and ligaments during manual handling activities in early life results in rheumatic disorders as people get older.

Safe manual handling

Injuries associated with manual handling of raw materials, people, animals, goods and other items are the principal form of injury at work. Such injuries include prolapsed intervertebral (slipped) discs, hernias, ligamental strains and various forms of physical injury. It is essential, therefore, that all people required to handle items be aware of the basic principles of safe manual handling.

The principles

The following principles should always be considered in handling activities and in the training of people in manual handling techniques.

Feet positions

Place feet hip breadth apart to give a large base. Put one foot forward and to the side of the object to be lifted. This gives better balance.

Correct grip

Ensure that the grip is by the roots of the fingers and palm of the hand. This keeps the load under control and permits the load to be better distributed over the body.

Arms close to body

This reduces muscle fatigue in the arms and shoulders and the effort required by the arms. It ensures that the load, in effect, becomes part of the body and moves with the body.

Flat back

This does not mean vertical but at an angle of approximately 15o. This prevents pressure on the abdomen and ensures an even pressure on the vertebral discs. The back will take the weight but the legs do the work.

Chin in

It is just as easy to damage the spine at the top as it is at the bottom. To keep the spine straight at the top, elongate the neck and pull the chin in. Do not tuck the chin on to the chest as this bends the neck.

Use of body weight

Use the body weight to move the load into the lifting position and to control movement of the load.

Planning the lift

When considering moving a load, make sure your route is unobstructed and that there are no obstructions or tripping hazards. Ensure there is an area cleared to receive the load. If your route requires you to wear a safety helmet, eye protection or hearing protection, put them on before you lift.

Assessing/testing the load

The majority of injuries occur when actually lifting the load. People involved in handling operations should be instructed to assess the following:

1. Are there any rotating or moving parts?

   If so, do not use them to lift with.

2. Is the load too big to handle?

   If so, get help.

3. Is the load too heavy?

   Rock the load. This will give a rough idea of its weight.

   If too heavy, get help.

Don't jerk. Carry out the lifting movement smoothly, keeping control of the load.

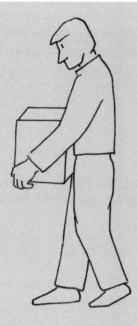

Move the feet. Don't twist the trunk when turning to the side.

Keep close to the load. Keep the load close to the trunk for as long as possible. Keep the heaviest side of the load next to the trunk. If a close approach to the load is not possible try sliding it towards you before attempting to lift it.

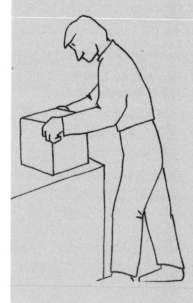

Put down, then adjust. If precise positioning of the load is necessary, put it down first, then slide it into the desired position.

Personal protective equipment

The provision and use of the correct PPE is an essential feature of safe manual handling. The following instructions should be incorporated in manual handling training and activities:

Hand protection

Examine the load for evidence of sharp edges, protruding wires, splinters or anything that could injure the hands. Wear the correct type of glove to prevent hand injury.

Feet protection

Wear footwear which is suitable for the job with:

a) steel toe caps to protect the feet against falling objects;

b) steel insoles to protect against protruding nails;

c) soles that will resist heat, oil and acid.

Two-person lift

Use all the principles involved in a one man lift, with one variation. The leading foot should point in the direction of travel. One person should give the order to lift, ensuring that his partner understands the order. It is vital that there be unison in the movement of both people and the load.

Manual Handling Operations Regulations 1992

Important definitions

Injury does not include injury caused by any toxic or corrosive substance which:

- has leaked or spilled from a load;
- is present on the surface of a load but has not leaked or spilled from it; or
- is a constituent part of a load.

Load includes any person and any animal.

Manual handling operations means any transporting or supporting of a load (including the lifting, putting down, pushing, pulling, carrying or moving thereof) by hand or bodily force.

Principal requirements of the regulations

1. Each employer shall:

    a) so far as is reasonably practicable, avoid the need for his employees to undertake any manual handling operations at work which involve a risk of their being injured;

    b) where it is not reasonably practicable to avoid the need for his employees to undertake any manual handling operations at work which involve a risk of their being injured;

- make a suitable and sufficient assessment of all such manual handling operations to be undertaken by them, having regard to the factors which are specified in column 1 of Schedule 1 to these Regulations and considering the questions which are specified opposite thereto in column 2 of that Schedule;

- take appropriate steps to reduce the risk of injury to those employees arising out of their undertaking any such manual handling operations to the lowest level reasonably practicable;

- take appropriate steps to provide any of those employees who are undertaking any such manual handling operations with general indications and, where it is reasonably practicable to do so, precise information on:

    – the weight of each load; and

    – the heaviest side of any load whose centre of gravity is not positioned centrally.

2. Any assessment such as is referred to in paragraph 1((b)(i) of this Regulation shall be reviewed by the employer who made it if:

a) there is reason to suspect it is no longer valid; or

b) there has been a significant change in the manual handling operations to which it relates;

and where as a result of any such review changes to an assessment are required, the relevant employer shall make them.

3. In determining for the purposes of this regulation whether manual handling operations at work involve a risk of injury and in determining the appropriate steps to reduce that risk regard shall be had in particular to:

- the physical suitability of the employee to carry out the operations;

- the clothing, footwear or other personal effects he is wearing;

- his knowledge and training;

- the results of any relevant risk assessment carried out pursuant to Regulation 3 of the MHSWR;

- whether the employee is within a group of employees identified by that assessment as being especially at risk; and

- the results of any health surveillance provided pursuant to Regulation 6 of the Management of Health and Safety at Work Regulations 1999.

4. Each employee while at work shall make full and proper use of any system of work provided for his use by his employer in compliance with Regulation 4(1)(b) of these Regulations.

Manual handling risk assessment

An employer must take into account the factors detailed in Schedule 1 when undertaking a manual handling risk assessment.

Example of an assessment checklist

Manual handling of loads

EXAMPLE OF AN ASSESSMENT CHECKLIST

Note: This checklist may be copied freely. It will remind you of the main points to think about while you:
- consider the risk of injury from manual handling operations
- identify steps that can remove or reduce the risk
- decide your priorities for action.

SUMMARY OF ASSESSMENT	Overall priority for remedial action: Nil / Low / Med / High*
Operations covered by this assessment:	Remedial action to be taken: ....
....	....
....	....
Locations:	Date by which action is to be taken: ....
Personnel involved:	Date for reassessment: ....
Date of assessment:	Assessor's name: .... Signature: ....

*circle as appropriate

Section A - Preliminary:

Q1 Do the operations involve a significant risk of injury?   Yes / No*

      If 'Yes' go to Q2. If 'No' the assessment need go no further.

      If in doubt answer 'Yes'. You may find the guidelines in Appendix 1 helpful.

Q2 Can the operations be avoided / mechanised / automated at reasonable cost?   Yes / No*

      If 'No' go to Q3. If 'Yes' proceed and then check that the result is satisfactory.

Q3 Are the operations clearly within the guidelines in Appendix 1?   Yes / No*

      If 'No' go to Section B. If 'Yes' you may go straight to Section C if you wish.

Section C - Overall assessment of risk:

Q What is your overall assessment of the risk of injury?   Insignificant / Low / Med / High*

      If not 'Insignificant' go to Section D. If 'Insignificant' the assessment need go no further.

Section D - Remedial action:

Q What remedial steps should be taken, in order of priority?

    i ....

    ii ....

    iii ....

    iv ....

    v ....

And finally:

    - complete the SUMMARY above

    - compare it with your other manual handling assessments

    - decide your priorities for action

    - TAKE ACTION.................AND CHECK THAT IT HAS THE DESIRED EFFECT

Section B - More detailed assessment, where necessary:

Questions to consider: (If the answer to a question is 'Yes' place a tick against it and then consider the level of risk)		Level of risk: (Tick as appropriate)			Possible remedial action: (Make rough notes in this column in preparation for completing Section D)
	Yes	Low	Med	High	
The tasks - do they involve:					
◆ holding loads away from trunk?					
◆ twisting?					
◆ stooping?					
◆ reaching upwards?					
◆ large vertical movement?					
◆ long carrying distances?					
◆ strenuous pushing or pulling?					
◆ unpredictable movement of loads?					
◆ repetitive handling?					
◆ insufficient rest or recovery?					
◆ a workrate imposed by a process?					
The loads - are they:					
◆ heavy?					
◆ bulky/unwieldy?					
◆ difficult to grasp?					
◆ unstable/unpredictable?					
◆ intrinsically harmful (eg sharp/hot?)					
The working environment - are there:					
◆ constraints on posture?					
◆ poor floors?					
◆ variations in levels?					
◆ hot/cold/humid conditions?					
◆ strong air movements?					
◆ poor lighting conditions?					
Individual capability - does the job:					
◆ require unusual capability?					
◆ hazard those with a health problem?					
◆ hazard those who are pregnant?					
◆ call for special information/training?					
Other factors - Is movement or posture hindered by clothing or personal protective equipment?					

Deciding the level of risk will inevitably call for judgement. The guidelines in Appendix 1 may provide a useful yardstick.
When you have completed Section B go to Section C.

Table 8: Manual handling risk assessment

See:

- *Ergonomics*
- *Health surveillance and health protection*
- *Information, instruction and training*
- *Personal protective equipment*
- *Risk assessment*

Mechanical handling

A wide range of machinery and equipment, such as elevators, hoists, trucks and conveyors is used in mechanical handling operations. The selection of a mechanical handling system will depend on a range of factors, such as the size, weight, shape, distance and frequency of movement of loads, together with ancillary factors, such as space and height restrictions, storage arrangements and the nature of the material to be handled.

Fixed handling equipment

This term is generally taken to include conveyors, elevators, fixed cranes and lifts, used for the transfer of products, raw materials and other items.

Conveyors

These may take the form of belt conveyors, roller conveyors, chain conveyors, screw conveyors and slat conveyors. Hazards vary for different types of conveyor, but the principal hazards with conveyors can be outlined below:

a) traps or 'nips' between moving parts, e.g. between a moving belt and rollers;

b) traps between moving and fixed parts, e.g. between the screw of a screw conveyor (auger) and the edge of a feed opening;

c) hazards associated with sharp worn edges, e.g. on worn conveyor chains;

d) traps and nips created by drive mechanisms, e.g. V-belts and pulleys; and

e) traps created at transfer points between two conveyors, e.g. between a belt conveyor and a roller conveyor.

Conveyors should be appropriately guarded, including the installation of fixed guards at trapping points or, in certain cases, interlocking guards. In addition:

a) arrangements should be made for lubrication with the guards in position, where practicable;

b) to minimize the risk of conveyed items jamming or falling off the conveyor, the radius of all bends should be maximized;

c) all fixed support members, including guide rails, should be free from sharp edges;

d) where conveyors rise one metre above floor or walkway level, suitable rails or side members should be provided to a sufficient height to contain the top item of the load being conveyed; and

e) emergency stop buttons located at operator positions, or a continuous stop wire, provided on long conveyors.

Elevators

Fixed elevators may operate vertically or at an angle, usually between floors of a building. They may take the form of:

a) bucket elevators for transferring loose materials, such as grain; and

b) bar elevators, on which items are placed or hung, e.g. sacked or boxed items.

The elevator is generally contained inside a fixed shaft, hoistway or enclosure and may be continuous in operation, often being linked with horizontal conveyors at each end.

When conveying loose materials, such as grain or flour, the potential for dust explosions is significant. Thus, in flour and agricultural mills, the installation of explosion reliefs at elevator heads is a basic safety requirement. Hoistways and floor openings should also be fire-proofed to provide a notional period of fire resistance of 30 minutes.

Fixed guards, e.g. tunnel guards, must be installed at trapping points, e.g. at the entrance to an elevator, where a trap is created between the elevator and the hoistway or enclosure.

Fixed cranes

These are a common installation in loading bays, wharves, docks and rail sidings. They may incorporate a fixed angle jib or variable angle jib and rotate through a full circle. Crane failures result in crane collapse are commonly associated with:

a)   overloading of the crane;

b)   failure to lift vertically;

c)   the use of a fixed crane to drag a load sideways; and

d)   the 'snatching' of loads, as opposed to operating a slow and steady lifting action.

With variable angle jib cranes, operators must be trained to recognize the reduction in the SWL as the jib moves towards the horizontal position.

Lifts

The principal hazards associated with lifts for the carriage of both people and/or goods are:

a)   total failure of the lift, resulting in the car dropping vertically to the base of the shaft;

b)   inadequate mechanical and electrical maintenance causing faults in operation, including the risk of people being trapped inside a car;

c) the risk of people falling down liftways due to the gates being open when the car is at another point in the liftway;

d) overloading; and

e) people coming into contact with moving parts of a lift or lift mechanism, e.g. maintenance personnel.

Mobile handling equipment

Within this heading can be included mobile cranes, overhead travelling cranes, various forms of lift truck and pedestrian-operated stacking trucks.

Mobile cranes

This form of crane, mounted, in many cases, on a purpose-built road vehicle, may incorporate a variety of features, such as a fixed or variable angle jib telescopic or articulated boom, and rotation through a full circle. Much will depend on the tasks undertaken, from vehicle recovery to the lifting of loads into position in construction operations.

The principal hazards, as with any crane, are that of overloading and the use of incorrect lifting techniques. The procedures relating to jib angles in relation to loads lifted are similar as those for fixed cranes. With a mobile crane, it is vital that any lift takes place on solid ground using, where fitted, the vehicle's outriggers fully extended to spread the load. The use of mobile cranes on sloping, soft or uneven ground, where the centre of gravity of the load combined with that of the crane has fallen outside the wheel base of the vehicle, inevitably results in a mobile crane failing and, in many cases, overturning.

Overhead travelling cranes

This type of crane, which runs along a fixed traverse, is commonly used in foundries and in engineering fabrication shops. The crane may have a fixed operating position or rotate through a full circle.

Derailment is the principal hazard with such cranes, which may be caused by:

a) overloading;

b) 'snatching' and dragging of loads;

c) obstructions on the traverse; and

d) the absence of adequate stop devices at each end of the traverse.

In the case of rail-mounted cranes, the crane should be fitted with an effective braking system or controlled through the use of sprags, scotches or chocks.

Absolute duties on employers with regard to the safe use of overhead travelling cranes are incorporated generally in the Provision and Use of Work Equipment Regulations 1998 and, more specifically, in the Lifting Operations and Lifting Equipment Regulations 1998.

Lift trucks

There are numerous variations of this type of mobile handling equipment, including pedestrian operated stacking trucks, reach trucks, counterbalance fork trucks, narrow aisle trucks and order pickers. Whilst their design features may vary, they all fundamentally operate on the same principles and for the same purposes, namely that of transferring commodities both vertically and horizontally, and for the placing in, and removal from, storage of loads.

Unsafe driving of lift trucks is the principal cause of fatal and major injury accidents, together with damage to premises, plant, products and the truck itself. To ensure safe operation of trucks, the following points must be considered:

In the case of the **lift truck itself**, the following points must be stressed:

- only trained and authorized personnel should operate such equipment;

- drivers should not leave trucks unattended unless the forks are lowered, the truck immobilized and the starter key removed;

- the maximum rated load capacity, as stated on the manufacturer's identification plate should never be exceeded;

- on no account should passengers be carried, unless in a properly constructed cage or platform;

- when used on a public highway, they must comply with the Road Traffic Acts in terms of the provision of adequate brakes, lights and steering;

- the keys must be kept in a secure place when the truck is not in use;

- the truck must be adequately maintained and subject to a regular servicing programme; and

- lifting chains should be inspected on an annual basis at least.

The design and layout of **operating areas** should incorporate the following:

- floors and roadways should be of adequate load-bearing capacity, well-maintained, smooth-surfaced and level;

- ramps should be installed at changes of road or floor level;

- gradients should not exceed 10%;

- bridge plates should incorporate an adequate safety margin to support loaded equipment;

- aisles should be of adequate width and overhead clearance to facilitate turning and safe movement;

- lighting should be adequate with a minimum overall illuminance level of 100 Lux; extra lighting on the truck may be necessary for external work; (see Lighting at work)

- clear direction signs, marked barriers, electrically-operated warning devices and convex mirrors should be used to prevent pedestrian contact with lift trucks;

- where pedestrians and trucks use the same route between parts of a building, separate pedestrian access doors should be available and the pedestrian route protected by steel barriers;

- in truck battery charging areas, permanent natural ventilation should be sufficient to prevent concentrations of hydrogen gas developing; and

- refuelling of petrol driven trucks should be located in the open air.

In the case of **truck operators**:

- a highly level of supervision should be maintained;

- drivers should be physically and mentally fit;

- they should be trained by trained trainers and subject to a formal test prior to formal authorization as truck operators;

- they should be provided with appropriate personal protection including, as appropriate, safety footwear, safety helmet and protective clothing to suit weather and/or temperature conditions.

(See further HSC Approved Code of Practice and Supplementary Guidance *Rider-operated Lift Trucks: Operator Training*)

The use of lift trucks with working platforms

Lift trucks are commonly used, in conjunction with a purpose-designed working platform fitted to the forks of the truck, for high level work, such as inspection and maintenance, fault-finding, redecoration and repair work.

The following precautions are necessary to ensure safe working:

- the manufacturer's view of the suitability of the truck for use with a working platform should be obtained;

- the vertical movement of the platform should be under the control of the person using the platform;

- the weight of the platform and total superimposed load should be less than 50% of the truck's rated capacity;

- the platform should be firmly fixed to the forks and should incorporate a 1m high safety rail with either an intermediate rail and toe board or steel mesh infill below the safety rail;

- a locking device should be fitted to ensure the mast remains vertical;

- where controls are located on the working platform, they should be of the 'dead man's handle' type;

- the parking brake should be applied before elevating the platform and a notice to this effect displayed on the truck;

- no person should remain on the platform during movement of the truck;

- the truck should only be used for this purpose on level and well-maintained floors; and

- all trapping points on the truck should be adequately fenced or screened.

Motor vehicles

A wide range of commercial vehicles operate in and around workplaces. Many of the requirements for lift trucks outlined above apply in the case of motor vehicles, in particular the need to regulate speed with visibility and comply with designated speed limits. In particular:

- loads should be secure;

- reversing and manoeuvring activities should be undertaken with the aid of traffic marshals where there is serious congestion;

- vehicles should be maintained, with particular attention to brakes, lights and steering; and

- drivers should adhere to designated traffic routes, including one-way systems, and park only in identified parking areas.

See:

- *Chains, ropes and lifting tackle*

- *Construction safety*

- *Contractors and visitors on site*

- *Lifting operations, machinery and equipment*

- *Lifts*

- *Mobile work equipment*

- *Powered working platforms*

Method statements

A method statement is, fundamentally, a written safe system of work, or series of safe systems of work, agreed between:

- a client and principal contractor; or

- a principal contractor and contractor,

and produced where work with a foreseeably high hazard content is to be undertaken.

Under the CDM Regulations, the requirement for the principal contractor to produce method statements prior to high risk operations should be incorporated in the Pre-Tender Stage Health and Safety Plan.

A method statement should specify the activities to be undertaken on a stage-by-stage basis and the precautions necessary to protect site operators, the client's employees and members of the public who could be affected by site activities. In certain cases, model method statements may be produced and agreed between a client and principal contractor for a range of high risk activities prior to commencement of work.

Typical situations where a method statement may be required include work involving:

- the use of hazardous substances in large quantities;

- the use of explosives;

- lifting operations;

- demolition; and

- potential exposure to hazardous dusts and asbestos.

What goes into a method statement?

Whilst there is no standard format for a method statement, the following aspects may need consideration:

- working systems to be used;
- arrangements for access e.g. to roofs;
- methods for safeguarding existing structures;
- segregation of certain areas;
- structural stability precautions, e.g. temporary shoring arrangements;
- arrangements for protecting the safety of members of the public;
- plant and equipment to be used;
- health protection arrangements, such as the use of local exhaust ventilation and respiratory protection, where hazardous dusts and fumes could be created;
- procedures to prevent local pollution;
- segregation of specific areas; and
- procedures to ensure compliance with legal requirements under, for instance, the Noise Act, Control of Lead at Work Regulations and Construction (Health, Safety and Welfare) Regulations.

The method statement may also incorporate information and specific requirements laid down by clients, enforcement officers, the police, local Fire Authority, manufacturers and suppliers of plant, equipment and substances and health and safety specialists. In certain cases, the method statement may identify training needs for contractors' employees and the use of competent persons or specially-trained operators for certain activities.

See:

- Asbestos
- Confined spaces
- Construction safety
- Contractors and visitors on site
- Lifting operations, machinery and equipment
- Shared workplaces
- Work at height

Mobile work equipment

Four specific aspects need consideration in preventing accidents associated with internal transport, namely the driver, the truck, the working environment and the system of work. The close co-ordination of these aspects is vital for maintaining high levels of lift truck safety.

The driver

Fitness

Drivers should be in a good state of health, with particular reference to vision and hearing. They should be subject to a pre-employment health examination by an occupational physician or occupational health nurse prior to appointment, with follow up health examinations at annual intervals. Drivers should be over 18 years.

Training

All drivers should be trained according to the standards and criteria outlined in the HSC ACOP and Supplementary Guidance *Rider-operated Lift Trucks –Operator Training*. This document distinguishes between three areas of training, that is basic training, specific job training and familiarization training, and provides guidance on such aspects as selection of trainees, accrediting bodies for instructor training, test of operator skills, training records and programmes.

Personal protective equipment

Operators should be provided with safety footwear and a safety helmet and, where appropriate, hearing protection, together with protective clothing appropriate to weather and/or temperature conditions.

Supervision

Line managers should ensure that all drivers work safely, that supervision is efficient and frequent, that they are undertaking the appropriate checks on their truck and that the system for reporting deficiencies in trucks is being used.

The truck

Maintenance

Trucks come within the definition of 'mobile work equipment' under PUWER. 'Mobile work equipment' is defined as 'any work equipment which carries out work while it is travelling or which travels between different locations where it is used to carry out work'.

Trucks should be subject to a clearly defined maintenance programme based on the manufacturer's recommendations for inspection, maintenance and servicing. Servicing records should be maintained and kept up to date. Apart from daily checks undertaken by operators, weekly maintenance on the truck should incorporate an operational examination of steering gear, lifting gear, battery, masts, forks, attachments and of any chains or ropes used in the lifting mechanism. There should be a formal system for operators to report truck defects.

Trucks should also be subject to six monthly and annual examinations. In the case of the six monthly examination (or 1,000 running hours) all parts of the truck should be examined by either a trained fitter or a representative of the manufacturer and a certificate issued by the examiner to the effect that the truck is safe to use. Lifting chains should be inspected on an annual basis and certificated as safe for use.

Lift trucks also come under the Lifting Operations and Lifting Equipment Regulations (LOLER).

Working platforms

Where a working platform is used in conjunction with a truck, e.g. for high level maintenance and cleaning, such platforms should be specifically designed for use with the truck.

Roll-over protection

Every employer shall ensure that a fork lift truck which carries an employee is adapted or equipped to reduce to as low as is reasonably practicable the risk to safety from its overturning. This Regulation applies to trucks fitted with vertical masts, which effectively protect seated operators from being crushed between the truck and the ground in the event of roll-over, and other trucks fitted with a roll-over protective structure, for example, rough terrain variable reach trucks that are used with fork lift attachments.

The working environment

Structural aspects

Well-designed layout and regular maintenance of operating areas is crucial to safe truck operation. Floors should be of adequate load-bearing capacity, reasonably smooth-surfaced and level. The edges of loading bays should be protected when not in use and 'tiger-striped' to warn the driver of such hazards. Sharp bends and overhead obstructions, such as pipes and cables, should be eliminated. Ramps should be installed to prevent displacement of the load at changes in floor level. Bridge plates should incorporate an adequate safety margin to support loaded equipment. Aisles should be of an adequate width and overhead clearance to facilitate turning and safe movement, and should be kept clear at all times. Where speed ramps are installed, a bypass for trucks should be provided.

Lighting

Lighting should be adequate, that is a minimum of 100 Lux internally and 50 Lux externally. If a permanent level of 100 Lux is not available in working areas, auxiliary lighting should be installed on the truck and so arranged to avoid glare to pedestrians and other truck operators.

Battery charging

In truck battery-charging bays, ventilation should be sufficient to prevent accumulations of hydrogen gas. Smoking and the use of naked lights in these areas should be prohibited. Refuelling areas for petrol-driven trucks should be located outside the building.

The system of work

Safe working

Many accidents, particularly to other persons, and damage to vehicles and structures, are associated with the absence of, or failure to, follow safe systems of work. Typical causes of overturning of trucks are due to drivers exceeding the maximum rated load capacity or failing to place the load dead centre. Where loads are being carried by the use of slings, slinging should be at designated slinging points on the truck. The movement of unsafe loads and the use of defective or under-strength pallets is a common cause of pallet loads collapsing during movement. Movement of trucks in unlit or badly lit external areas can result in accidents involving people and property. Convex mirrors should be installed prior to bends and junctions.

When powered industrial trucks are used on public highways, they must comply with the Road Traffic Acts and Regulations, particularly with regard to brakes, lights and steering.

Operator safety rules

The following safety rules should be enforced, including taking disciplinary action where necessary. These rules should be incorporated in the Permit to Drive issued to all approved truck drivers.

- Regulate speed with visibility

- Use the horn wherever necessary, but particularly at blind corners

- Pay particular attention to pedestrians and other vehicles

- Travel with the forks down; no movement of the forks when in motion

- Drive in reverse when the load obscures vision

- Use the prescribed truck routes; no short cuts

- Take care when reversing, using the horn where necessary

- Passengers must not be carried at any time

- Adhere to the speed limit e.g. 10 mph

- Slow down on wet or bad surfaces; no quick turns

- No parking in front of fire exits or equipment

- Use the handbrake and tilt mechanism correctly

- Take care on ramps; no turning on ramps

- When leaving the truck at any time, follow the procedure below:
    - controls in NEUTRAL;
    - forks down;
    - power off;
    - brakes on; and
    - remove the key or connector plug.

Table 9: Lift truck operator safety rules

The operator should carry out the daily check prior to starting or handover, namely brakes, lights, horn, steering, battery, hydraulics, speed controls, and any defects immediately to the manager responsible.

See:

- *Lifting operations, machinery and equipment*
- *Machinery and work equipment*
- *Mechanical handling*
- *Powered working platforms*

N

Negligence

Negligence comes within the area of law that deals with torts. A tort is, fundamentally, a 'civil wrong'. Negligence is broadly defined as 'careless conduct injuring another'. The majority of personal injury claims brought by employees and other persons, such as members of the public and non-employees, are based on negligence.

Case law has defined the three principal elements of a claim for negligence thus:

- the existence of a duty of care owed by the defendant to the claimant, for example, by an employer towards an employee or by a manufacturer of a product towards the user of that product;

- breach of that duty by commission or omission; and

- a consequential damage to the claimant i.e. injury, damage or loss, resulting from, or caused by, that breach.

    [Lochgelly Iron & Coal Co.Ltd. v M'Mullan (1934) AC1]

These three elements must be established by the injured party before he is entitled to bring a claim for damages. It is essential to establish that the breach of duty caused the injury or ill-health. Breach of duty need not be the exclusive cause. However, it must constitute a substantial part of same, in that it materially contributes to the injury or ill-health condition.

The legal procedure involving negligence is for a claimant, the injured person or his dependants, to sue a defendant, such as his employer, the occupier of premises or the manufacturer of a product, for some form of remedy. In most cases, this remedy is an award of damages, financial compensation for loss of life, pain and suffering, loss of future employment prospects, etc suffered by the claimant.

Defences

A defendant presented with a claim based on his negligence may submit a number of defences.

Volenti non fit injuria

'To one who is willing, no harm is done' (voluntary assumption of risk) is a complete defence, implying that no damages are payable to the claimant.

This defence is a complete defence but is rarely successful. It applies to situations or circumstances where the claimant, being fully aware of the risks he is taking in not following safety procedures or meeting his own safety duties, after being informed, instructed, trained and supervised with respect to the hazards that could arise during the work, suffers injury or ill-health as a result.

In this case, it is open to a defendant, such as his employer, to argue that the claimant, of his own volition, agreed to accept the risk involved. Fundamentally, a person who consents to run a risk has no legal remedy if injuries result and, where such a defence is successful, the defendant will not be required to pay damages.

Contributory negligence

The defence of contributory negligence is a partial defence and implies the claimant's damages could be reduced to the extent to which the claimant is considered by a court to be to blame, or at fault, for the injury or ill-health sustained.

The Law Reform (Contributory Negligence) Act 1945 states:

> Where any person suffers damage as the result partly of his own fault and partly of the fault of any other person or persons, a claim in respect of that damage shall not be defeated by reason of the fault of the person suffering the damage, but the damages recoverable in respect thereof shall be reduced to such extent as the court thinks just and equitable having regard to the claimant's share in the responsibility for the damage.

Thus, where injury is caused by two or more persons, liability or fault and, in consequence, any damages awarded, must be apportioned on the basis of individual blame or fault. In cases, for instance, where an employee is injured and it is established that both the employer and the employee were at fault, for example, in breach of specific regulations, when sued for damages by the injured employee, the employer is entitled to plead that the employee, as a result of his own negligence in failing to protect himself, should be held partly to blame. Where such pleading is successful, damages are reduced on the basis of the percentage blameworthiness.

In *Uddin v Associated Portland Cement Manufacturers Ltd (1965) 2 AER 213*, a machine minder, Mr Uddin, in trying to catch a pigeon roosting in the dust-extracting plant, an area to which he was not allowed access, leaned across a revolving shaft and lost his arm as a result. His employment was confined to the cement packing area. He sued his employer for a breach of Section 14 of the Factories Act 1937 which was concerned with the guarding of moving machinery.

It was held that the employer was liable under that section of the Factories Act, but that Mr Uddin's damages be reduced by 80% to account for his own contributory negligence.

Breach of statutory duty

The courts have sometimes recognized that a breach of a duty imposed by a statute may give rise to civil liability in terms of a claim for damages. This situation applies in cases where a statute may impose criminal duties but makes no reference to civil liability for injury, loss or damage arising from the breach of the statute. In these cases, the approach of the courts has been that of ascertaining whether the duty imposed by the statute was for the protection of a particular class of persons, such as employees, for the general public.

The courts have viewed the safety provisions of the Factories Acts, particularly those relating to the safeguarding of machinery, as being protective of a particular class of persons and, in many cases, have allowed a civil action for damages by a claimant belonging to that particular class who has been injured as a result of that breach of statutory duty.

See:

- *Common law liability*
- *Duty of care*
- *Insurance*
- *Occupiers' liability*
- *Vicarious liability*

New or expectant mothers

The MHSWR define a 'new or expectant mother' as an employee who is pregnant; who has given birth within the previous six months; or who is breastfeeding. 'Given birth' means delivered a living child or, after 24 weeks of pregnancy, a stillborn child.

Risk assessment

Employers must undertake the risk assessment process in respect of new or expectant mothers thus:

Where:

a) the persons working in an undertaking include women of child-bearing age; and

b) the work is of a kind which would involve risk, by reason of her condition, to the health and safety of a new or expectant mother, or to that of her baby, from any processes or working conditions, or physical, biological or chemical agents, including those spec-ified in Annexes I and II of Council Directive 92/85/EEC on the introduction of measures to encourage improvements in the safety and health at work of pregnant workers and workers who have recently given birth or are breastfeeding,

the assessment required by Regulation 3(1) shall also include an assessment of such risk.

- Where, in the case of an individual employee, the taking of any other action the employer is required to take under the relevant statutory provisions would not avoid the risk referred to in paragraph 1 the employer shall, if it is reasonable to do so, and would avoid such risks, alter her working conditions or hours of work.

- If it is not reasonable to alter the working conditions or hours of work, or if it would not avoid such risk, the employer shall, subject to section 67 of the 1996 Act suspend the employee from work for so long as is necessary to avoid such risk.

- References to risk, in relation to risk from any infectious or contagious disease, are references to a level of risk at work which is in addition to the level to which a new or expectant mother may be expected to be exposed outside the workplace.

- Where:
  a) a new or expectant mother works at night; and
  b) a certificate from a registered medical practitioner or a registered midwife shows that it is necessary for her health or safety that she should not be at work for any period of such work identified in the certificate,

  the employer shall, subject to section 67 of the 1996 Act, suspend her from work for so long as is necessary for her health or safety.

- Nothing shall require the employer to take any action in relation to an employee until she has notified the employer in writing that she is pregnant, has given birth within the previous six months, or is breastfeeding.

See:

- *Risk assessment*

Noise

Definitions

Noise is defined as 'unwanted sound'. Exposure to noise from machinery and equipment in the workplace can result in several forms of hearing impairment.

'Sound' is defined as any pressure variation in air, water or some other medium that the human ear can detect. 'Noise' on the other hand, is defined as 'unwanted sound'.

Noise nuisance

Noise may be a nuisance at common law and under statute law, such as the Environmental Protection Act 1990 and Noise Act 1996. This form of nuisance, such as noise from a nearby disco, results in disturbance and loss of enjoyment of life, loss of sleep and fatigue.

Noise and accidents

Noise can distract attention and concentration, mask audible warning signals or interfere with work, thereby becoming a causative factor in accidents.

Hearing impairment

Exposure to noise may result in hearing impairment.

The nature of sound

Sound comprises a series of pressure waves impinging on the ear (sound waves). The sound waves of everyday life are composed of a mixture of many simple sound waves.

Sound is generated by the vibration of surfaces or turbulence in an air stream which sets up rapid pressure variations in the surrounding air. The rate at which variations occur (frequency) is expressed in cycles per second or Hertz (Hz).

The human ear is sensitive to frequencies between 20 Hz and 20,000 Hz, being particularly sensitive in the range 1,000 Hz to 4,000 Hz (the frequencies of interest and progressively less sensitive at higher and lower frequencies. This fact is very important when measuring sound since two sounds of equal intensity, but of different frequency, may appear subjectively to be of different loudness.

Sound may be pure tone, i.e. of one frequency only, such as that produced by a tuning fork. Some industrial noise may be pure tone, but most is highly complex with components being distributed over a wide range of frequencies. Noise of this type is referred to as broad band noise, common examples being that produced by looms, air jets and printing presses.

Industrial noise is commonly produced by impact between metal parts. Where this features many impacts per second, as in riveting machines, the noise is generally treated as broad band noise. However, if the noise is produced by widely spaced impacts, as from a drop hammer or cartridge-operated tool, the noise is referred to as impulse noise. This presents special difficulties in measurement and in assessing the risk to hearing.

Noise-induced hearing loss

Exposure to excessive noise can result in hearing impairment, the condition known as 'noise-induced hearing loss' or 'occupational deafness'. Where the intensity and duration of exposure are sufficient, even 'wanted sound', such as loud music, can lead to hearing impairment.

Occupational deafness is a prescribed occupational disease which is described thus:

> 'substantial sensorineural hearing loss amounting to at least 50 dB in each ear, being due in the case of at least one ear to occupational noise, and being the average of pure tone loss measured by audiometry over the 1, 2 and 3 KHz frequencies'.

Under the Social Security (Industrial Injuries)(Prescribed Diseases) Regulations, this definition goes on to state a wide range of activities and occupations associated with exposure to noise whereby industrial injuries benefit may be payable.

Exposure to noise

Noise dose

For most steady types of industrial noise, intensity and duration of exposure, i.e. the dose of noise, are the principal factors in the degree of noise-induced hearing loss (sociocusis). Hearing ability also deteriorates with age (presbycusis), and it is sometimes difficult to distinguish between the effects of noise exposure and normal age-related deterioration in hearing.

The risk of noise-induced hearing loss can be related to the total amount of noise energy taken in by the ears over a working lifetime.

The effects of noise exposure

Exposure to noise can affect hearing in three ways:

Temporary threshold shift

This is the short-term effect, that is, a temporary reduction in hearing acuity, which may follow exposure to noise. The condition is reversible and the effect depends, to some extent, on an individual's susceptibility to noise.

Permanent threshold shift

This takes place when the limit of tolerance is exceeded in terms of time, the level of noise and individual susceptibility to noise. Recovery from permanent threshold shift will not proceed to completion, but will effectively cease at some particular point in time after the end of the exposure.

Acoustic trauma

This condition involves ear damage from short-term intense exposure or even from one single exposure. Explosive pressure rises are often responsible, such as that from gun fire, major explosions or even fireworks.

Symptoms of noise-induced hearing loss

Symptoms vary according to whether the hearing loss is mild or severe.

Mild form of hearing loss

Typical symptoms include a difficulty in conversing with people and the wrong answers may be given occasionally due to the individual missing certain key elements of the question. Speech on television and radio seems indistinct. There may also be difficulty in hearing normal domestic sounds, such as a clock ticking.

Severe form of hearing loss

Here there is difficulty in discussion, even when face-to-face with people, as well as hearing what is said at public meetings, unless sitting right at the front. Generally, people seem to be speaking indistinctly and there is an inability to hear the normal sounds of the home and street.

What is important is that it is often impossible for someone with this level of hearing loss to tell the actual direction from which a source of noise is coming and to assess the actual distance from that noise. This can be a contributory factor in accidents and, in particular, pedestrian-related road accidents.

In the most severe cases, there is the sensation of whistling or ringing in the ear (tinnitus).

The human hearing system

The human ear incorporates:

- the outer ear, incorporating the external pinna and the auditory canal terminating at the ear drum;

- the middle ear, which comprises a chamber containing ossicles, i.e. three linked bones, the malleus, incus and stapes (hammer, anvil and stirrup bones); and

- the inner ear, which houses the cochlea, the important organ of hearing and which is, fundamentally, a coiled fluid-filled tube incorporating the Organ of Corti.

Sound is conveyed via the auditory canal to the ear drum and ossicles to the cochlea, and from the cochlea via the auditory nerve to the brain where the sensation of sound is perceived. Hearing loss takes place in the Organ of Corti and this may be measured by audiometry.

Noise control

In any strategy to reduce or control noise, two factors must be considered, that is:

- the actual source or sources of noise e.g. machinery, ventilation systems; and

- the transmission pathway taken by the noise to the recipient.

The design stage

The first consideration must be that of tackling a potential noise hazard at the design stage of new projects, rather than endeavouring to control noise once the machinery or noise-emitting plant is installed.

Manufacturers, suppliers and importers of machinery and plant must be required to give an indication of anticipated sound pressure levels from their equipment once installed, and of the measures necessary to reduce noise emission, prior to the ordering of the equipment. Ensuring appropriate reduction of noise emission by manufacturers, suppliers and importers of plant and machinery should feature in any contract to supply.

Existing machinery and plant

In this case, a range of methods of noise control are suitable for dealing with identified sources of noise and the stages in the transmission pathway. These methods are summarized in the Table below: Methods of noise control.

SOURCES AND PATHWAYS	CONTROL MEASURES
Vibration produced through machinery operation	Reduction at source, e.g. substitution of metal components by nylon components; use of tapered tools on power presses
Structure-borne noise (vibration)	Vibration isolation e.g. use of resilient mounts and connections, anti-vibration mounts
Radiation of structural vibration	Vibration damping to prevent resonance
Turbulence created by air or gas flow	Reduction at source or the use of silencers
Airborne noise pathway	Noise insulation – reflection; use of heavy barriers
	Noise absorption – no reflection; use of porous lightweight barriers

Table 10: Methods of noise control

Control of the main or primary pathway is the most important strategy in noise control and to ensure compliance with the Noise at Work Regulations 1989.

Hearing protection

Where it is not reasonably practicable to control noise by recognized engineering methods, some form of hearing protection must be provided for operators exposed to noise. Hearing protection takes a number of forms:

Glass down material

Disposable; fine fibres of glass down; machine-dispensed from a roll or in individual packs; one per ear; risk of ear infection if not changed regularly; can break off and be retained in the ear canal; effectiveness relies heavily on operators using and inserting the material correctly.

Plastic or rubber ear plugs

Disposable and non-disposable types; range of sizes available; must be individually fitted by a specialist to be effective; some manufacturers and suppliers do not make this fact known.

Moulded ear plugs

In effect 'made to measure' ear plugs; non-disposable; moulded to the individual's left and right auditory canals; need regular sanitization and correct storage in a sealed container.

Ear muffs

A cup incorporating plastic absorption foam material; annular seal between the cup and the head filled with viscous fluid or polyurethane foam; headband to provide tension and maintain the seal over the ears.

High hysteresis plus

A half inch by three quarter inch long plug of material with the end pinched to form a cone; inserted into the auditory canal and, in endeavouring to return to its original shape, moulds itself to the contours of the canal, thereby sealing it off.

Limitations in the use of hearing protection

The use of hearing protection, such as ear plugs, ear defenders and acoustic wool may go some way towards preventing people from going deaf at work, but such a strategy must be regarded as secondary since it relies too heavily on exposed persons wearing potentially uncomfortable and inconvenient protection for all the time they are exposed to noise. The majority of employees simply will not do this! It may also limit or reduce the input of information to individuals, thereby becoming a contributory feature of accidents.

Noise at Work Regulations 1989

These regulations are accompanied by a number of Noise Guides issued by the HSE.

Important definitions

Daily personal noise exposure means level of daily personal noise exposure of an employee ascertained in accordance with Part 1 of the Schedule to the Regulations, but taking no account of the effect of any personal ear protector used.

Exposed means exposed whilst at work, and **exposure** shall be construed accordingly.

The **first action level** means a daily personal noise exposure of 85 dB(A).

The **peak action level** means a peak sound pressure of 200 pascals.

The **second action level** means a daily personal noise exposure of 90 dB(A).

Principal requirements of the regulations

- Every employer shall, when any of his employees is likely to be exposed to the first action level or above or to the peak action level or above, ensure that a competent person makes a noise assessment which is adequate for the purposes of:

  a) identifying which of his employees are so exposed; and

  b) providing him with such information with regard to the noise to which those employees may be exposed as will facilitate compliance with his duties.

- The above noise assessment shall be reviewed when:

  a) there is reason to suspect that the assessment is no longer valid; or

  b) there has been a significant change in the work to which the assessment relates,

    and where as a result of the review changes in the assessment are required, those changes shall be made.

- Following any noise assessment, the employer shall ensure that an adequate record of the assessment and of any review thereof carried out, is kept until a further noise assessment is made.

- ·Every employer shall reduce the risk of damage to the hearing of his employees from exposure to noise to the lowest level reasonably practicable.

- Every employer shall, when any of his employees is likely to be exposed to the second action level or above or to the peak action level or above, reduce, so far as is reasonably practicable, (other than by the provision of ear protectors), the exposure to noise of that employee.

- Every employer shall ensure, so far as is practicable, that when any of his employees is likely to be exposed to the first action level or above in circumstances where the daily personal noise exposure of that employee is likely to be less than 90 db(A), that employee is provided, at his request, with suitable and sufficient personal ear protectors.

- When any of his employees is likely to be exposed to the second action level or above or to the peak action level or above, every employer shall ensure, so far as is practicable, that that employee is provided with suitable ear protectors which, when properly worn, can reasonably be expected to keep the risk of damage to that employee's hearing to below that arising from exposure to the second action level or, as the case may be, to the peak action level.

- Employers must ensure the demarcation and identification of ear protection zones, i.e. areas where employees must wear ear protection.

- Every employer shall, in respect of any premises under his control, ensure, so far as is reasonably practicable, that:

  a) each ear protection zones is demarcated and identified by means of the sign specified in paragraph A.3.3 of Appendix A to Part 1 of BS 5878, which sign shall include such text as indicates:

     i) that it is an ear protection zone; and

     ii) the need for his employees to wear personal ear protectors whilst in any such zone; and

  b) none of his employees enters any such zone unless that employee is wearing personal ear protectors.

- In this Regulation, 'ear protection zone' means any part of the premises referred to above where any employee is likely to be exposed to the second action level or above or to the peak action level or above, and Part 1 of BS 5378 has the same meaning as in Regulation 2(1) of the Safety Signs Regulations 1980.

- Every employer shall:

  a) ensure, so far as is practicable, that anything provided by him to, or for the benefit of, an employee is compliance with his duties (other than personal ear protectors provided pursuant to Regulation 8) is fully and properly used; and

  b) ensure, so far as is practicable, that anything provided by him in compliance with his duties under these Regulations is maintained in an efficient state, in efficient working order and in good repair.

- Every employee shall, so far as is practicable, fully and properly use personal ear protectors when they are provided by his employer pursuant to Regulation 7 and any other protective measures provided by his employer in compliance with his duties under these Regulations; and if the employee discovers any defect therein, he shall report it forthwith to his employer.

- Every employer shall, in respect of any premises under his control, provide each of his employees who is likely to be exposed to the first action level or above or to the peak action level or above with adequate information, instruction and training on:

  a) the risk of damage to that employee's hearing that such exposure may cause;

  b) what steps that employee can take to minimize that risk;

  c) the steps that the employee must take in order to obtain the personal ear protectors; and

  d) that employee's obligations under these Regulations.

- The duties under Section 6 of HSWA on the part of manufacturers, designers, etc. include a duty to ensure that, where any such article is likely to cause any employee to be exposed to the first action level or above or to the peak action level or above, adequate information is provided concerning the noise likely to be generated by that article.

See:

- *Health surveillance and health protection*

- *Information, instruction and training*

- *Occupational diseases and conditions*

- *Risk assessment*

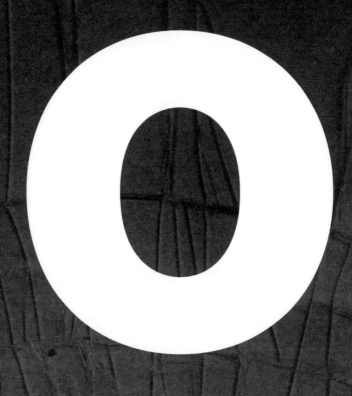

O

Occupational diseases and conditions

Occupational diseases and conditions are classified according to their causative factors and the type of work undertaken. These factors may be of a physical, chemical, biological or work-related origin. Exposure to physical phenomena, such as noise for instance, may result in workers suffering noise-induced hearing loss. On the other hand, people handling hazardous chemical substances may contract dermatitis and those involved in stripping asbestos could suffer from asbestosis.

Since the Industrial Revolution many diseases and conditions have been associated with a range of employment activities. For instance, coal worker's pneumoconiosis is commonly associated with the coal mining industry, byssinosis with the cotton industry, phosphorus poisoning with the manufacture of matches, and brucellosis with people such as stockmen, herdsmen, veterinary surgeons and others working with livestock in agriculture.

Occupational diseases and conditions are therefore those diseases and conditions contracted or caused as a result of a particular employment.

The classification of occupational diseases and conditions is generally based on the agents causing the disease and the work activities undertaken. These causative agents may be of a physical, chemical, biological or work-related nature.

Physical agents

Physical phenomena such as radiation, noise, vibration, heat and pressure will, after prolonged or even short exposure, cause ill-health.

Radiation

Workers dealing with, or coming into contact with, particularly, unsealed sources of radiation may suffer a range of symptoms from hair loss and fibrosis of the skin following local exposure or, more seriously, chronic anaemia and leukaemia as a result of general exposure to small doses over a period of time.

Noise

Noise-induced hearing loss (occupational deafness) is a well-established occupational condition in the ship-building, mining and quarrying industries. Workers may contract occupational deafness through being exposed to continuous sound pressure levels above 90 dBA or suffer acoustic trauma as a result of one single exposure to, for instance, an explosion.

Vibration

The condition known as 'vibration-induced white finger' is commonly associated with the use of compressed air-operated equipment and electrically-operated hand tools, such as rotary sanders and chain saws. Drivers of, for instance, earth moving equipment may suffer the ill effects arising from whole-body vibration.

Heat

Working in high temperatures, as with foundry work, can result in heat stroke and heat cramps.

Pressure

Decompression sickness is commonly associated with those working under water, such as divers, and people working in pressurized environments, for instance in a caisson, an underwater working chamber.

Chemical agents

Many hazardous substances are used in manufacturing, processing and servicing industries. These may include acids, alkalis, organic solvents and carcinogenic substances. These substances may have toxic, corrosive, harmful, irritant or other harmful effects on those exposed. The majority of these substances are defined as 'substances hazardous to health' under the COSHH Regulations and are classified according to their health effects under the Chemicals (Hazard Information and Packaging for Supply) (CHIP) Regulations.

Dermatitis

The most common occupational disease associated with exposure to chemical agents is dermatitis. These agents may be classed as primary irritants, such acids and alkalis, or secondary cutaneous sensitisers, such as nickel.

Occupational cancers

Exposure to a number of organic substances, such a beta-naphthylamine and vinyl chloride monomer (VCM), may result in a range of cancers in different body organs, such as the bladder and liver. As with most forms of cancer, the tumour involved may develop secondary growths, or metastases, which can be spread to other parts of the body via the circulatory or lymphatic systems.

Chemical poisoning

The form taken by a chemical agent, e.g. a dust, gas, vapour, fume, mist or fog, is significant in the potential for harm of that agent. Exposure to a range of gases, such as ammonia and chlorine, fume, such as lead fume, and chromic acid mist can result in damage to specific body organs.

Biological agents

Biological agents may be human-borne, animal-borne and vegetable-borne. This includes bacteria, certain dusts and viruses.

Bacterial and other agents

Certain bacteria, viruses and micro-organisms hazardous to health are listed in the ACOP *Control of Biological Agents* issued by the HSC in conjunction with the COSHH Regulations. Most prominent of these biological agents is Legionella pneumophila, the agent responsible for legionellosis or Legionnaires' disease.

Zoonoses

Biological agents further include that range of micro-organisms that are transmissible from animal to man, including the agents responsible for the range of diseases known as zoonoses. Classic examples are brucellosis, leptospirosis and Q-fever.

Vegetable-borne agents

Certain airborne agents, particularly dusts and spores arising from vegetables and cereals, can have serious effects on people. These include aspergillosis or farmer's lung, an influenza-like hypersensitive pulmonary condition associated with exposure to the dust and spores from mouldy hay.

Work-related factors

The type of work that people undertake is a common causative factor in the development of a range of ill-health conditions, particularly that group of disorders known as the 'beat' disorders, various work-related upper limb disorders and cramp conditions arising from work movements.

The beat disorders

Beat knee and beat elbow, commonly referred to as 'housemaid's knee' and 'tennis elbow' respectively, are two painful conditions caused by inflammation of the joint which may be followed by suppuration due to infection entering the joint.

These disorders are frequently associated with people involved in manual labour, such as paviors, gardeners and horticultural workers, where the work causes severe or prolonged friction or pressure at or about the joint.

Work-related upper limb disorders

These disorders include that group of disorders known as 'repetitive strain injury', (RSI) including tenosynovitis, carpal tunnel syndrome and Dupuytren's contracture. In most cases, the disorders are associated with tasks requiring the repetitive movement of the hand, elbow and/or forearm coupled with the application of force. Common symptoms include local pain, swelling, tenderness and inflammation which is aggravated by pressure or movement.

Cramps

Most people will have suffered the painful condition known as 'writer's cramp' on a temporary basis, perhaps after a series of written examinations or intensive note-taking sessions. The condition soon fades, however, after completion of the writing task.

Some occupations, however, may entail prolonged periods which require repetitive movements of the hand or arm.

Reportable diseases and prescribed diseases

Provisions relating to reportable diseases are covered in the Reporting of Injuries, Diseases and Dangerous Occurrences Regulations (RIDDOR) 1995.

Schedule 3 to RIDDOR

This Schedule classifies reportable diseases on the basis of the listed disease or condition and the activities undertaken. The disease or condition, as described, must fit the work activity for it to be reportable.

Reportable diseases are classified thus:

- Part I: Occupational diseases
- Part II: Diseases additionally reportable in respect of offshore workplaces

Occupational diseases are sub-classified as:

- Conditions due to physical agents and the physical demands of work
- Infections due to biological agents
- Conditions due to substances

Prescribed diseases

The Social Security Act 1975 states that a disease may be prescribed for the purposes of industrial injuries benefit if:

a) it ought to be treated, having regard to its causes and incidence and other relevant considerations, as a risk of occupation and not a risk common to all persons; and

b) it is such that, in the absence of special circumstances, the attribution of particular cases to the nature of the employment can be established with reasonable certainty (Section 76(2)).

Social Security (Industrial Injuries) (Prescribed Diseases) Regulations 1985

These Regulations contain a comprehensive code relating to claims for special industrial injuries benefits which are payable by the State under the National Insurance scheme to those who, subject to certain conditions, have contracted a disease which is prescribed for that occupation.

A classification of prescribed diseases and appropriate occupations is contained in Schedule 1 Part 1 of the regulations. These diseases are sub-classified thus:

- Group A: Conditions due to physical agents
- Group B: Conditions due to biological agents
- Group C: Conditions due to chemical agents
- Group D: Miscellaneous conditions

See:

- Accident and ill health costs
- Accident and ill health data
- Asbestos
- Biological agents
- Dermatitis
- Display screen equipment
- Hazardous substances
- Health risk assessment
- Health surveillance and health protection
- Information, instruction and training
- Lead at work

continued over

See *continued*:

- Manual handling operations
- New or expectant mothers
- Noise
- Occupational exposure limits
- Occupational hygiene
- Radiation and radiological protection
- Reportable and prescribed diseases
- Smoking at work
- Stress at work
- Toxicology

Occupational exposure limits

Threshold limit values

Threshold Limit Values (TLVs) are values published by the American Conference of Government Industrial Hygienists and adopted for use in the UK by the HSE. They refer to airborne concentrations of substances and represent conditions under which it is believed that nearly all workers may be repeatedly exposed, day after day, without adverse effect. TLVs refer to time-weighted average concentrations for a seven or eight hour work day and a 40-hour working week. (The term was replaced by *Occupational exposure limits – OELs*).

HSE Guidance Note EH40 *Occupational Exposure Limits* gives details of OELs which should be used for determining the adequacy of control of exposure by inhalation to substances hazardous to health. These limits form part of the requirements of the COSHH Regulations.

The advice given in Guidance Note EH40 should be taken in the context of the requirements of the COSHH Regulations, especially in relation to health risk assessments, control of exposure, use and maintenance of control measures and monitoring of exposure. Additional guidance may be found in the COSHH General ACOP *Substances Hazardous to Health*.

Legal requirements

Regulation 2(1) of COSHH states that:

'the **maximum exposure limit**' for a substance hazardous to health means the maximum exposure limit for that substance set out in

Schedule 1 in relation to the reference period specified therein when calculated by a method approved by the HSC;

'the **occupational exposure standard**' for a substance hazardous to health means a standard approved by the HSC for that substance in relation to a specified reference period when calculated by a method approved by the HSC.

Regulation 7(4) of COSHH requires that where there is exposure to a substance for which an **MEL** is specified in Schedule 1, the control of exposure, so far as inhalation of that substance is concerned, shall only be treated as being adequate if the level of exposure is reduced so far as is reasonably practicable and in any case below the MEL.

Regulation 7(5) of COSHH requires that, without prejudice to the generality of regulation 7(1), where there is exposure to a substance for which an **OES** has been approved, the control of exposure shall, so far as inhalation of that substance is concerned, be treated as being adequate if:

a)   the OES is not exceeded; or

b)   where the OES is exceeded, the employer identifies the reasons for the standard being exceeded and takes appropriate action to remedy the situation as soon as is reasonably practicable.

Units of measurement

The lists of OELs given in the Guidance Note, unless otherwise stated, relate to personal exposure to substances hazardous to health in the air of the workplace.

Concentrations of gases and vapours in air are usually expressed as parts per million (ppm), a measure of concentration by **volume**, as well as in milligrams per cubic metre of air (mg m³), a measure of concentration by **mass**.

Concentrations of airborne particles (fume, dust, etc.) are usually expressed in milligrams per cubic metre, with the exception of mineral fibres, which are expressed as fibres per millilitre of air.

Maximum exposure limits and occupational exposure standards

Maximum exposure limits (MELs)

MELs are listed in both Schedule 1 of the COSHH Regulations and Table 1 of Guidance Note EH40.

An MEL is the maximum concentration of an airborne substance, averaged over a reference period, to which employees may be exposed by inhalation under any circumstances and is specified, together with the appropriate reference period, in Schedule 1 of the COSHH Regulations.

Regulation 7(4) of COSHH, when read in conjunction with Regulation 16, imposes a duty on the employer to take all reasonable precautions and to exercise all due diligence to achieve these requirements.

In the case of substances with an eight hour long-term reference period, unless the assessment carried out in accordance with regulation six shows that the level of exposure is most unlikely ever to exceed the MEL, to comply with this duty the employer should undertake a programme of monitoring in accordance with Regulation 10 so that he can show, if it is the case, that the MEL is not normally exceeded. That is, that an occasional result above the MEL is without real significance and is not indicative of a failure to maintain adequate control.

Some substances measured in Schedule 1 of the COSHH Regulations have been assigned short-term MELs, i.e. a 15 minute reference period. These substances give rise to acute effects and the purpose of limits of this kind is to render insignificant the risks to health resulting from brief exposure to the substance. For this reason short-term exposure limits should never be exceeded.

In determining the extent to which it is reasonably practicable to reduce exposure further below the MEL, as required by Regulation 7(4), the nature of the risk presented by the substance in question should be weighed against the cost and the effort involved in taking measures to reduce the risk.

Occupational exposure standards (OESs)

An OES is the concentration of an airborne substance, averaged over a reference period, at which, according to current knowledge, there is no evidence that it is likely to be injurious to employees if they are exposed by inhalation day after day to that concentration and which is specified in a list approved by the HSC.

OESs are approved by the HSC following a consideration of the often limited available scientific data by the Working Group on the Assessment of Toxic Chemicals (WATCH).

For a substance which has been assigned an OES, exposure by inhalation should be reduced to that standard. If exposure by inhalation exceeds the OES, then control will still be deemed to be adequate provided that the employer has identified why the OES has been exceeded, and is taking appropriate steps to comply with the OES as soon as is reasonably practicable. In such a case, the employer's objective must be to reduce exposure to the OES, but the final achievement of this objective may take some time. Factors which need to be considered in determining the urgency of the necessary action include the extent and cost of the required measures in relation to the nature and degree of the exposure involved.

Long-term and short-term exposure limits

Substances hazardous to health may cause adverse effects, e.g. irritation of the skin, eyes and lungs, narcosis or even death after short-term exposure, or via long-term exposure through accumulation of substances in the body or through the gradual development of increased risk of disease with each contact.

It is important to control exposure so as to avoid both short-term and long-term effects. Two types of exposure limit are therefore listed in Guidance Note EH40.

- The long-term exposure limit (LTEL) is concerned with the total intake over long periods and is therefore appropriate for protecting against the effects of long-term exposure.

- The short-term exposure limit (STEL) is aimed primarily at avoiding acute effects, or at least reducing the risk of the occurrence. Specific STELs are listed for those substances for which there is evidence of a risk of acute effects occurring as a result of brief exposures.

For those substances for which no STEL is listed, it is recommended that a figure of three times the LTEL averaged over a 15 minute period be used as a guideline for controlling exposure to short-term excursions.

Both LTELs and STELs are expressed as airborne concentrations averaged over a specified reference period. The period for the LTEL is normally eight hours: when a different period is used, this is stated. The averaging period for a STEL is normally 15 minutes, such a limit applying to any 15 minute period throughout the working shift.

'Skin' annotation

Certain substances listed in Guidance Note EH40 carry the skin annotation (Sk). This implies that the substance can be absorbed through the skin. This fact is important when undertaking health risk assessments under the COSHH Regulations.

Examples of OELs

Table 10 (over) gives some examples of substances listed in Guidance Note EH40.

Substance	Formula	LTEL		STEL		Notes
		ppm	mg/m³	ppm	mg/m³	
Acrylonitrile	$CH_2=CHCN$	2	4	–	–	Skin
Carbon disulphide	CH_2	10	30	–	–	Skin
Isocyanates		–	0.02	–	0.07	
Trichloroethylene	$CCl_2=CHCl$	100	535	150	802	Skin
OCCUPATIONAL EXPOSURE STANDARDS						
Ammonia	NH_3	25	18	35	27	
Sulphur dioxide	SO_3	2	5	5	13	
Chloroform	$CHCl_3$	10	50	50	225	
Disulphur decafluoride	S_2F_{10}	0.025	0.025	0.075	0.075	
Mercury compounds Hg (except mercury alkyls)		–	0.05	–	0.15	

Table 11: Typical occupational exposure limits

See:

- *Hazardous substances*
- *Health risk assessment*
- *Safety data (hazardous substances)*
- *Toxicology*

Occupational hygiene

Occupational hygiene is an area of health protection concerned with identification, measurement, evaluation and control of airborne contaminants and other phenomena, such as noise and radiation, which would have otherwise unacceptable adverse effects on the health of people exposed to them.

As such, it is concerned with the identification, measurement, evaluation, prevention or control of a wide range of environmental stressors of a physical, chemical or biological nature. These can include, for instance, bacteria, chemical agents, which may take the form of gases, fumes, fogs, mists and dusts, and physical phenomena, such as noise, vibration and radiation, which can affect the health of people at work.

Occupational hygiene practice takes a number of clearly identified stages, thus:

- identification of the stressor, such as noise, hazardous substance;

- measurement of the extent of the stressor using prescribed sampling techniques;

- evaluation of the risks by reference to established criteria, such as Occupational Exposure Limits;

- selection of a particular prevention or control strategy, such as the substitution of a less hazardous substance, the installation of a local exhaust ventilation (LEV) system to remove dust from a process or the enclosure of a particular source of noise;

- implementation of that strategy;

- monitoring of the working environment through the taking of air samples, measurement of sound pressure levels or assessing the efficiency of an LEV system to ensure the prevention or control strategy installed remains effective.

See:

- *Hazardous substances*

- *Health risk assessment*

- *Lead at work*

- *Noise*

- *Occupational exposure limits*

- *Radiation and radiological protection*

- *Safety data (hazardous substances)*

- *Temperature control in the workplace*

- *Toxicology*

- *Ventilation in the workplace*

Occupiers' liability

People in control of premises

People who occupy land and premises, such as private individuals, local authorities, organizations and companies, shop keepers and operators of licensed premises have a range of liabilities. Their land and premises are visited by people for a variety of purposes, such as to undertake work, provide goods and services, settle accounts, etc. The HSWA requires those people in control of premises to take reasonable care towards these other persons, and failure to comply with this duty can lead to prosecution and a fine on conviction.

Moreover, anyone who is injured while visiting or working on land or premises may be in a position to sue the occupier for damages, even though the injured person may not be their employee. Lord Gardner in the case *Commissioner for Railways v McDermott [1967] 1AC 169* explained the position thus:

> "Occupation of premises is a ground of liability and is not a ground of exemption from liability. It is a ground of liability because it gives some control over and knowledge of the state of the premises, and it is natural and right that the occupier should have some degree of responsibility for the safety of persons entering his premises with his permission... there is proximity between the occupier and such persons and they are his 'neighbours'. Thus arises a duty of care..."

Thus, occupier's liability is a branch of civil law concerned with the duties of occupiers of premises to all those who may enter on to those premises. The legislation covering this area of civil liability is the Occupiers'

Liability Act (OLA) 1957 and, specifically in the case of trespassers, the Occupiers' Liability Act 1984.

Occupier's Liability Act 1957

Under the OLA an occupier owes a common duty of care to all lawful visitors. This common duty of care is defined as

'a duty to take such care as in all the circumstances of the case is reasonable to see that the visitor will be reasonably safe in using the premises for the purposes for which he is invited or permitted by the occupier to be there'.

Section 1 of the Act defines the duty owed by occupiers of premises to all persons lawfully on the premises in respect of 'dangers due to the state of the premises or to things done or omitted to be done on them'.

The Act regulates the nature of the duty imposed in consequence of a person's occupation of premises. The duties are not personal duties but rather, are based on the occupation of premises, and extend to a person occupying, or having control over, any fixed or movable structure, including any vessel, vehicle or aircraft.

Visitors

Protection is afforded to all lawful visitors, whether they enter for the occupier's benefit, such as customers or clients, or for their own benefit, for instance, a police officer, though not to persons exercising a public or private right of way over premises.

Warning notices

Occupiers have a duty to erect notices warning visitors of imminent danger, such as an uncovered pit or obstruction. However, Section 2(4) states that a warning notice does not, in itself, absolve the occupier from liability, unless, in all the circumstances, it was sufficient to enable the visitor to be reasonably safe.

Furthermore, while an occupier, under the provisions of the Act, could have excused his liability by displaying a suitable prominent and carefully worded notice, the chance of such avoidance is not permitted as a result of the Unfair Contract Terms Act 1977. This Act states that it is not permissible to exclude liability for death or injury due to negligence by a contract or by a notice, including a notice displayed in accordance with Section 2(4) of the OLA.

Trespassers

A trespasser is defined in common law as a person who:

a) goes on premises without invitation or permission;

b) although invited or permitted to be on premises, goes to a part of the premises to which the invitation or permission does not extend;

c) remains on premises after the invitation or permission to be there has expired;

d) deposits goods on premises when not authorized to do so.

Occupier's Liability Act 1984

Section 1 of this Act imposes a duty on an occupier in respect of trespassers, namely 'persons who may have a lawful authority to be in the vicinity or not, who may be at risk of injury on the occupier's premises'

Warning notices

This duty can be discharged by issuing some form of warning such as the display of hazard warning notices, but such warnings must be very explicit.

For example, it is insufficient to display a notice that merely states:

> **SLIPPING HAZARD**

where there may be a risk to people of slipping on a floor.

A suitable notice in such circumstances might read:

> **RISK OF SLIPPING ON FLOOR**
>
> **FOLLOW THE PRESCRIBED PEDESTRIAN ROUTE ONLY**

It is not good enough, however, to merely display a notice. The requirements of notices must be actively enforced by management.

Generally, the displaying of a notice, the clarity, legibility and explicitness of such a notice, and evidence of regularly reminding people of the message outlined in the notice, may count to a certain extent as part of a defence when sued for injury by a simple trespasser under the Act.

Under the Act there is no duty on the part of occupiers to persons who willingly accept risks [Section 2(5)]. Further, the fact that an occupier has taken precautions to prevent persons going in to his premises or on to his land, where some form of danger may exist, does not mean that the occupier has reason to believe that someone would be likely to come into the vicinity of the danger, thereby owing a duty to the trespasser under the OLA 1984.

Children

Generally from a legal viewpoint children have always been deemed to be less responsible than adults. The OLA 1957 is quite specific on this matter. Section 2(3)(a) requires an occupier to be prepared for children to be less careful than adults. Where, for instance, there is something, or a situation, on the premises that is a lure or attraction to a child, such as a pond, an old motor car, a derelict building or scaffolding, this can constitute a trap as far as a child is concerned. Should a child be injured as a result of this trap, the occupier could then be liable. Much will depend upon the location of the premises, for instance, whether or not it is close to houses or a school or is in an isolated location, such as a farmyard deep in the countryside but, in all cases, occupiers must consider the potential for child trespassers and take appropriate precautions.

Contractors and their employees

The relationship between occupiers and contractors has always been a tenuous one. Section 2(3)(b) of the OLA 1957 states that an occupier may expect that a person, in exercising their calling, such as a window cleaner, bricklayer or painter, will appreciate and guard against any risks ordinarily incident to that calling, for instance the risk of falling, so far as the occupier gives them leave to do so. This means that the risks associated with the system of work on a third party's premises are the responsibility of the contractor's employer, not the occupier. (It should be appreciated, however, that while the above may be the case at civil law, the situation at criminal law, namely the duties of employers towards non-employees under Section 3 of the HSWA, is quite different.)

Where work is being carried out on a premises by a contractor, the occupier is not liable if he:

a)   took care to select a competent contractor; and

b)   satisfied himself that the work was being properly done by the contractor [Section 2(4)(b)].

However, in many cases, an occupier may not be competent or knowledgeable enough to ascertain whether or not the work is being properly done. For instance, an occupier may feel that an unsafe system of work adopted by a contractor's employee, such as cleaning the external window surfaces to fourth floor offices without using any form of access equipment, such as a suspended scaffold or a safety line, is standard practice amongst window cleaners! In such cases, the occupier might need to be advised by a surveyor, architect or health and safety consultant in order to be satisfied that the work is being done properly and safely.

This relationship between occupiers and contractors has been substantially modified through the CDM Regulations.

See:

- *Common law liability*
- *Contractors and visitors on site*
- *Courts and tribunals*
- *Negligence*
- *Safety signs*

P

Passport schemes

Many employees work away from their main workplace, such as those involved in contracting activities involving the servicing of plant and equipment, construction, stripping of asbestos, contract catering and cleaning activities. Apart from the general duty on employers under the HSWA for such employees to be provided with health and safety training, many regulations, such as the COSHH Regulations and the CDM Regulations, lay down specific requirements for the training of employees.

So how does a client, in selecting a competent contractor for construction work at his premises, or prior to taking on a contract catering service, ensure that the employees of that contractor are adequately trained in health and safety procedures and the precautions necessary to ensure safe working? One of the ways is through the operation of a Safety Passport Scheme.

Passport schemes ensure that workers have received health and safety awareness training, and are particularly useful for workers and contractors who work in more than one industry or organization. Passport schemes operate in a number of ways. In the majority of cases, such schemes are driven by a particular industry based on the need to ensure that the employees in that industry, suppliers of services, contractors, self-employed persons and agency staff meet a particular training standard. On this basis, the industry may decide:

- what training is required, particularly core syllabus requirements;

- the qualifications and resources needed by trainers;

- how training will be delivered and assessed, perhaps through passing an accredited training course;

- for how long a Passport will be valid;

- the need for refresher training before renewal; and

- the system for keeping records.

Following the development of the training course, courses are offered to workers who must pass some form of assessment before a Passport is issued. On satisfactory completion of the course, the worker is issued with a card, similar to a photocard driving licence, bearing his photograph, signature and a date of expiry of the card.

After the Passport Scheme has come into operation, only those holding a valid Passport are allowed access to workplaces or construction sites. In some cases, clients insist that all contractors' employees hold Passports, before completing the selection process for a principal contractor.

Outcome of a passport training scheme

On completion of training, Passport holders should know:

- the hazards and risks they may face;

- the hazards and risks they can cause for other people;

- how to identify relevant hazards and potential risks;

- how to assess what to do to eliminate the hazards and control the risk;

- how to take steps to control the risks to themselves and others;

- their safety and environmental responsibilities, and those of the people they work with;

- where to find extra information they need to do their job safely; and

- how to follow a safe system of work.

Co-operation between organizations

The HSE encourages organizations to co-operate in this scheme whereby one scheme recognizes the core training of other schemes. This means that Passport holders do not have to repeat the core syllabus if they move from one employer or contract to another. They will simply need site and/or activity specific training.

Monitoring

It is important that supervisors monitor Passport holders on a day-to-day basis by asking people about their work, checking whether people are following procedures and observing their work. The standard of training should further be monitored by clients.

See further *Passport Schemes for Health, Safety and the Environment: a Good Practice Guide INDG381* HSE Books.

See:

- Construction safety
- Contractors and visitors on site

Permit to work systems

Section 2(2)(a) of the HSWA places a duty on employers to provide and maintain plant and systems of work that are, so far as is reasonably practicable, safe and without risks to health.

A Permit to Work system is a formally documented safe system of work designed to prevent accidental injury to operators and damage to plant, premises and product where work with a foreseeably high level of risk is to be undertaken. Such a system is operated, for instance, where people may be entering confined spaces, using highly flammable substances or working on electrical systems.

A Permit to Work is a document which sets out the work to be done and the precautions to be taken. It predetermines a safe procedure and is a clear record that all foreseeable risks have been considered in advance and that all precautions are specified and taken in the correct sequence. It does not, in itself, make the job safe but is dependent for its effectiveness on trained persons undertaking the work conscientiously with a high degree of supervision and control.

An effective Permit to Work system

A Permit to Work system must be formal but, on the other hand, comprehensible to those operating same. Permit to work systems will involve many groups of staff, including engineering staff, production staff, laboratory personnel, health and safety specialists and, perhaps, contractors.

The following principles should be observed in the operation of Permit to Work systems:

- The Permit to Work must provide concise and accurate information about the work to be undertaken, the period of time in which the work must be completed and individual responsibilities for the various stages of the operation.

- It must be considered as the principal instruction and, until the permit to work is cancelled, it overrides all other instructions.

- No one must, under any circumstances, work at a place or on equipment not indicated as safe in the Permit to Work.

- No one must carry out any work which is not indicated and described in the Permit to Work. Where a change in the work programme is indicated, the Permit to Work should be amended by the originator or, preferably, cancelled and a new Permit to Work issued.

- Only the originator, for instance, a senior manager, may amend or cancel the Permit to Work.

- Anyone taking over responsibility for the operation of a Permit to Work system, either as a matter of routine or in an emergency situation, must be adequately briefed.

- The person accepting the Permit to Work is, from that moment, responsible for the safe conduct of the work within the limits of the Permit to Work. He must make himself fully conversant with its terms and requirements, and must give sufficient instructions to persons working under his control.

- The boundary or limits of the working area should be clearly defined.

- Special care must be taken to ensure that contractors, who may be engaged to undertake specific tasks, are included in the Permit to Work system. Contractors' employees and other persons may be completely unaware of the nature of any particular risks inherent in process plant, inexperienced in the use of safety equipment and ignorant of safety and rescue procedures. Such persons must be trained in the procedure and instructed in the risks prior to commencing activities.

- Management should make the observance of safety rules and procedures, including the operation of, and participation in, Permit to Work systems, a condition of the contract for the work, underwriting this with training, advice and staff assistance where necessary.

Permit to Work situations

The decision to operate a Permit to Work system is dependent on the risks inherent in the work involved. Typical Permit to Work situations include:

a) entry into confined spaces, closed vessels and vessels containing agitators;

b) work involving the breaking of lines or the opening of plant containing steam, hazardous substances, such as chlorine and ammonia, hot substances or vapours, gases and liquids under pressure;

c) work on electrical systems;

d) welding and cutting operations in areas other than workshops;

e) work in isolated locations, locations with difficult access or at high level;

f) work in the vicinity of, or requiring the use of, highly flammable, explosive or toxic substances;

g) work resulting in possible atmospheric pollution of the workplace;

h) certain fumigation activities using potentially hazardous chemical substances in the form of a gas, mist, fog, vapour or dust; and

i) work involving contractors in any of the above activities.

Operation of the system

The system should be operated in a number of clearly defined stages.

Assessment

The first and most important step is the assessment of the situation. This should be undertaken by a manager or person with specific authority who is experienced in the work and, where specialized plant is concerned is familiar with the relevant scientific and engineering requirements. The person undertaking the assessment should be allowed sufficient time to consider each task and personally check each stage of the action required in the issue of the permit to work.

The process of assessment should involve consideration of the work necessary, the methods by which this work can be carried out and the hazards that could arise. The ultimate objective of this assessment stage is the determination of the steps to be taken to make the job safe and the precautions to be taken during the actual working.

Withdrawal from service

Before plant is prepared for work identified in the Permit to Work, it should be withdrawn from service. This may entail physical locking off of valves and other items of machinery to prevent other persons from opening these valves or activating the machinery whilst others are working on or inside same. When the withdrawal procedure has been completed, the person supervizing the operation should certify to that effect on the Permit to Work. The entry should also confirm that all operators have been advised of the withdrawal. Warning notices and safety signs should be displayed at this stage.

Isolation

After withdrawing the plant from service, it should be physically isolated by means of barriers displaying appropriate warning notices and mechanically and electrically isolated. A declaration to this effect should be made on the Permit to Work certificate. In certain cases, it may be necessary to undertake atmospheric testing where personnel may be required to enter confined spaces.

Cancellation of the permit to work

When the operations as specified in the Permit to Work have been completed, the permit to work should be cancelled by completion of the appropriate section. The cancellation section should incorporate a declaration to the effect that all personnel and equipment have been removed from the plant and area in question. The Permit to Work should then be returned to the originator.

Return to service

Following completion of the work and cancellation of the Permit to Work certificate, the plant can be returned to service. The person in charge of the process or operation should ensure that the Permit to Work has been cancelled and make the final entry to the effect that he accepts responsibility for the same.

Administrative procedures

A Permit to Work must be raised before the work, or a particular phase of the work requiring a Permit to Work, is commenced by the senior person responsible for undertaking the work. Work should be carefully pre-planned to cause the least possible interference with other work. In some cases it may be necessary to refer to specialist sources of advice. Under no circumstances should Permits to Work be issued, even in an emergency situation, without careful consideration of the risks and precautions necessary.

In some cases, it is advisable to prepare check lists for identified types of work to provide guidance on expected hazards and the preventive and protective measures necessary. Where an isolation procedure is particulary complicated, it is common practice to attach the formal isolation procedure to the Permit to Work certificate.

Authority for the issue of permits to work should be restricted to named senior managers, a list of such persons being shown as an Appendix to the Statement of Health and Safety Policy. The criteria for authorization must be based on a detailed knowledge of all aspects of that individual's areas of responsibility, competence and skill.

Documentation

Permit to work forms should be printed in triplicate, self-carbonned and serial numbered, with different colours for the original, first copy and second copy.

Distribution should be thus:

a) Original – person undertaking the work;

b) First copy – person responsible for the area/department where the work is being carried out.

c) The second copy is retained by the originator.

On completion of the work and final clearance of the Permit to Work, the original and first copy are returned to the originator.

Records

A record of Permits to Work issued should be maintained. This provides useful feedback for the future design of safe systems of work, specification of plant and equipment and in the identification of training needs. Completed permits to work should be retained for not less than two years.

Training

Staff involved in the implementation of Permit to Work systems should receive thorough training prior to operation of same. Competent supervision is also necessary to ensure all stages of the operation are completed according to the details outlined in the Permit and any supporting documentation, such as isolation check lists.

See:

- *Confined spaces*
- *Electrical installations*
- *Health and Safety at Work etc Act 1974*
- *Safety management systems*
- *Welding and similar operations ('Hot work')*
- *Work at height*

Personal protective equipment

This term includes equipment worn and used by people at work to protect them from both general and specific risks.

'Personal protective equipment' is defined as meaning 'all equipment (including clothing affording protection against the weather) which is intended to be worn or held by a person at work and which protects him against one or more risks to his health or safety, and any addition or accessory designed to meet that objective'.

The range of PPE

A wide range of personal protective equipment (PPE) is available for use by people at work. This includes:

Head protection

Industrial safety helmets, various forms of riding helmets, industrial scalp protectors (bump caps) and caps and hair nets.

Eye protection

Safety spectacles, eye shields, safety goggles and face shields.

Face protection

Face shields which can be hand-held, fixed to a helmet or strapped to the head.

Respiratory protection

General purpose dust respirators, positive pressure powered dust respirators, helmet-contained positive pressure respirators, gas respirators, emergency escape respirators, air-line breathing apparatus, self-contained breathing apparatus.

Hearing protection

Ear plugs, ear defenders, muffs and pads, ear valves, acoustic wool.

Body protection

One-piece and two-piece overalls, donkey jackets, rubber and PVC-coated aprons, vapour suits, splash-resistant suits, warehouse coats, body warmers, thermal and weather protection overclothing, oilskin overclothing, high visibility clothing, personal buoyancy equipment, such as life jackets.

Hand and arm protection

General purpose fibre gloves, PVC fabric gauntlets, leather gloves and sleeves, wrist protectors, chain mail hand and arm protectors.

Leg and foot protection

Safety boots and shoes, wellington boots, clogs, foundry boots, anti-static footwear, together with gaiters and anklets.

Limitations in the use of PPE

The use of any form of PPE should, in the majority of cases, be seen either as:

a) an interim measure until an appropriate 'safe place' strategy e.g. machine guarding, can be implemented; or

b) the last resort, when all other protection strategies have failed.

Mere provision of PPE is never the perfect solution to protecting people from hazards due to the need for users to wear or use the equipment all the time they are exposed to such hazards. People simply do not do this for a number of reasons. For instance:

a) it may create discomfort, restrict movement and be difficult to put on or remove;

b) it may obscure vision;

c) it may reduce their perception of hazards;

d) it may be inappropriate to the risk, for example, where unsuitable respiratory protection is provided;

e) it requires, in many cases, frequent cleaning, replacement of parts, maintenance or some form of regular attention by the user, which he may see as a chore; and

f) some people perceive the use of PPE as unnecessary, a sign of immaturity or yet another management imposition.

On the whole there is a general reluctance on the part of operators to wear or use PPE for a variety of reasons.

Selection of PPE

A systematic approach to the selection of PPE is essential to ensure that workers at risk are adequately protected. Generally, PPE must be 'suitable', in terms of preventing or controlling exposure to a risk and for the work being undertaken.

When considering the type and form of equipment to be provided, and its relative suitability, the following factors are relevant:

a) the needs of the user in terms of comfort, ease of movement, convenience in putting on, use and removal, and individual suitability;

b) the ergonomic requirements and state of health of the persons who may use that PPE;

c) the capability of the PPE to fit the wearer correctly, if necessary, after adjustments within the range for which it is designed;

d) the number of personnel exposed to a particular hazard, for instance, noise, dust or risk of hand injury;

e) the risk or risks involved, the conditions at the place where the exposure to risk may occur, and the relative appropriateness of the PPE in protecting operators against, for example, fume and dust inhalation or molten metal splashes;

f) its relative effectiveness to prevent or adequately control the risk or risks without increasing overall risk;

g) the scale of the hazard;

h) standards representing recognized 'safe limits' for the hazard e.g. HSE Guidance Notes, British Standards;

i) specific Regulations currently in force;

j) specific job requirements or restrictions e.g. work in confined spaces, roof work;

k) the presence of environmental stressors which will affect the individual wearing or using the equipment e.g. extremes of temperature, inadequate ventilation, background noise; and

l) the ease of cleaning, sanitization, maintenance and replacement of equipment and/or its component parts.

Personal Protective Equipment at Work Regulations 1992

Principal requirements of the regulations

- Every employer shall ensure that suitable PPE is provided to his employees who may be exposed to a risk to their health and safety while at work except where and to the extent that such risk has been adequately controlled by other means which are equally or more effective.

- Every employer shall ensure that where the presence of more than one risk to health or safety makes it necessary for his employee to wear or use simultaneously more than one item of PPE, such equipment is compatible and continues to be effective against the risk or risks in question.

- PPE shall not be suitable unless:

  a) it is appropriate for the risk or risks involved, the conditions at the place where exposure to the risk may occur, and the period for which it is worn;

  b) it takes account of ergonomic requirements and the state of health of the person or persons who may wear it, and of the characteristics of the workstation of each such person;

  c) it is capable of fitting the wearer correctly, if necessary, after adjustments within the range for which it is designed;

  d) so far as is practicable, it is effective to prevent or adequately control the risk or risks involved without increasing overall risk;

  e) it complies with any enactment (whether in Act or instrument) which implements in Great Britain any provision on design or manufacture with respect to health or safety of any of the relevant Community directives listed in Schedule 1 which is applicable to that item of PPE.

- Where it is necessary to ensure that PPE is hygienic and otherwise free of risk to health, every employer and every self-employed person shall ensure that PPE provided under this regulation is provided to a person for use only by him.

- Before choosing any personal protective equipment which he is required to provide, an employer or self-employed person shall make an assessment to determine whether the PPE he intends to provide is suitable.

- The assessment shall comprise:

  a) an assessment of any risk or risks which have not been avoided by other means;

b) the definition of the characteristics which PPE must have in order to be effective against the risks referred to above, taking into account any risks which the equipment itself may create;

c) comparison of the characteristics of the PPE available with the characteristics referred to in (b) above; and

d) an assessment as to whether the PPE is compatible with other PPE which is in use and which an employee would be required to wear simultaneously.

- The assessment shall be reviewed forthwith if:

    a) there is reason to suspect that any element of the assessment is no longer valid; or

    b) there has been a significant change in the work to which the assessment relates;

    and where, as a result of the review, changes in the assessment are required, these changes shall be made.

- Every employer and every self-employed person shall ensure that any PPE provided by them is maintained in relation to any matter which it is reasonably foreseeable will affect the health and safety of any person in an efficient state, in efficient working order, in good repair and in hygienic condition.

- Every employer and every self-employed person shall ensure that appropriate accommodation is provided for PPE when it is not being used.

- Where an employer is required to provide PPE to an employee, the employer shall provide that employee with such information, instruction and training as is adequate and appropriate to enable the employee to know:

    a) the risk or risks which the PPE will avoid or limit;

    b) the purpose for which, and the manner in which, the PPE is to be used; and

    c) any action to be taken by the employee to ensure that the PPE remains in an efficient state, in efficient working order, in good repair and in hygienic condition, and shall ensure that such information is kept available to employees.

- The employer shall, where appropriate, and at suitable intervals, organize demonstrations in the wearing of PPE.

- Every employer who provides any PPE shall take all reasonable steps to ensure that it is properly used.

- Every employee and self-employed person who has been provided with PPE shall:

  a) make full and proper use of the PPE; and

  b) take all reasonable steps to ensure it is returned to the accommodation provided for it after use.

- Every employee who has been provided with PPE by his employer shall forthwith report to his employer any loss of, or obvious defect in, that PPE.

Guidance on the regulations

Detailed HSE guidance is provided on the requirements of the Regulations.

Table 12: Specimen risk survey table for the use of personal protective equipment

| | | | Risks |||||||||||||||||||||| |
| | | | Mechanical ||||| Thermal || | | | | | | | | | | | | | | |
			Falls from a height	Blows, cuts, impact, crushing	Stabs, cuts, grazes	Vibration	Slipping, falling over	Scalds, heat, fire	Cold	Immersion	Non-ionising radiation	Electrical	Noise	Ionising radiation	Dust fibre	Fume	Vapours	Splashes, spurts	Gases, vapours	Harmful bacteria	Harmful viruses	Fungi	Non-micro biological antigens
P	Head	Cranium																					
A		Ears																					
R		Eyes																					
T		Respiratory tract																					
S		Face																					
of		Whole head																					
the	Upper limbs	Hands																					
B		Arms (parts)																					
O	Lower limbs	Foot																					
D		Legs (parts)																					
	Various	Skin																					
		Trunk/abdomen																					
Y		Whole body																					

The PPE at Work Regulations 1992 apply except where the Construction (Head) Protection Regulations 1989 apply

The CLW, IRR, CAW, COSHH and NAW Regulations[1] will each apply to the appropriate hazard

(1) The Control of Lead at Work Regulations 2002; The Ionising Radiations Regulations 1999; The Control of Asbestos at Work Regulations 2002; The Control of Substances Hazardous to Health Regulations 2002; The Noise at Work Regulations 1989.

See:

- *Accidents and accident prevention*
- *Noise*
- *Safety signs*

Portable electrical appliances

A substantial number of deaths and injuries are associated with portable electrical tools and equipment, such as drills, saws, and grinders and a wide range of domestic equipment, such as electric blankets, kettles, heaters and radios.

Hazards vary from the risk of electrocution and death to burns, shocks, eye injuries (from arc welding) and the ever-constant risk of explosion and fire due to the presence, as in battery charging, of hydrogen gas.

Fires can result through the emission of sparks, arcing, short circuits, over-loading of circuits or the breakdown of insulation on old wiring resulting in short circuiting.

Precautions

The precautions necessary in the use of portable electrical equipment can be related principally to the risk of injury to people and that of fire.

Risk of injury

The following precautions are essential:

a) earthing of supply circuit;

b) earthing of equipment;

c) insulation of all live conductors and equipment; and

d) the use of low voltage circuits (not exceeding 110 volts) and equipment.

Supply circuit design

The supply circuit should incorporate:

a) fusing;

b) current-operated circuit breakers;

c) voltage-operated circuit breakers; and

d) thermal trip devices.

Working systems

The following matters must be considered:

a) use of protective equipment e.g. rubber gloves and insulated tools/appliances;

b) use of rubber mats;

c) isolation and locking off of circuits prior to work;

d) portable step-down transformers and low voltage equipment;

e) trained and competent staff; and

f) use of a safe system of work/Permit to Work system.

Fire and explosion

The principles of isolation, insulation, circuit protection and minimizing supply and equipment voltages apply equally in the prevention of fire and explosion.

In certain cases further protection from potentially flammable atmospheres, using flameproof or sparkproof equipment, may be necessary.

Portable equipment: Basic preautions

The following precautions must be taken with portable equipment and should be considered in the inspection of same by a competent person.

1. Flexible leads should be protected from mechanical damage.

2. The outer covering of a flexible lead should be firmly clamped at its end terminations to relieve strain on the inner conductors.

3. Apparatus should never be pulled or suspended from its lead.

4. The inner conductors of a flexible lead should always be properly connected into the appliance or into a plug or approved type of connector.

5. Any exposed metalwork on a portable appliance should normally be firmly connected to earth. A three core flexible lead is essential. (Where the apparatus is of the double-insulated or all-insulated type an earthing terminal is not necessary.)

7. As far as possible reduced voltage portable appliances should be used i.e. 110/55 volts or, in the case of hand lamps, 25/12.5 volts. The reduced voltage will reduce the severity of an electric shock.

6. Portable hand tools should be regularly inspected and tested by a competent person, using a standard test set.

(See HSE Guidance Note PM32 *The Installation, Use and Maintenance of Portable and Mobile Electrical Apparatus.*)

Testing of portable electrical appliances

Approximately 25% of accidents involving electricity are associated with portable electrical appliances. To ensure compliance with the general provisions of the Electricity at Work Regulations 1989, there is an implied duty on employers, in particular, to undertake some form of testing of electrical equipment. Further guidance and information on portable appliance testing is incorporated in the Memorandum of Guidance which accompanies the Regulations and HSE Guidance Note PM 32.

Electrical equipment is very broadly defined in the Regulations as including anything used, intended to be used or installed for use, to generate, provide, transmit, transform, rectify, convert, conduct, distribute, control, store, measure or use electrical energy. **Portable appliances** include such items as electric drills, kettles, floor polishers and lamps, in fact any item that will connect into a 13 amp socket. 110 volt industrial portable electrical equipment should also be considered as portable appliances.

Safety of appliances

The operator or user of an electrical appliance is protected from the risk of electric shock by insulation and earthing of the appliance, which prevent the individual from coming into contact with a live electrical part. For insulation to be effective it must offer a high resistance at high voltages. In the case of earthing, it must offer a low impedance to any potentially high fault current that may arise.

A principal of electrical safety is that there should be two levels of protection for the operator or user and this results in two classes of appliance.

- **Class 1** appliances incorporate both earthing and insulation (earthed appliances), whereas

- **Class 2** appliances are doubly insulated. The testing procedures for Class 1 and Class 2 appliances differ according to the type of protection provided.

Appliance testing programmes

Testing should be undertaken on a regular basis and should incorporate the following:

a) inspection for any visible signs of damage to or deterioration of the casing, plug terminals and cable sheath;

b) an earth continuity test with a substantial current capable of revealing a partially severed conductor; and

c) high voltage insulation tests.

The test results should be recorded, thus enabling future comparisons to determine any deterioration or degradation of the appliance.

Control system

The control system should include:

a) clear identification of the specific responsibility for appliance testing;

b) maintenance of a log listing portable appliances, date of test and a record of test results; and

c) a procedure for labelling appliances when tested with the date for the next inspection and test.

Any appliance that fails the above tests should be removed from use.

Frequency of testing

An estimation of the frequency of testing must take into account the type of equipment, its usage in terms of frequency of use and risk of damage, and any recommendations made by the manufacturer/supplier.

The use of portable appliance testing equipment

Electrical tests of appliances should confirm the integrity or otherwise of earthing and insulation. To simplify this task a competent person may use a proprietary portable appliance testing (PAT) device. In this case, the unit under test is plugged into the socket of the testing device. Some tests are carried out through the plug, others through both the plug and an auxiliary probe to the casing of the appliance.

The tests

Two basic tests are offered by a PAT device, namely:

Earth bond test

This applies a substantial test current, typically around 25 amps, down the earth pin of the plug to an earth test probe which should be connected by the user to any exposed metalwork on the casing of the unit under test. From this the resistance of the earth bond is determined by the PAT device.

Insulation test

This applies a test voltage, typically 500 volts DC, between the live and neutral terminals bonded together and earth, from which the insulation resistance is calculated by the PAT device.

Other tests

Flash test

This tests the insulation at a higher voltage, typically 1.5 kV for Class 1 appliances and 3 kV for Class 2 appliances. From this test the PAT device derives a leakage current indication. This is a more stringent test of the insulation that can provide an early warning of insulation defects developing in the appliance. It is recommended that this test should not be undertaken at a greater frequency than every three months to avoid overstressing the insulation.

Load test

This test measures the load resistance between live and neutral terminals to ensure that it is not too low for safe operation.

Operation test

This is a further level of safety testing which proves the above tests were valid.

Earth leakage test

This is undertaken during the operation test as a further test of the insulation under its true working conditions. It should also ensure that appliances are not responsible for nuisance tripping of residual current devices (RCDs).

Fuse test

This will indicate the integrity of the fuse and that the appliance is switched on prior to other tests.

Earthed Class 1 appliances

The following tests are undertaken:

a) earth bond test;

b) insulation test; and

c) in certain cases, flash test.

Double-insulated Class 2 appliances

The following tests are undertaken:

a) insulation test; and

b) flash test.

See:

- *Electrical installations*

- *Welding and similar operations ('Hot work')*

Powered working platforms

A powered working platform (PWP) comprises:

- a fenced platform capable of supporting people and equipment;
- a powered device which supports the platform and is instrumental in the movement of the platform, and
- a self-propelled chassis supporting the platform and device.

PWPS: Two categories

PWPs are of two main types where:

a) the platform can be manoeuvred universally relative to the support vehicle, using telescoping or articulating rotating jibs or booms;

b) only vertical and, on some models, rotational movement of the platform can be made using:

   i)   scissor mechanisms;

   ii) hydraulic or pneumatic rams;

   iii) screw jacks; or

   iv) racks and pinions.

Hazards arising from the use of PWPs

The operation of PWPs can be particularly dangerous and many accidents are associated with their use, in particular:

- overturning of the equipment arising from:
  - use on uneven ground;
  - overloading of the platform with materials and equipment;
  - excessive wind loading;
  - movement on unsuitable gradients and terrain;
  - failure to install outriggers or stabilizers prior to use;
- falls of persons from the platform;
- collisions between the working platform and buildings, vehicles and other lifting appliances;
- trapping of operators in the raising, lowering, rotating or telescopic mechanism;
- failure of the platform supports, or the raising, lowering, rotating or telescopic mechanism;
- inadvertent or unexpected movement, arising from incorrect use of controls, brake failure, etc;
- electrical hazards, associated with contact with overhead cables, faults in circuits;
- other employees and members of the public being struck by the mobile platform.

Precautions

The following precautions are necessary to ensure the safe operation of PWPs:

- the maximum number of persons and the safe working load which may be carried should be clearly marked on the platform;
- guard rails at least 920mm high, with mid-rails or mesh infilling, and toe boards at least 150mm high, should be provided at the

edges of the platform; alternatively, solid enclosures at least 920mm in height should be provided;

- access gates to the platform should not open outwards and should return automatically to the closed and fastened position;

- guards should be installed to prevent access to dangerous parts of PWPs;

- safety devices should be fitted to prevent uncovenanted movement of the platform in the event of failure of the systems used to support and/or manoeuvre the platform;

- the maximum permissible wind speed in which the PWP may operate or remain raised or extended should be specified;

- the maximum gradient on which a PWP may operate should be clearly marked on the platform and inclinometers should be provided to enable the operator to establish platform slope;

- stabilizers/outriggers should be provided with suitable sole plates for use on soft ground;

- interlocking systems should be provided to ensure that when necessary, stabilizers/outriggers are used;

- stabilizers/outriggers should be so designed so that only stowed and fully extended positions are available and angular positioning cannot make the machine unstable;

- only trained and authorized operators should use a PWP;

- the person(s) on the platform should be in control of all movements;

- controls for a PWP should be:
    - clearly marked to indicate their function and mode of operation;
    - of the dead-man's handle type;
    - designed and installed so that unintentional operation is prevented; two-hand controls should be used to reduce the risk;

- emergency lowering controls should be provided at ground level;

- PWPs should not travel with the platform elevated unless this is approved by the manufacturer; such travelling should be limited to the minimum distances necessary to complete the work in hand.

- Electrically-operated PWPs and/or control circuits should meet strict electrical safety standards.

See:

- *Machinery and work equipment*

- *Mobile work equipment*

- *Work at height*

Power presses

A power press is defined in PUWER as 'a press or press brake for the working of metal by means of tools, or for die proving, which is power driven and which embodies a flywheel and clutch'.

Power presses have, in the past, been responsible for many fatal accidents and serious accidents involving amputations of arms, hands and fingers. As such, they have always been subject to extensive regulation, including the need for regular maintenance, examination and testing by a competent person.

Legal requirements for power presses

General and specific requirements relating to power presses are incorporated in Part IV of PUWER (Regulations 31 to 35) and Schedules 2 and 3. Further information is available in the ACOP and Guidance *Safe Use of Power Presses* and HSE Guidance HS(G)236 *Power Presses: Maintenance and Thorough Examination,* HSE Guidance HS(G)180 *Application of Electro-Sensitive Protective Equipment Using Light Curtains and Light Beam Devices to Machinery* and HSE Guidance INDG316 *Procedures for Daily Inspection and Testing of Mechanical Power Presses and Press Brakes.*

Employers have a duty to ensure:

- power presses are maintained in an efficient state, in efficient working order and in good repair;

- power presses and all their guards, the control systems and ancillary equipment (e.g. automatic feed systems) are maintained so that they do not put people at risk;

- maintenance work on power presses is carried out safely, i.e. the machinery is shut down and isolated, and undertaken by people who have the right skills and knowledge;

- training is provided for the 'appointed person', i.e. the person designated by an employer to inspect and test guards and safety devices every day they are in use and after setting, resetting or adjustment of the tools;

- the appointed person is trained and competent to carry out the work on each type of press; and

- an independent competent person, i.e, one with the appropriate skill, knowledge and experience, is appointed to undertake thorough examination and test of a power press, its guard(s) and/or protection devices on initial installation of the press and at designated periods afterwards.

See:

- *Competent persons*

- *Electrical installations*

- *Information, instruction and training*

- *Machinery and work equipment*

- *Risk assessment*

Pressure systems

Pressure vessels

Traditionally, pressure vessels have been associated with death and serious injuries arising from explosions. The hazards arising from the storage and use of steam, gases and liquids under pressure in pressure vessels, such as steam boilers, are principally associated with overheating in boilers and boiler corrosion.

Overheating in pressure vessels may arise as a result of:

- lack of testing and maintenance of controls and alarms, leading to malfunction; and

- in some cases, inadequate standards of control.

The long-term effects of boiler corrosion can be both explosions and boiler failure.

Pressure systems

Pressure systems incorporate one or more pressure vessels, pipework and a range of protective devices fitted to pressure vessels, such as a high and low water alarm, water gauges, safety valves, pressure gauge, stop valve and anti-priming pipe, all of which are installed to ensure maximum safety of operation.

Pressure Systems Regulations 2000

Important definitions

Pressure system is defined as meaning:

a) a system comprising one or more pressure vessels of rigid construction, any associated pipework and protective devices;

b) the pipework with its protective devices to which a transportable pressure receptacle is, or is intended to be, connected; or

c) a pipeline and its protective devices,

which contains a relevant fluid, but does not include a transportable pressure receptacle.

Relevant fluid means:

a) steam;

b) any fluid or mixture of fluids which is at a pressure greater than 0.5 bar above atmospheric pressure, and which fluid or mixture of fluids is:

   i) a gas, or

   ii) a liquid which would have a vapour pressure greater than 0.5 bar above atmospheric pressure when in equilibrium with its vapour at either the actual temperature of the liquid or 17.5 degrees Celsius; or

   a gas dissolved under pressure in a solvent contained in a porous substance at ambient temperature and which could be released from the solvent without the application of heat.

Principal requirements of the regulations

- Any person who designs, manufactures, imports or supplies any pressure system or any article which is intended to be a component part of any pressure system shall ensure that:

   a) the pressure system or article is properly designed and constructed from suitable material, so as to prevent danger;

b) the pressure system or article is so designed and constructed that all necessary examinations for preventing danger can be carried out;

c) where the pressure system has any means of access to its interior, it is so designed and constructed as to ensure, so far as is practicable, that access can be gained without danger; and

d) the pressure system is provided with such protective devices as may be necessary for preventing danger; and any such device designed to release contents shall do so safely, so far as is practicable.

- Anyone who designs, supplies, modifies or repairs any pressure system must provide sufficient written information to enable the requirements of the regulations to be complied with.

- Any person who manufactures a pressure vessel shall ensure that it is correctly marked.

- The employer of a person who installs a pressure system shall ensure that nothing about the way in which it is installed gives rise to danger or otherwise impairs the operation of any protective device or inspection facility.

- The user of an installed pressure system and owner of a mobile system shall not operate the system or allow it to be operated unless he has established the safe operating limits of that system.

- The user of an installed system and owner of a mobile system shall not operate the system or allow it to be operated unless he has a written scheme for the periodic examination, by a competent person, of the following parts of the system:

a) all protective devices;

b) every pressure vessel and every pipeline in which (in either case) a defect may give rise to danger; and

c) those parts of the pipe work in which a defect may give rise to danger,

- and such parts of the system shall be identified in the scheme.

- The competent person must prepare a written report of the examination to a format prescribed in the regulations, including details of any repairs, modifications and changes in the safe operating limits of the system deemed necessary to prevent danger or ensure the safe operation of the system.

- Where a competent person carrying out an examination of a pressure system is of the opinion that it will give rise to imminent danger unless certain repairs or modifications are carried out, or unless suitable changes to the operating conditions have been made, he shall forthwith make a written report to the user, and within 14 days of the completion of the examination send a written report containing the same particulars to the enforcing authority.

- The user of a pressure system shall provide for any person operating the system adequate and suitable instructions for:

  a) the safe operation of the system; and

  b) the action to be taken in the event of emergency.

- The user shall ensure that the system is not operated except in accordance with the instructions provided.

- The user shall ensure that the system is properly maintained in good repair, so as to prevent danger.

- The employer of a person who modifies or repairs a pressure system shall ensure that nothing about the way it is modified or repaired gives rise to danger or otherwise impairs the operation of any protective device or inspection facility.

- The user of an installed system and owner of a mobile system must keep a record of the report of the last examination by a competent person, information from suppliers and any agreement relating to postponement of examination by a competent person.

- Where a person is charged with an offence under the regulations, it shall be a defence for the person charged to prove:

  a) that the commission of the offence was due to the act or default of another person not being one of his employees; and

  b) that he took all reasonable precautions and exercised all due diligence to avoid the commission of the offence.

See:

- *Competent persons*
- *Information, instruction and training*
- *Machinery and work equipment*
- *Product liability*
- *Risk assessment*

Product liability

Product liability is an area of the law concerned with both the criminal and civil liabilities of all those who design, manufacture, import, install and sell products.

Criminal liability

Health and Safety at Work Act 1974

Sec 6: General duties of manufacturers, etc. as regards articles and substances for use at work:

1. It shall be the duty of any person who designs, manufactures, imports or supplies any article for use at work:

   a) to ensure, so far as is reasonably practicable, that the article is so designed and constructed as to be safe and without risks to health when properly used;

   b) to carry out and arrange for the carrying out of such testing and examination as may be necessary for the performance of the duty imposed on him by (a) above;

   c) to take such steps as are necessary to secure that there will be available in connection with the use of the article at work adequate information about the use for which it is designed and has been tested, and about any conditions necessary to ensure that when put to that use, it will be safe and without risks to health.

2. It shall be the duty of any person who undertakes the design or manufacture of any article for use at work to carry out or arrange for the carrying out of any necessary research with a view to the discovery and, so far as is reasonably practicable, the elimination or minimization of any risks to health or safety to which the design or article may give rise.

3. It shall be the duty of any person who erects or installs any article for use at work in any premises where that article is to be used by persons at work to ensure, so far as is reasonably practicable, that nothing about the way in which it is erected or installed makes it unsafe or a risk to health when properly used.

4. Where a person designs, manufactures, imports or supplies an article for, or to another, on the basis of a written undertaking by that other to take specified steps sufficient to ensure, so far as is reasonably practicable, that the article will be safe and without risks to health when properly used, the undertaking shall have the effect of relieving the first-mentioned person from the duty imposed by sub-section 1 above to such extent as is reasonable having regard to the terms of the undertaking.

Section 6 of the HSWA is concerned with the criminal liability of all persons involved in the production and supply chain of articles and substances for use at work. Generally, it is a term used to indicate the duties, responsibilities and liabilities of all who play a part in the creation, production, distribution or servicing of products towards all who suffer, or may suffer, damage as a result of a product defect.

Civil liability

Where a person suffers injury, damage or loss as a result of a defective or dangerous product, he may be in a position to sue the supplier for negligence.

The chain of supply

The following organizations and persons have varying degrees of responsibility within the chain of supply:

a) corporate bodies, directors and managers;

b) designers;

c) proof houses and other testing organizations;

d) standards institutes;

e) manufacturers of components and suppliers of ingredients;

f) assemblers and producers of finished products, installers and erectors;

g) purveyors of natural commodities and raw materials;

h) importers;

j) packagers;

k) providers of storage and transport facilities;

l) distributors;

m) retailers;

n) advertising, marketing and promotion specialists;

o) insurers;

p) lawyers;

q) trade union specialists/worker representatives; and

r) employees.

Principal liability rests with manufacturers, designers, importers and suppliers, secondary liability with erectors, installers, assemblers, distributors, advertisers and support services, such as lawyers, insurers and promotion specialists. Liability may be of a criminal and/or civil nature.

Information and instruction requirements

Delivery, collection and loading

Adequate information and instruction should be provided for all persons involved in delivery, collection and loading, indicating the hazards associated with such tasks and the precautions necessary.

Assembly or erection of buildings

Detailed information and instruction is required in the case of employed assemblers and erectors who have a duty to follow the assembly/erection instructions provided by their employer, the manufacturer or supplier.

Where assembly/erection is on a contracted basis, manufacturers and suppliers should ensure that such persons are competent to follow the written instructions for erection/assembly. In certain cases, a written undertaking from a contractor to assemble/erect according to a manufacturer's instructions may give some degree of protection in the event of incorrect or dangerous assembly/erection. Liability would hinge around whether the instructions and information were reasonable in the circumstances, and very much a matter for a court to decide.

Product liability insurance

Many organizations take out a form of product liability insurance to give cover against claims for defective products. In the case of portable buildings, cover would be provided against both a defective building or part of same and defective erection or assembly. However, the emphasis must be on prevention sooner than protection.

Preventing product liability incidents

Prevention of such incidents must be through:

a) the provision of training for all persons involved in the supply chain;

b) documentation of information and procedures in company manuals and instruction booklets;

c) regular supervision and control to ensure the manufacturer/ supplier's instructions are being followed implicitly; and

d) regular liaison between manufacturers, designers, erectors, installers and others involved in the supply chain.

See:

- *Common law liability*

- *Hazardous substances*

- *Health and Safety at Work etc Act 1974*

- *Information sources*

- *Negligence*

- *Safety data (hazardous substances)*

R

Radiation and radiological protection

Radiation is a form of energy and can be a source of danger in uncontrolled situations.

Radiation energy is released in the form of waves, the length and frequency of the wave depending upon how much energy the atom is releasing. The length and frequency of the waves control the form of energy and its effects on the human body.

Energy types can be listed in increasing wavelength as shown in Table 13 below.

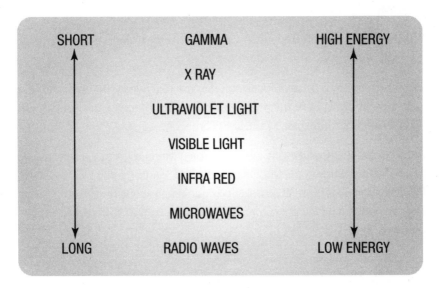

Table 13: The electromagnetic spectrum

The most important division in the spectrum is between ionising and non-ionising radiation. (An ion is a charged atom or group of atoms.)

Ionising radiation can produce chemical changes as a result of ionising molecules upon which it is incident. Non-ionising radiation does not, however, have this effect and is usually absorbed by the molecules upon which it is incident, with the result that the material will heat up, as in the case of microwaves.

Radiation hazards

To assess the hazard associated with radiation, it is necessary to consider:

a)   the type of radiation;

b)   the energy;

c)   the extent of penetration of tissue; and

d)   the duration of exposure.

Exposure to radiation

Effects on the human body may vary according to the type of exposure i.e. local or general, and the duration of exposure.

The most common form of local exposure results in reddening of the skin with ulceration. Where there is a small dose but of long duration, loss of hair, atrophy and fibrosis of the skin can occur.

Acute general exposure can have variable results mild nausea to severe illness, with vomiting, diarrhoea and collapse, leading ultimately to death. Where exposure is in small doses, chronic anaemia and leukaemia can result. The ovaries and testes are vulnerable and this can lead to reduced fertility and sterility.

Radiological radiation

In considering radiological protection strategies, it is necessary to distinguish between sealed and unsealed sources of radiation.

Sealed sources

The source is contained in such a way that the radioactive material cannot be released, e.g. X-ray machines. The source of radiation can be a piece of radioactive metal, such as cobalt, which is sealed in a container or held in another material which is not radioactive. It is usually solid and the container and any bonding material are regarded as the source.

Unsealed sources

Unsealed sources may take a variety of forms – gases, liquids and particulates. Because they are unsealed, entry into the body is comparatively easy.

Criteria for radiological protection

The basic criteria for radiological protection rest on three specific considerations: time, distance and shielding. The principle is to ensure that no one receives a harmful dose of radiation.

- Radiation workers may be protected on a time basis by limiting the duration of exposure to certain predetermined limits.

- Alternatively, they may be protected by ensuring that they do not come within certain distances of radiation sources. This may be achieved by the use of restricted areas, barriers and similar controls. The Inverse Square Law applies in this case.

- They may be shielded by the use of absorbent material, such as lead or concrete, between themselves and the source to reduce the level of radiation to below the maximum dose level. The quality and quantity (thickness) of shielding varies for the radiation type and energy level and varies from no shielding through lightweight shielding (e.g. 1cm thick Perspex) to heavy shielding (e.g. centimetres of lead or metres of concrete).

Further protection procedures

Radiological protection procedures may also include:

a) pre-employment and subsequent medical examinations;

b) appointment of a responsible trained person;

c) maintenance of individual dose records;

d) full training and employee awareness;

e) continuous and spot-check radiation (dose) monitoring by the use of personal dosemeters, such as film badges;

f) adherence to maximum permissible dose levels.

ADDITIONALLY for unsealed sources:

g) provision and use of appropriate protective clothing;

h) efficient ventilation;

i) enclosure of sources (containment);

j) use of impervious working surfaces;

k) immaculate working techniques; and

l) the use of remote control facilities.

The central objective is the avoidance of radioactive contamination.

Ionising Radiations Regulations 1999

These regulations impose duties on employers to protect employees and other persons against ionising radiation arising from work with radioactive substances and other sources of ionising radiation.

Principal requirements of the regulations

- Certain specified practices are prohibited without the authorization of the HSE.

- Specified work with ionising radiation must be notified to the HSE.

- Employers must make a prior assessment of the risks arising from their work with radiation, an assessment of the hazards likely to arise from that work, and prevent and limit the consequences of identifiable radiation accidents.

- Employers must take all necessary steps to restrict so far as is reasonably practicable the extent to which employees and other persons are exposed to ionising radiation.

- Respiratory protective equipment must conform to agreed standards, and personal protective equipment and other controls must be regularly examined and properly maintained.

- Limits of doses of ionising radiation which people may receive per calendar year are:

  – 20 millisieverts for employees of 18 years of age or above;

  – 6 millisieverts for trainees aged under 18 years;

  – 1 millisievert for any other person, including members of the public.

- In certain circumstances, employers must prepare contingency plans for radiation accidents (Regulation 12).

- Employers must consult radiation protection advisers in respect of certain matters and provide adequate information, instruction and training to employees and other persons.

- Employers must designate controlled or supervised areas where there may be a need to restrict exposure, or where employees are likely to receive more than specified doses of radiation, set out appropriate local rules for these areas, appoint radiation protection supervisors and monitor radiation levels in these areas.

- Where employees are likely to receive more than specified does of ionising radiation they must be designated as classified persons, doses received by such persons must be assessed by an HSE-approved dosimetry service, and appropriate dose records maintained.

- Radioactive substances used as a source of ionising radiation must, whenever reasonably practicable, be in the form of a sealed source.

- Employers must make specific arrangements for the control of radioactive substances, articles and equipment.

- Employees:

    a) must not knowingly expose themselves or other persons to ionising radiation to an extent greater than is reasonably necessary;

    b) must exercise reasonable care while carrying out such work;

    c) make full and proper use of any PPE; and

    d) report defects in their PPE to their employer.

See:

- *Health surveillance and health protection*

- *Occupational diseases and conditions*

- *Risk assessment*

Risk assessment

Principles of risk assessment

A risk assessment is carried out to identify the risks to employees and any other persons arising out of, or in connection with, work or the conduct of an undertaking. It should identify how the risks arise and how they impact on those affected. This information is needed to make decisions on how to manage those risks so that decisions are made in an informed, rational and structured manner, and the action taken is proportionate.

What is risk assessment?

Risk assessment involves:

- the identification of hazards at work;
- the weighing up of the risks from the hazards;
- deciding how to control the risks; and
- implementing a control strategy.

A risk assessment has three purposes:

- to identify all the factors which may cause harm to employees and others (the hazards);
- to consider the chance of that harm actually befalling anyone in the circumstances of a particular case, and the possible consequences that could come from it (the risks); and
- to enable employers to plan, introduce and monitor preventive measures to ensure that the risks are adequately controlled at all times.

Without effective assessment there can seldom be effective control.

EXTRACT FROM THE ACOP TO THE MHSWR

'Hazard' and 'risk' – the distinction

'Hazard'

A hazard is something with the potential to cause harm. This can include articles, substances, plant or machines, methods of work, the working environment and other aspects of work organization.

'Risk'

A risk is the likelihood of potential harm from that hazard being realized. The extent of the risk will depend on:

- the likelihood of that harm occurring;

- the potential severity of that harm, i.e. of any resultant injury or adverse health effect; and

- the population which might be affected by the hazard, i.e. the number of people who might be exposed.

The purpose of the risk assessment is to help the employer or self-employed person to determine what measures should be taken to comply with the employer's or self-employed person's duties under the relevant statutory provisions. This covers the general duties in the HSWA and more specific duties in the regulations (including these Regulations) associated with the HSWA.

Once the measures have been determined in this way, the duty to put them into effect will be defined in the statutory provisions. For example a risk assessment on machinery would be undertaken under these Regulations, but the Provision and Use of Work Equipment Regulations (PUWER 1998) determine what precautions must be carried out.

Suitable and sufficient

A suitable and sufficient risk assessment should be made. 'Suitable and sufficient' is not defined in the Regulations. In practice it means the risk assessment should do the following:

- The risk assessment should identify the risks arising from or in connection with work; the level of detail in a risk assessment should be proportionate to the risk and the level of risk arising from the work activity should determine the degree of sophistication of the risk assessment.

- Employers and the self-employed are expected to take reasonable steps to help themselves identify risks, e.g. by looking at appropriate sources of information, such as relevant legislation, appropriate guidance, supplier manuals and manufacturers' instructions and reading trade press, or seeking advice from competent sources. The risk assessment should include only what an employer or self-employed person could reasonably be expected to know; they would not be expected to anticipate risks that were not foreseeable.

- The risk assessment should be appropriate to the nature of the work and should identify the period of time for which it is likely to remain valid.

- For activities where the nature of the work may change fairly frequently or the workplace itself changes and develops (such as a construction site), or where workers move from site to site, the risk assessment might have to concentrate more on the broad range of risks that can be foreseen.

Risk assessment in practice

There are no fixed rules about how a risk assessment should be carried out; indeed it will depend on the nature of the work or business and the types of hazards and risks.

In some cases employers may make a first rough assessment to eliminate from consideration those risks on which no further action is needed. This should show where a fuller assessment is needed, if appropriate, using more sophisticated techniques.

Employers who control a number of similar workplaces containing similar activities may produce a 'model' (or 'generic') risk assessment reflecting the core hazards and risks associated with those activities. 'Model' assessments may also be developed by trade associations, employers' bodies or other organizations concerned with a particular activity. Such 'model' arrangements may be applied by employers or managers at each workplace, but only if they:

a)   satisfy themselves that the 'model' assessment is appropriate to their type of work;

and

b)   adapt the 'model' to the detail of their own actual work situations, including any extension necessary to cover hazards and risks not referred to in the 'model'.

A risk assessment should:

- ensure the significant risks and hazards are addressed;

- ensure all aspects of the work activity are reviewed, including routine and non-routine activities;

- take account of non-routine operations, e.g. maintenance, cleaning operations, loading and unloading of vehicles, changes in production cycles, emergency response arrangements;

- take account of the management of incidents such as interruptions to the work activity, which frequently cause accidents, and consider what procedure should be followed to mitigate the effects of the incident;

- be systematic in identifying hazards and looking at risks, whether one risk assessment covers the whole of the work activity or the assessment is divided up;

- take account of the way in which the work is organized, and the effects this can have on health;

- take account of risks to the public;

- take account of the need to cover fire risks. (See the guide *Fire Safety: An Employer's Guide*)

Stages of the risk assessment process

- Identify the hazards

- Identify who might be harmed and how

- Evaluate the risks from the identified hazards

- Record the significant findings

Recording

The significant findings of a risk assessment should include:

- a record of the preventive and protective measures in place to control the risks;

- what further action, if any, needs to be taken to reduce risk sufficiently;

- proof that a suitable and sufficient risk assessment has been made.

Review and revision

Risk assessments should be subject to review and revision, in circumstances where, for example:

- the nature of the work changes; and/or

- developments suggest that it may no longer be valid.

Assessment under other regulations

The requirements of, for example, the COSHH Regulations, may need to be considered in conjunction with a work activity risk assessment.

STEP 1: HAZARD

Hazard means anything that can cause harm.

Look only for hazards which you could reasonably expect to result in *significant* harm under the conditions in your workplace. Use the following examples as a guide.

- slipping
- fire
- chemicals
- moving parts of machinery
- work at height
- ejection of material
- pressure systems
- vehicles
- electricity
- dust/fumes
- manual handling
- noise
- poor lighting
- low temperature

STEP 2: WHO MIGHT BE HARMED?

There is no need to list individuals by name. Just think about the groups of people doing similar work or who may be affected, e.g.

- office staff
- maintenance personnel
- contractors
- people sharing your workplace
- operators
- cleaners
- members of the public

Pay particular attention to:

- staff with disabilities
- visitors
- inexperienced staff

- lone workers
- pregnant workers
- young persons

They may be more vulnerable.

STEP 3: IS MORE NEEDED TO CONTROL THE RISKS?

Risk is the chance, high or low, that somebody will be harmed by the hazard. For the hazards listed, do the precautions already taken:

- meet the standards set by a legal requirement?
- comply with a recognized industry standard?
- represent good practice?
- reduce risk so far as is reasonably practicable?

Have you provided:

- adequate information, instruction and training?
- adequate systems or procedures?

If so, then the risks are adequately controlled, but you need to indicate the precautions you have in place. (You may refer to procedures, company rules, etc.)

Where the risk is not adequately controlled, indicate what more you need to do (the 'action list').

STEP 4: RECORD YOUR FINDINGS

_____

_____

_____

_____

_____

_____

_____

_____

STEP 5: REVIEW AND REVISION

Set a date for a review of the assessment.

On review, check that the precautions for each hazard still adequately control the risk. Note the outcome. If necessary complete a new page for your risk assessment.

Making changes in your workplace, e.g. when bringing in new:

- machines
- substances
- procedures

may introduce significant new hazards. Look for them and follow the five steps.

RISK ASSESSMENT

Risk assessment for	Assessment undertaken	Assessment review
Company name	Date	Date
Company address	Signed	
	Date	
Post Code		

STEP 1	STEP 2	STEP 3
List significant hazards here	List groups of people who are at risk from the risk from the significant hazards you have identified	List existing controls or note where the information may be found. List risks which which are not adequately controlled and the action needed

Fig 11: HSE guidance: five steps to risk assessment

See:

- *Accidents and accident prevention*

- *Children at work*

- *Display screen equipment*

- *Health risk assessment*

- *Lead at work*

- *Manual handling operations*

- *Noise*

- *New and expectant mothers*

- *Safety management systems*

- *Stress at work*

- *Work at height*

- *Vibration*

- *Young persons*

S

Safety budgets

Traditionally, as far as health and safety at work is concerned, organizations have taken the view 'Comply with the law but no more!'. Compliance with the law has always been seen as the ultimate goal. What they fail to consider, however, are the economic costs and losses associated with accidents, ill health and loss-producing incidents (see *Accident costs*). Moreover, health and safety improvement has always been viewed as something of an en-cost, with no specific provision being made in budgets. As a result, when improvement is required a 'robbing Peter to pay Paul' approach has had to be taken with existing budgets.

However, with the operation of various forms of safety monitoring, including risk assessment, it should be possible for organizations to identify future health and safety improvements and make provision in budgets for these improvements. Very few organizations, however, have specific safety budgets. Much of the information relating to the costs of accidents and ill-health can be identified through the operation of accident costing systems. From these systems, a better knowledge of the main costs of accidents, both direct and indirect, can be ascertained which, in turn, contributes to future decision making with regard to machinery and plant acquisition, structural improvements and management systems.

There are good reasons for operating specific safety budgets, namely:

- to make provision for future improvements arising as a result of:
  - impending or new legislation; and
  - recommendations from safety monitoring activities, risk assessment and accident investigations;

- to ensure managers pay sufficient attention to the subject and in assessing future workplace safety provisions;

- to make provision, for example, for the replacement of worn-out guards to machinery, refurbishment of amenities, provision of PPE, health surveillance and environmental monitoring.

On this basis, health and safety improvement should feature in the standard budget-setting process for an organization, whether this is done as specific safety budgets or as a safety element of a manager's budget.

See:

- *Accident and ill health costs*

- *Safety management systems*

Safety committees

In conjunction with the Safety Representatives and Safety Committees Regulations 1977, the HSE published guidance on the objectives, function, membership and conduct of health and safety committees.

Basic objectives

- The promotion of co-operation between employers and employees in instigating, developing and carrying out measures to ensure the health and safety at work of employees.

- To act as a focus for employee participation in the prevention of accidents and the avoidance of industrial diseases.

Specific functions of health and safety committees

- The study of accident and notifiable disease statistics and trends, so that reports can be made to management on unsafe and unhealthy conditions and practices, together with recommendations for corrective action.

- Examination safety audit reports on a similar basis.

- Consideration of reports and factual information provided by inspectors of the enforcing authority appointed under the Health and Safety at Work Act.

- Assistance in the development of workplace safety rules and safe systems of work.

- A watch on the effectiveness of safety content of employee training.

- A watch on the adequacy of safety and health communication and publicity in the workplace.

- The provision of a link with the appropriate enforcing authority.

In certain cases safety committees may consider it useful to carry out an inspection by the committee itself. But it is management's responsibility to take executive action and to have adequate arrangements for regular and effective checking of health and safety precautions and for ensuring that the declared health and safety policy is being fulfilled. The work of the safety committee should supplement these arrangements; it cannot be a substitute for them.

Membership of safety committees

The membership and structure of safety committees should be settled in consultation with management and the trade union representatives concerned through the use of the normal machinery. The aim should be to keep the total size as reasonably compact as possible and compatible with the adequate representation of the interests of management and of all the employees, including safety representatives. The number of management representatives should not exceed the number of employees' representatives.

Management representatives should not only include those from line management but such others as engineers and personnel managers. The supervisory level should also be represented.

Management representation should be aimed at ensuring:

a) adequate authority to give proper consideration to view and recommendations; and

b) the necessary knowledge and expertise to provide accurate information to the committee on company policy, production needs and on technical matters in relation to premises, processes, plant, machinery and equipment.

Conduct of safety committees

Safety committees should meet as often as necessary. The frequency of meetings will depend upon the volume of business, which in turn is likely to depend on local conditions, the size of the workplace, numbers employed, the kind of work carried out and the degree of risk inherent. Sufficient time should be allowed during each meeting to ensure full discussion of all business.

Meetings should feature an agenda and minutes of the meeting should be circulated as soon as possible to all members, together with the most senior executive responsible for health and safety.

Arrangements should be made to ensure that the Board of Directors is kept informed generally of the work of the committee.

See:

- *Consultation on health and safety*

Safety culture

All organizations incorporate a set of cultures which have developed over a period of time. They are associated with the accepted standards of behaviour within that organization and the development of a specific culture with regard to, for instance, quality, customer service and written communication is a continuing quest for many organizations.

Establishing a safety culture

With the greater emphasis on health and safety management, attention should be paid by managers to the establishment and development of the correct safety culture within the organization. Both the HSE and the CBI have provided guidance on this issue.

The main principles, which involve the establishment of a safety culture, accepted and observed generally, are:

a) the acceptance of responsibility at and from the top, exercised through a clear chain of command, seen to be actual and felt through the organization;

b) a conviction that high standards are achievable through proper management;

c) setting and monitoring of relevant objectives/targets, based upon satisfactory internal information systems;

d) systematic identification and assessment of hazards and the devising and exercise of preventive systems which are subject to audit and review; in such approaches, particular attention is given to the investigation of error;

e) immediate rectification of deficiencies; and

f) promotion and reward of enthusiasm and good results.

Rimington JR (1989): *The Onshore Safety Regime*, HSE Director General's Submission to the Piper Alpha Inquiry, December 1989

Developing a safety culture

(Excerpt from *Developing a Safety Culture*, CBI (1991):

Several features can be identified from the study which are essential to a sound safety culture. A company wishing to improve its performance will need to judge its existing practices against them.

1. Leadership and commitment from the top which is genuine and visible. This is the most important feature.

2. Acceptance that it is a long-term strategy which requires sustained effort and interest.

3. A policy statement of high expectations, conveying a sense of optimism about what is possible supported by adequate codes of practice and safety standards.

4. Health and safety should be treated as other corporate aims, and properly resourced.

5. It must be a line management responsibility.

6. 'Ownership' of health and safety must permeate at all levels of the workforce. This requires employee involvement, training and communication.

7. Realistic and achievable targets should be set and performance measured against them.

8. Incidents should be thoroughly investigated.

9. Consistency of behaviour against agreed standards should be achieved by auditing and good safety behaviour should be a condition of employment.

10. Deficiencies revealed by an investigation or audit should be remedied promptly.

11. Management must receive adequate and up-to-date information to be able to assess performance.

The role of management

Legal requirements have moved away from the setting of prescriptive standards for health and safety to a more management and human factors orientated approach. On this basis, the role of senior management in developing and sustaining an appropriate safety culture has become increasingly significant. What must managers do then to encourage a positive safety culture?

Firstly, the Board must clearly state their intentions, expectations and beliefs in relation to health and safety at work. In other words, they must state where they want the organization to be in terms of health and safety, and formulate action plans for achieving these objectives.

Adequate resources, in terms of financial resources, time and effort must be made available in order to translate these plans and objectives into effective action. In particular, managers at all levels must be made accountable and responsible for their performance, as with other areas of performance, as part of this process. This should take place through routine performance monitoring and review, such performance being related to the reward structure of the organization. On the job performance monitoring should take into account the human decision-making components of a job, in particular the potential for human error.

Above all, senior managers and directors must be seen by all concerned to be taking an active and continuing interest in the development and implementation of health and safety improvements. On this basis, they should reward positive achievement in order to reinforce their message to subordinates that health and safety is of prime importance in the activities of the organization.

In the same way, the various lower levels of management must be actively involved. They must accept their responsibilities for maintaining health and safety standards as line managers and ensure that health and safety keeps a high profile within their area of responsibility. This will entail vigilance on their part to ensure, for instance, that safe systems of work are being followed, that people under their control are wearing the appropriate personal protective equipment and that unsafe practices by workers are being adopted. They must show that deviations from recognized health and safety standards will not be tolerated but, in doing so, it is important for line managers to recognize that they will receive backing from senior managers where such deviations actually occur. It is vitally important that senior management demonstrate their commitment.

See:

- *Human factors and safety*
- *Safety incentive schemes*
- *Safety management systems*

Safety data (hazardous substances)

Appendix 1 of the ACOP *Safety Data Sheets for Substances and Prepara-tions Dangerous for Supply,* issued by the HSC in conjunction with the CHIP Regulations, lists the following headings which must be incorpo-rated in a Safety Data Sheet provided by a supplier, thus:

The safety data sheet referred to in Regulation 6(1) should contain the following obligatory headings, as stated in Schedule 6 to the Regulations.

1. Identification of the substance/prepa-ration and company

2. Composition/information on ingredi-ents

3. Hazards identification

4. First aid measures

5. Fire fighting measures

6. Accidental release measures

7. Handling and storage

8. Exposure controls/personal protection

9. Physical and chemical properties

10. Stability and reactivity

11. Toxicological information

12. Ecological information

13. Disposal considerations

14. Transport information

15. Regulatory information

16. Other information

Table 14: Headings on the safety data sheet

It is incumbent on the person responsible for supplying the substance or preparation to supply information specified under these headings.

See:

- *Fire prevention*
- *First aid*
- *Hazardous substances*
- *Health risk assessment*
- *Occupational exposure limits*
- *Product liability*
- *Toxicology*

Safety incentive schemes

Safety incentive schemes have a number of purposes, for example, to increase the awareness of employees with respect to safe working practices, to compare performance across different parts of the organization, to reward good performance and to raise the profile of health and safety. Safety incentive schemes take many forms but, fundamentally, should reflect what goes on in the organization, such as manufacturing and, to be successful, must have the full support and co-operation of directors and senior managers.

Award schemes

One way of raising the profile of health and safety in an organization is through the operation of a health and safety award scheme. The aims and objectives of such a scheme are outlined below.

Awards

1. Three Awards (Gold, Silver and Bronze) would be presented initially for the best health and safety performance by individual units during the year under review.

2. After the first year of the Award Scheme coming into operation, an Award for Most Improved Performance would be added to the three Awards.

3. Each Award could take the form of a shield with badgelets, the shield passing from one winner to another on a yearly basis. The name of the winning unit each year would be engraved on a badgelet

on the shield. The winner of the Gold Award could also be provided with a specially-designed flag to fly during the following year.

4. Each Award would be accompanied by a framed certificate to be retained at the unit.

Selection

5. Six finalists would be nominated by senior/area managers and a judging panel or group would visit each finalist unit with a view to assessing the winners and runners-up for the Awards.

Recognition of achievement

6. Maximum publicity would be given by the organization to the Health and Safety Award Scheme through the use of posters and other means of raising awareness, and to the winners and finalists on a yearly basis.

7. Some form of recognition for Award-winning units, by way of a special party, dinner, evening out for staff and partners, or by giving Christmas hampers, should be made.

8. Directors and senior management should show commitment to the Award Scheme by direct encouragement, identification personally with the Award Scheme and by attendance at Award-winners' functions.

Lack of commitment

9. Where there is clear evidence of lack of commitment to the Award Scheme by managers, which may be shown by a continuing deterioration in performance shown in the assessments, some form of stimulation, and even disciplinary action, may be necessary.

See:

- *Accident and ill health costs*
- *Safety monitoring systems*

Safety management systems

BS 8800 – Guide to occupational health and safety management systems

BS 8800: 2004 offers an organization the opportunity to review and revise its current occupational health and safety arrangements against a standard that has been developed by industry, commerce, insurers, regulators, trade unions and occupational health and safety practitioners.

The aims of the standard are "to improve the occupational health and safety performance of organizations by providing guidance of how management of occupational health and safety may be integrated with the management of other aspects of the business performance in order to:

- minimize risks to employees and others;
- improve business performance; and
- assist organizations to establish a responsible image in the workplace.

In order to achieve positive benefits, health and safety management should be an integral feature of the undertaking contributing to the success of the organization.

Status review

In any status review of the health and safety management system, BS 8800 recommends the following headings:

1. Requirements of relevant legislation dealing with health and safety management issues.

2. Existing guidance on health and safety management within the organization

3. Best practice and performance in the organization's employment sector and other appropriate sectors e.g. from relevant HSC's industry advisory committees and trade association guidelines.

4. Efficiency and effectiveness of existing resources devoted to health and safety management.

Policies

BS 8800 identifies nine key areas that should be addressed in a policy, each of which allows visible objectives and targets to be set:

- recognizing that occupational health and safety is an integral part of its business performance;

- achieving a high level of health and safety performance, with compliance to legal requirements as the minimum and continual cost effective improvement in performance;

- provision of adequate and appropriate resources to implement the policy;

- the publishing and setting of health and safety objectives, even if only by internal notification;

- placing the management of health and safety as a prime responsibility of line management, from most senior executive to first-line supervisory level;

- ensuring understanding, implementation and maintenance of the policy statement at all levels in the organization;

- employee involvement and consultation to gain commitment to the policy and its implementation;

- periodic review of the policy, the management system and audit of compliance to policy;

- ensuring that employees at all levels receive appropriate training and are competent to carry out their duties and responsibilities.

The models

There are two recommended approaches depending upon the organizational needs of the business and with the objective that such an approach will be integrated into the total management system, namely:

a) one based on *Successful Health and Safety Management* [HS(G)65]; and

b) one based on ISO 14001, which is compatible with the environmental standard.

Failure mode and effect analysis

This technique is based on identifying the possible failure modes of each component of a system and predicting the consequences of that failure. For example, if a safety device linked to a machinery guard fails, it could result in the operator being exposed to danger.

As a result, attention is paid to those consequences at the design stage of the machinery safety system and in the preparation of the planned preventive maintenance procedure for the machine.

Fault tree analysis

A form of safety management technique which begins with the consideration of a chosen 'top event', such as a pressure vessel explosion, and then assesses the combination of failures and conditions which could cause this event to take place.

This technique is used widely in quantitative risk analysis, particularly where control over process controls is critical to meeting safety standards.

Event tree analysis

This technique is similar to Fault Tree Analysis, working from a selected 'initiating event', such as an electrical fault in a manufacturing system. Basically it is a systematic representation of all the possible states of the processing system conditional to the specific initiating event and relevant for a certain type of outcome, such as a major fire or unsafe feature of the manufacturing system.

Consequence analysis

Consequence analysis is a feature of risk analysis which considers the physical effects of a particular process failure and the damage caused by these effects. It is undertaken to form an opinion on potentially serious hazardous outcomes of accidents and their possible consequences for people and the environment. The technique should be used as a tool in the decision-making process in a safety study which incorporates the following features:

a) description of the process system to be investigated;

b) identification of the undesirable events;

c) determination of the magnitude of the resulting physical effects;

d) determination of the damage;

e) estimation of the probability of the occurrence of calculated damage; and

f) assessment of the risk against established criteria.

The outcome of consequence analysis is:

a) for the chemical and process industries, to obtain information about all known and unknown effects that are of importance when something goes wrong in the plant and to obtain information on measures for dealing with catastrophic events;

b) for the designing industries, to obtain information on how to mini-mize the consequences of accidents;

c) for the operators in the processing plant and people living in the immediate vicinity, to give them an understanding of their personal situation and the measures being taken to protect them; and

d) for the enforcement and legislative authorities, to provide them with information on measures being taken to ensure compliance with current legal requirements.

Consequence analysis is generally undertaken by a team of specialists, including chemists and safety technologists experienced in the actual prob-lems of the system concerned.

ISO 14001: Environmental Management Systems

This Standard provides a model for health and safety management systems. Implementation of the Standard takes place in a number of clearly defined stages, thus:

Initial status review

This stage entails a review and assessment of the current 'state of play' with regard to health and safety management systems. Proactive factors to be considered include the presence of written safe systems of work, joint consul-tation procedures, an integrated approach to risk assessment, documented planned preventive maintenance systems and a procedure for providing information, instruction and training at all levels within the organization.

Reactive management systems include those for accident and incident reporting, recording and investigation, accident and incident costing and means for the provision of feedback following the investigation of acci-dents, incidents and occupational ill health.

Occupational health and safety policy

A review of the current Statement of Health and Safety Policy and other sub-policies covering, for example, stress at work, contractors' activities and the provision of personal protective equipment, takes place at this stage.

Planning

Feedback from the initial status review and assessment of the effectiveness of the Statement of Health and Safety Policy will identify areas for planning for future actions. This stage may entail the establishment of management systems to cover:

a) future safety monitoring operations;

b) the preparation of rules for the safe conduct of project work (contractors' regulations)

c) systems for raising the awareness of employees;

d) the provision of information, instruction and training;

e) planned preventive maintenance;

f) health surveillance of specific groups of employees; and

g) a review of risk assessment procedures.

Implementation and operation

Once the strategies and objectives for future health and safety activities have been established at the planning stage, the process of implementing these objectives must be put into operation, perhaps on a phased basis. The written objectives should specify:

a) the actual objective;

b) the manager responsible for achieving this objective;

c) the financial arrangements where appropriate;

d) the criteria for assessing successful achievement of the objective; and

e) a date for completion of the objective.

Checking and corrective action

Procedures should be established for ensuring that agreed objectives are being achieved within the timescale allocated and for ensuring specific corrective action is taken in the event of failure or incomplete fulfilment of the objective.

Management review

Any phased programme of improvement must be subject to regular management review. The timescale for review, and the management responsible for same, should be established before the implementation stage. In most cases a review team would assess the success in achievement of the pre-determined objectives and make recommendations for future action, including any safety monitoring arrangements necessary.

Continual improvement

As a result of undertaking this phased approach to health and safety management, there should be continual improvement in health and safety performance including:

    a) improved attitudes and awareness on the part of management and employees;

    b) greater commitment to, and recognition of, the need to incorporate health and safety in management procedures;

    c) regular revisions of policy based on feedback from reviews;

    d) a developing health and safety culture within the organization;

    e) improved systems for ensuring corrective action is dealt with quickly; and

    f) ease of integration of environmental management systems with health and safety management systems.

Management oversight and risk tree (MORT)

MORT is defined as 'a systemic approach to the management of risks in an organization'. It was developed by the United States Department of Energy during the period 1978 – 83, and incorporates methods aimed at increasing reliability, assessing the risks, controlling losses and allocating resources effectively.

The MORT philosophy is summarized in the following points:

Management takes risks of many kinds

Specifically, these risks are classified in the areas of:

a) product quantity and quality;

b) cost;

c) schedule;

d) environment, health and safety.

Risks in one area affect operations in other areas

Management's job may be viewed as one of balancing risks. For instance, to focus only on safety and environmental issues would increase the risk of losses from deficiencies, schedule delays and costs.

Risks should be made explicit where practicable

Since management must take risks, it should know the potential consequences of those risks.

Risk management tools should be flexible enough to suit a variety of diverse situations

While some analytical tools are needed for complex situations, other situations require simpler and quicker approaches. The MORT system is designed to be applied to all of an organization's risk management concerns, from simple to complex.

The MORT Process

The acronym, MORT, carries two primary meanings:

a) the MORT 'tree' or logic diagram, which organizes risk, loss and safety programme elements and is used as a master worksheet for accident investigations and programme evaluations; and

b) the total safety programme, seen as a sub-system to the major management system of an organization.

The MORT process includes four main analytical tools:

Change analysis

This is based on the Kepner-Tregoe method of rational decision-making. Change analysis compares a problem-free situation with a problem (accident) situation in order to isolate causes and effects of change. It is especially useful when the decision-maker needs a quick analysis, when the cause is obscure, and when well-behaved personnel behave differently from past situations, as with the Three Mile Island incident.

Energy trace and barrier analysis (ETBA)

ETBA is based on the notion that energy is necessary to do work, that energy must be controlled, and that uncontrolled energy flowing in the absence of adequate barriers can cause accidents. The simple 'energy-barrier-targets' concept is expanded with the details of specific situations to answer the question "What happened?" in an accident. ETBA may be performed very quickly or applied meticulously as time permits.

MORT tree analysis

This is the third and most complex tool, combining principles from the fields of management and safety. It uses fault tree methodology with a view to assisting the investigator to ascertain what happened and why it happened. The MORT tree organizes over 1500 basic events (causes) leading to 98 generic events (problems). Both specific control factors and management system factors are analysed for their contributions to the accident.

People, procedures and hardware are considered separately, and then together, as key system safety elements.

Positive (success) tree design

This technique reverses the logic of fault tree analysis. In positive tree design, a system for successful operation is comprehensively and logically laid out. The positive tree is an excellent planning and assessment tool because it shows all that must be performed and the proper sequencing of events needed to accomplish an objective.

Objectives of the MORT technique

MORT is, fundamentally, an analytical technique or procedure to determine the potential for downgrading incidents in situations. It places special emphasis on the part that management oversight plays in allowing untoward or adverse events to occur. The MORT system is designed to:

a)   result in a reduction in oversights, whether by omission or commission, that could lead to downgrading incidents if they are not corrected;

b)   determine the order of risks and refer them to the proper organizational level for corrective action;

c)   ensure best allocation and use of resources to organize efforts to prevent or reduce the number and severity of adverse incidents.

OHSAS 18001 – A pro-active approach to health and safety management

This standard specifies a staged approach for developing and implementing a plan, incorporating key stages, thus:

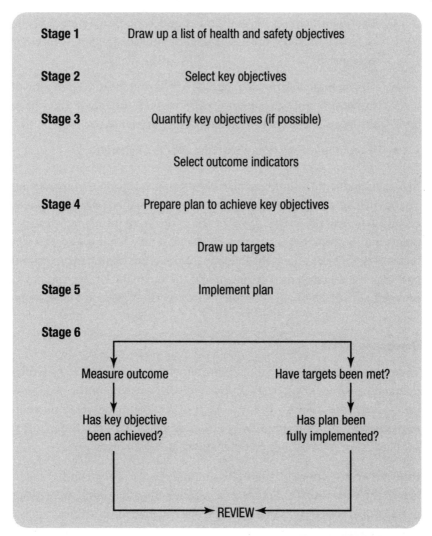

Fig 12: OHSAS 18001.

Note: This diagram covers both the planning and implementation stages to indicate the complete process. Planning involves Stages 1 to 4.

Risk management

Risk management is variously defined as:

- The minimization of the adverse effects of pure and speculative risks within a business.

- The identification, measurement and economic control of the risks that threaten the assets and earnings of a business or other enterprise.

- The identification and evaluation of risk and the determination of the best financial solution for coping with the major and minor threats to a company's earnings and performance.

- A technique for coping with the effects of change.

Risk management techniques have the principal objective of producing savings in insurance premiums by first defining and then minimizing areas of industrial and other risk. It seeks not to discredit insurance arrangements but to promote the concept of insuring only what is necessary in terms of risk. On this basis the manageable risks are identified, measured and either eliminated or controlled, and the financing of the remaining or residual risks, normally through insurance, takes place at a later stage.

Categories of risk

There are two main areas of risk, namely catastrophic risk, which demands insurance, and risks associated with wastage of the organization's assets. The latter is where the scope of self-insurance and diminution of risk is most evident, and is why organizations appoint risk managers, in some cases establishing risk management subsidiaries.

Risks may be of a pure or speculative nature. *Pure risks* can only result in loss to the organization. *Speculative risks*, on the other hand, may result in either gain or loss. Within the context of a risk management programme, risk may be defined as 'the chance of loss', and the programme is therefore geared to safeguarding the organization's assets, namely manpower, materials, machinery, methods, manufactured goods and money.

The risk management process

This takes place in a series of stages:

a) identification of the exposure to risk, such as that arising from fire, storm and flood, accidents, human error, theft or fraud, breach of legislation, etc.;

b) analysis and evaluation of the identified exposures to risk;

c) risk control, using a range of protective measures; and

d) financing of the risk at the lowest cost.

Risk control strategies

Risk avoidance

This strategy involves a conscious decision on the part of the organization to completely avoid a risk by discontinuing the operation or circumstances that produces the risk.

Risk retention

In this case, the risk is retained within the organization where any consequent loss is financed by that organization.

Risk transfer

This is the legal assignment of the costs of certain potential losses from one party to another, e.g. from a company to an insurance company.

Successful health and safety management [HS(G)65]

This HSE publication specifies elements of successful health and safety management within five main areas:

Policy

Organizations which are successful in achieving high standards of health and safety have health and safety policies which contribute to their business performance, while meeting their responsibilities to people and the environment in a way which fulfils both the spirit and the letter of the law. In this way they satisfy the expectations of shareholders, employees, customers and society at large. Their policies are cost effective and aimed at achieving the preservation and development of physical and human resources and reductions in financial losses and liabilities. Their health and safety policies influence all their activities and decisions, including those to do with the selection of resources and information, the design and operation of working systems, the design and delivery of products and services, and the control and disposal of waste.

Organizing

Organizations which achieve high health and safety standards are structured and operated so as to put their health and safety policies into effective practice. This is helped by the creation of a positive culture which secures involvement and participation at all levels. It is sustained by effective communication and the promotion of competence which enables all employees to make a responsible and informed contribution to the health and safety effort. The visible and active leadership of senior managers is necessary to develop and maintain a culture supportive of health and safety management. Their aim is not simply to avoid accidents, but to motivate and empower people to work safely. The visions, values and beliefs of leaders become the shared 'common knowledge' of all.

Planning

These successful organizations adopt a planned and systematic approach to policy implementation. Their aim is to minimize the risks created by work activities, products and services. They use risk assessment methods to decide priorities and set objectives for hazard elimination and risk reduction. Performance standards are established and performance is measured against them. Specific actions needed to promote a positive health and safety culture and to eliminate and control risks are identified. Wherever possible, risks are eliminated by the careful selection and design of facilities, equipment and processes or minimized by the use of physical control measures. Where this is not possible, systems of work and personal protective equipment are used to control risks.

Measuring performance

Health and safety performance in organizations which manage health and safety successfully is measured against pre-determined standards. This reveals when and where action is needed to improve performance. The success of action taken to control risks is assessed through active self-monitoring involving a range of techniques. This includes an examination of both hardware (premises, plant and substances) and software (people, procedures and systems), including individual behaviour. Failures of control are assessed through reactive monitoring which requires the thorough investigation of accidents, ill-health and incidents with the potential to cause harm or loss. In both active and reactive monitoring the objectives are not only to determine the immediate causes of sub-standard performance but, more importantly, to identify the underlying causes and the implications for the design and operation of the health and safety management systems.

Auditing and reviewing performance

Learning from all relevant experience and applying the lessons learned are important elements in effective health and safety management. This needs to be done systematically through regular reviews of performance based on data both from monitoring activities and from independent audits of the whole health and safety management system. These form the basis of self-regulation and for securing compliance with Sections 2 to 6 of the Health and Safety at Work etc Act 1974. Commitment to continuous improvement involves the constant development of policies, approaches to implementation and techniques of risk control. Organizations which achieve high standards of health and safety assess their health and safety performance by internal reference to key performance indicators and by external comparison with the performance of business competitors. They often also record and account for their performance in their annual reports.

See Fig 13: Key elements of successful health and safety management

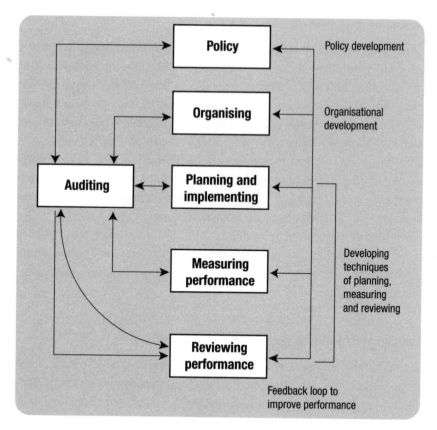

Fig 13: Key elements of successful health and safety management

Technique for human error rate probability (THERP)

Many accidents are associated with human error. THERP is a technique for predicting the potential for human error in a work activity. It evaluates quantitatively the contribution of the human error element in the development of an untoward incident.

The technique uses human behaviour as the basic unit of evaluation. It involves the concept of a basic error rate that is relatively consistent between tasks requiring similar human performance elements in different situations. Basic error rates are assessed in terms of contributions to specific systems failures.

The methodology of THERP entails:

a) selecting the system failure;

b) identifying all behaviour elements;

c) estimating the probability of human error; and

d) computing the probabilities as to which specific human error will produce the system failure.

Following classification of probable errors, specific corrective actions are introduced to reduce the likelihood of error.

The major weakness in the use of the THERP technique, however, is the lack of sufficient error rate data.

Total loss control

Total Loss Control is a management system developed in the 1960s by Frank Bird. It is defined as a programme designed to reduce or eliminate all accidents which downgrade the system and which result in wastage of an organization's assets. An organization's assets are:

1. **Manpower**

2. **Materials**

3. **Machinery**

4. **Manufactured goods**

5. **Money**

The five 'Ms'

Within the Total Loss Control concept a number of definitions are important.

Incident

An undesired event that could, or does, result in loss

or

An undesired event that could, or does, downgrade the efficiency of the business operation.

Accident

An undesired event that results in physical harm or damage to property. It is usually the result of contact with a source of energy (i.e. kinetic, electrical, thermal, ionising, non-ionising radiation, etc) above the threshold limit of the body or structure.

Loss control

An intentional management action directed at the prevention, reduction or elimination of the pure (non-speculative) risks of business.

Total loss control

The application of professional management techniques and skills through those programme activities (directed at risk avoidance, loss prevention and loss reduction) specifically intended to minimize loss resulting from the pure (non-speculative) risks of business.

Total loss control programmes

Total Loss Control is commonly run as a programme over a period of, for example, five years. The various stages are outlined below:

Injury prevention

This stage is concerned with the humanitarian and, to some extent, legal aspects of employee safety and employees' compensation costs. It normally incorporates a range of features, such as machinery safety, joint consultation, safety training, cleaning and housekeeping, safety rules, etc.

Damage control

This part of the programme covers the control of accidents which cause damage to property and plant and which might, conceivably, cause injury. Essential elements of this stage are damage reporting, recording and costing.

Total accident control

This stage of the programme is directed at the prevention of *all* accidents resulting in personal injury and/or property damage. Three important aspects of this stage are spot checking systems, reporting by control centres and health and safety audits.

Business interruption

This entails the incorporation in the programme of controls over all situations and influences which downgrade the system and result in interruption of the business activities, e.g. fire prevention, security procedures, product liability, pollution prevention. Business interruption results in lost money, e.g. operating expenses, lost time, reduced production and lost sales.

Total loss control

This is the control of all insured and uninsured costs arising from any incidents which downgrade the system.

The various stages of Total Loss Control are shown in Figure 14.

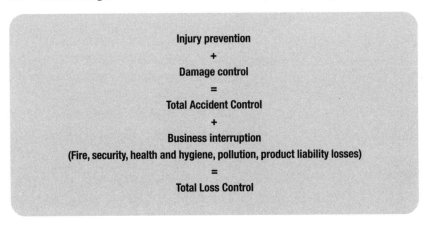

Fig 14: Total loss control stages

See:

- *Accident and ill-health costs*
- *Accident reporting, recording and investigation*
- *Benchmarking*
- *Documentation requirements*
- *Employee handbooks*
- *Job safety analysis*
- *Passport schemes*
- *Safety budgets*
- *Safety incentive schemes*
- *Safety monitoring systems*
- *Statements of health and safety policy*

Safety monitoring systems

Safety monitoring is a pro-active strategy aimed at assessing and evaluating health and safety performance. The outcome generally features a series of recommendations for future action to improve safety performance and meet the requirements of the law.

Safety monitoring may take a number of forms.

Safety inspections

This is generally taken to mean a scheduled inspection of a workplace or part of a workplace, such as a factory, office, workshop, construction site or a public building. It can be undertaken by a manager, safety adviser or representative of employee safety.

Whilst the principal objective of a safety inspection is to identify hazards and assess the remedial action necessary, this form of monitoring may also examine maintenance standards, working practices, environmental conditions and compliance with legal requirements and written safety procedures.

A safety inspection is, in effect, a general examination of a workplace at a specific point in time rather than the in-depth approach taken by a safety survey. As with any form of safety monitoring, it is vital that the objectives are clearly defined and the outcome of the inspection in terms of recommendations for action are acted upon promptly by management.

Safety surveys

A safety survey can take the form of an examination of a number of critical areas of operation, such as materials handling operations, or an in-depth study of all health and safety related activities in a workplace or an organization.

Safety surveys examine a range of issues, such as the effectiveness of the management of health and safety, environmental working conditions, health hazards, the very broad field of accident prevention and the current system for health and safety training. Evidence of compliance or otherwise with current health and safety legislation features strongly in a safety survey.

At the completion of the survey management are presented with a safety survey report incorporating immediate, short-term and long-term recommendations. Implementation of the recommendations is monitored on a regular basis by the safety surveyor and progress reports prepared and issued to management.

Safety audits

The HSE publication *Successful Health and Safety Management* (HS(G)65) defines the term 'safety audit' as 'the structured process of collecting independent information on the efficiency, effectiveness and reliability of the total safety management system and drawing up plans for corrective action'.

RoSPA define a safety audit as 'the systematic measurement and validation of an organization's management of its health and safety programme against a series of specific and attainable standards'. This form of monitoring subjects each area of an organization's activities to a systematic critical examination with the objective of minimizing injury and other forms of loss.

A safety audit can examine, for instance, the quality of health and safety documentation from the Statement of Health and Safety Policy to other documents, such as risk assessments, Permits to Work, contractors' regulations and employee health and safety information. It will also examine healthy and safety management systems, management and employee attitudes to health and safety, prevention and control procedures and training arrangements. Safety audits can be designed to cover areas of particular significance to an organization, e.g. management of hazardous substances, safety procedures for employees working away from base and specific health protection arrangements, in addition to those more general issues which apply to all workplaces.

Safety tours

A safety tour is an unscheduled examination of a workplace or work area, undertaken by a manager, possibly accompanied by employee representatives and/or safety committee members, to ensure, for instance, standards of housekeeping are at an acceptable level, fire protection measures are being observed or personal protective equipment is being correctly used or worn. A safety tour tends to be spontaneous as opposed to, for instance, an audit or survey, which may be planned some time ahead.

Safety sampling exercises

This technique is designed to measure, by random sampling, the accident potential in a specific workplace, or at a particular process or work activity, by identifying safety defects or omissions.

Safety sampling entails the use of a safety sampling form which lists specific aspects to be observed and assessed, e.g. machinery safety, electrical safety, housekeeping and personal protective equipment. Each of the areas for consideration is numerically graded according to its significance and a maximum number of points are awardable for each area of performance. Such a system monitors the effectiveness of the overall programme.

Safety sampling exercises are also used for comparing safety performance in an organization's workplaces where, for instance, the organization has offices, shops, workshops, manufacturing or service units at different locations.

A typical safety sampling sheet is shown at Figure 15.

SAFETY SAMPLING EXERCISE

		LOCATIONS				
		1	2	3	4	5
1.	Housekeeping	Max 20				
2.	Fire protection	Max 20				
3.	Machinery safety	Max 20				
4.	Electrical safety	Max 15				
5.	Internal storage arrangements	Max 10				
6.	Use of hazardous substances	Max 10				
7.	Manual handling operations	Max 10				
8.	Personal protection	Max 10				
9.	Welfare amenities	Max 10				
10.	Lift truck operations	Max 15				
11.	Lighting	Max 10				
12.	Access and egress	Max 10				
13.	Dust and fume control	Max 10				
14.	Hand tools	Max 10				
15.	Structural safety	Max 20				
TOTALS		**Max 200**				

ACTION PLAN

1.   Immediate action

2.   Short-term action (14 days)

3.   Medium-term action (six months)

4.   Long-term action (two years)

Sampling Officer _____ Date _____

Fig 15: Safety sampling

Checklist systems

Where there is a need to monitor safety standards on a regular basis, many organizations operate a simple check list system. In this case, a trained person, such as a supervisor, goes through the workplace or his department on a weekly basis using the check list. Such a system relies heavily on the conscientious use of the check list, regular revision of same, and on the effectiveness of action taken where there is a deviation from the requirements shown in the check list.

See:

- *Accident and ill health costs*
- *Accident and ill health data*
- *Benchmarking*
- *Hazard reporting*
- *Risk assessment*
- *Safety management systems*

Safety propaganda

'Safety propaganda' is a term used to describe the various forms of material directed at providing messages to employees on safe and healthy working practices. The use of safety propaganda is fundamentally concerned with:

- increasing the awareness of people to hazards and the precautions necessary;

- changing attitudes; and

- imparting information on health and safety-related issues.

It may include the use of:

a) safety publications;

b) safety posters;

c) slide/tape programmes; and

d) films and videos.

The relative usefulness of safety propaganda will depend, to a large extent, on the method of communication used.

There are a variety of media through which safety propaganda can be communicated:

a) publications, programmed learning;

b) taped commentaries, lectures;

c) slides, posters, viewfoils ;

d) films, videos, slide/tape programmes, on-line programmes,

e) discussion groups;

f) on the job training, simulation exercises, role playing.

Those techniques which encourage active participation by employees, such as role play exercises, have been found to best the best way of getting messages across to people.

Safety posters

The use of safety posters is, perhaps, the most common form of reminding employees to do, or not to do, certain things, such as 'Wear your ear protection' or 'No smoking on site'. One of the problems with safety posters is that after a time people no longer pay attention to them and the message that the poster is putting out can be lost. When displayed on general notice boards they can be covered by other material being displayed.

The most effective use of safety posters is through the operation of a weekly or monthly theme covering selected messages relevant to working practices and the workplace. On this basis, posters are displayed depicting the message for a week or month and them removed, being replaced with a new poster covering another health and safety-related message. There should be dedicated poster boards used solely for the display of safety posters and located in positions where they make a striking impact on employees and other people working on site.

See:

- *Information for employees*

Safety signs

The Safety Signs Regulations 1980 require that safety signs, other than those for fire fighting, rescue equipment and emergency exits, conform to a standard system with regard to colours and shapes.

Signs

Prohibition Signs

These are circular with a red band enclosing a crossed-out symbol on a white background e.g. "No smoking".

Warning signs

These signs are triangular in shape with a yellow background and black borders, symbols and text e.g. 'LPG – Highly Flammable'.

Mandatory signs

These are circular in shape incorporating a white mandatory symbol and/or text on a blue background e.g. 'Wear face shield'.

Safe condition signs

These are indicated by a green square or rectangle with symbols and lettering in white e.g. 'Emergency Stop'.

BS 5378: 1976

A safety sign giving health or safety information must comply with Part 1 of BS 5378: 1976 as must any strip of alternate colours used to identify a hazard e.g. 'tiger striping'.

- Part 1 of BS 5378 describes the safety colours as red, yellow, blue and green.
- RED is for STOP or PROHIBITION signs
- YELLOW is for CAUTION or RISK OF DANGER signs
- BLUE is for MANDATORY signs
- GREEN is for SAFE CONDITION signs

Additional information

If additional information is required, a supplementary test may be used in conjunction with the relevant symbol, provided that it is apart and does not interfere with the symbols. The text shall be in an oblong or square box of the same colour as the sign with the text in the relevant contrasting colour, or white with black text.

Fire safety signs

These are specified by BS 5499, which gives the characteristics of signs for fire equipment, precautions and means of escape in case of fire. It uses the basic framework concerning safety colour and design adopted by BS 5378.

Health and Safety (Safety Signs and Signals) Regulations 1996

These Regulations implement the Safety Signs Directive. They require employers to use a safety sign whenever there is a risk to health and safety that cannot be avoided or properly controlled by other means.

There is a general move towards symbol-based signs. The regulations extend the term 'safety sign' to include hand signals, pipeline markings, acoustic signals and illuminated signs.

Safety signs, including fire exit, fire fighting and fire alarm signs, need to convey the message instead of relying solely on text. Employers must display fire exit signs to incorporate the 'running man' pictogram. (The display of the sign FIRE EXIT without the pictogram is illegal.)

The Regulations also require the marking of pipework containing dangerous substances, by fixing labels or signs at sampling and discharge points. Small stores of dangerous substances must also be marked in a similar way.

See:

- *Information for employees*

- *Safety propaganda*

Shared workplaces

There are many situations where employers share workplaces, for example, in office blocks, industrial estates and, on a temporary basis, with construction sites. All the various groups of employees may be totally unaware of the processes and practices undertaken in other parts of the workplace and of the hazards to which they may be exposed from activities undertaken in these other parts of the workplace.

The legal situation relating to shared workplaces is dealt with in:

- **Health and Safety at Work etc Act 1974**

  Employers should be aware of their duties to non-employees under section 3 of the HSWA.

- **Management of Health and Safety at Work Regulations 1999**

  Regulation 13 deals with 'co-operation and co-ordination' between individual employers thus:

Where two or more employers share a workplace (whether on a temporary or a permanent basis) each employer shall:

a) co-operate with the other employers concerned so far as necessary to enable them to comply with the requirements and prohibitions imposed upon them by or under the relevant statutory provisions;

b) (taking into account the nature of his activities) take all reasonable steps to co-ordinate the measures he takes to comply with the requirements and prohibitions imposed upon him by or under the relevant statutory provisions with the measures the other employers concerned are taking to comply with the requirements and prohibitions imposed upon them by the legislation; and

c) take all reasonable steps to inform the other employers concerned of the risks to their employees' health and safety arising out of or in connection with the conduct by him of his undertaking.

> **See:**
>
> - Construction safety
>
> - Contractors and visitors on site
>
> - Risk assessment

Smoking at work

With the increasing attention that has been given to the risks associated with passive smoking, organizations must develop and implement policies on smoking at work.

The problem has been identified mainly in poorly ventilated open-plan offices and amongst employees who may suffer some form of respiratory complaint, e.g. asthma or bronchitis. Other people may complain of soreness of the eyes, headaches and stuffiness.

The HSE's booklet *Passive Smoking at Work* draws attention to the concept of passive smoking, where non-smokers inhale environmental tobacco smoke from burning cigarettes, cigars and pipes exhaled by smokers. Work carried out by the Independent Scientific Committee on Smoking and Health identified a small but measurable increase in risk from lung cancer for passive smokers of between 10% and 30%. The booklet also suggests that passive smoking could be the cause of one to three extra cases of lung cancer every year for each 100,000 non-smokers who are exposed throughout life to other people's smoke.

Policies on smoking at work

The first step is the development of a Policy on Smoking at Work. This should state the intention of the company to eliminate smoking in the workplace by a specific date, the legal requirements on the employer to provide a healthy working environment, and that smoking is bad for the health of smokers and non-smokers alike. The 'organization and arrangements' for implementing the policy should state the individual responsibilities of managers in supporting and implementing the various stages of the operation, and of the staff to comply with the policy.

On publication of the policy statement, the operation should proceed in clear stages, commencing with a questionnaire to all managers seeking information as to the number of employees on site, the number of smokers, the number who have given up in the last year, possible problems anticipated through operation of the eventual ban, local efforts made to assist smokers to give up smoking, facilities available to smokers, for example, designated smoking areas, and costs incurred in helping people to give up smoking e.g. counselling, hypnotherapy. Such collated information will give an indication of the current state of play on smoking in the organization.

Implementing the policy

The second stage is concerned with the provision of training, information, instruction, health education, therapy, propaganda and counselling on the health risks associated with smoking with a view to raising the awareness of all concerned. This should be backed up by marking of 'No Smoking' areas and the restriction of smoking to exempted rooms and areas. Job applicants should also be advised of the policy at the interview stage.

Some managers may be concerned at the risk of industrial action on declaration of the policy and of the problem of staff who persistently breach same. In certain extreme cases, dismissal may be the only solution. A recent industrial tribunal decision supports this view. In *Rogers v Wicks & Wilson* an employee, who subsequently resigned and claimed unfair dismissal when his employer announced a forthcoming ban on smoking, was held not to have been unfairly dismissed on the basis that employees do not have a contractual right to smoke. Moreover, where such bans are introduced with sufficient warning and consultation with staff, an employer cannot be said to have acted unreasonably.

See:

- *Health surveillance and health protection*

Statements of health and safety policy

Under section 2(3) of the HSWA every employer has a duty to prepare, and as often as appropriate, revise a written statement of his general policy with respect to the health and safety at work of his employees and the 'organization and arrangements' for the time being in force for carrying out that policy, and to bring the statement and any revision of it to the notice of his employees.

It is a technical offence under the HSWA for an employer not to have a written Statement of Health and Safety Policy, (except in the case where less than five employees are employed).

Importance of the statement

The Statement of Health and Safety Policy is the key document for detailing the management systems and procedures to ensure sound levels of health and safety performance. It should be revised at regular intervals, prior to, particularly, changes in the structure of the organization, the introduction of new articles and substances, and changes to legal requirements affecting the organization. Fundamentally, the Statement must be seen as a "living document" which reflects the current organizational requirements, the hazards and precautions necessary, the individual responsibilities of people and systems for monitoring performance. It should be reviewed on a regular basis, particularly following changes in the structure of an organization.

There is no standard format for a Statement of Health and Safety Policy. Much will depend upon the structure of the organization, the nature of the organization's activities, the hazards to which employees are exposed and the legislation currently applying to the organization.

Objectives of the Statement of Health and Safety Policy

There are a number of important objectives for a Statement.

- It should affirm long range purpose.
- It should commit management at all levels and reinforce this purpose in the decision-making process.
- It should indicate the scope left for decision-making by junior managers.

Scope of the Statement of Health and Safety Policy

A well-written Statement should cover the following aspects:

- Management intent.
- The 'arrangements' for implementing the Policy.
- Individual accountabilities of directors, line managers, employees and other groups, e.g. contractors.
- Details of the organization with respect to both line and staff functions.
- The role and function of health and safety specialists, e.g. health and safety advisers, occupational health nursing advisers, occupational hygienists, occupational health nurses, local safety officers, occupational physicians, company doctors and trade union-appointed safety representatives.

Principle features of a Statement of Health and Safety Policy

A Statement should incorporate the following features:

- A general statement of intent which states the basic objectives, supplemented by details of the 'organization and arrangements' (rules and procedures).

- Definition of both the duties and extent of responsibility at specified line management levels for health and safety, with identification made at the highest level of the individual with overall responsibility for health and safety.

- Definition of the functions of the safety adviser/officer/consultant and his relationship to senior and line management made clear.

- The system for monitoring safety performance and publishing of information about that performance.

- An identification and analysis of the hazards that may arise and the precautions necessary on the part of employees, contractors and visitors.

- An information system which will be sufficient to produce an identification of needs and which can be used as an indicator of the effectiveness of the policy.

- A policy on the provision of health and safety information, instruction and training for all levels of the organization.

- A commitment to consultation on health and safety and to a positive form of employee involvement.

- The Statement should bear the signature of the person with ultimate responsibility and accountability for health and safety at work, e.g. Chief Executive, Managing Director.

- It is common practice for Statements to incorporate a series of Appendices, such as:
  - current health and safety legislation (the 'relevant statutory provisions') applying to the organization;

- – duties and responsibilities for health and safety of individual levels of management;

- – role and function of the health and safety adviser and other health and safety specialists;

- – hazards and precautions necessary;

- – sub-policies covering:

  - smoking at work

  - alcohol at work

  - stress at work

  - bullying and harassment at work

  - the provision of personal protective equipment

  - joint consultation arrangements

  - risk assessment procedures.

See:

- • *Consultation on health and safety*

- • *Health and Safety at Work etc Act 1974*

- • *Health and safety practitioners*

- • *Information, instruction and training*

- • *Information sources*

- • *Personal protective equipment*

- • *Risk assessment*

- • *Smoking at work*

- • *Stress at work*

Stress at work

What is stress?

Stress has been variously defined as:

- the common response to attack (*Hans Selye The Stress of Life*)

- any influence that disturbs the natural equilibrium of the living body

- a feeling of sustained anxiety which, over a period of time, leads to disease.

Fundamentally, a stressor produces stress which, in turn, leads to some form of human stress response, such as anxiety or depression. What is important to recognize is that no two people necessarily exhibit the same response to a particular stressor.

Classic manifestations of stress are insomnia, tiredness, lack of motivation, behavioural changes, irritability, indecisiveness and absenteeism from work.

The more common occupational stressors

The causes of stress arising from work are diverse. They can be classified thus:

The physical environment

There may be poor working conditions associated with, for instance, insufficient space, lack of privacy, open plan office layouts, excessive noise, inadequate temperature and lighting arrangements.

The organization

The organization, its policies and procedures, culture and style of management may be considered unfriendly, lacking in compassion and praise for employees.

The way the organization is managed

Management styles, philosophies and work systems may feature inconsistencies in approaches and objectives, emphasis on competitiveness and 'crisis management' all the time.

Role in the organization

There may be inadequate or insufficient definition of the individual's role in the organization, too much or too little work or, in some cases, being 'a servant of two masters'.

Personal and social relationships

Poor relationships may exist between individuals, both on a personal and social basis, with inadequate opportunities for social contact while at work, sexism and sexual harassment, racism and racial harassment.

Career development

The individual may experience lack of career development and opportunities for same, lack of job security, under-promotion, over-promotion and thwarted ambitions.

Relations within the organization

Poor relations with superior managers, colleagues and subordinates due to, perhaps, difficulties in defining and delegating responsibility.

Equipment

Employees may have to work with inadequate, out-of-date and unreliable equipment which may not be suitable for the job and in poor condition.

Individual concerns

All people are different in terms of attitudes, motivation, personality and their ability to cope with work-related stressors. There may be difficulty in coping with change, lack of confidence in dealing with interpersonal problems or through not being assertive enough.

The effects of stress on job performance

This may include:

Absenteeism

Absenteeism, especially on Monday mornings, or in the taking of early or extended meal breaks, is a classic manifestation of stress.

Accidents

People working under stressful conditions may be more prone to the errors leading to accidents. Similarly, people who resort to excessive alcohol consumption, in particular, as a result of stress may suffer more accidents at work. Again, because of their depressed or reduced awareness, their actions may contribute to accidents.

Erratic job performance

Alternating between low and high productivity due, in some cases, to changes which have taken place outside the control of the individual, is a common manifestation of stress.

Loss of concentration

Stressful events in people's lives commonly result in a lack of the ability to concentrate on the task in hand, the individual is easily distracted and there is an inability to complete one task at a time.

Loss of short-term memory

This leads to arguments about who said, did or decided what.

Mistakes

Stress is a classic cause of errors of judgement which can result in accidents, wastage and rejected products. Such errors are commonly blamed on others.

Poor personal appearance

Becoming abnormally untidy, perhaps smelling of alcohol, is a common manifestation of a stressful state.

Poor employee relations

People undergoing a stressful period in their lives may become irritable and sensitive to criticism. This may be accompanied by 'Jekyll and Hyde' mood changes, all of which have a direct effect on relationships with others.

The legal situation

Employers need to consider both their criminal and civil liabilities towards their employees with respect to stress-induced injury.

Criminal liability

Employers must consider their duties under the HSWA to protect the health of their employees, which includes their mental health. This may entail the need to consider the potential for stress amongst employees, or certain groups of employees, such as those dealing with clients and members of the public, when undertaking a risk assessment under the MHSWR.

Employees may also be subject to violence, bullying and harassment at work. Employers need to be aware of this problem and take immediate action where such situations arise. Further advice on this matter is available in *The ACAS Advisory Handbook: Discipline at Work.*

Another cause of stress at work may be discrimination on the grounds of race or ethnic or national origin. Employers need to be aware, therefore, of their duties under the Race Relations Act 1976 and Race Relations Regulations 2003 which make harassment on the basis of these grounds a separate unlawful act.

(See further *Tackling Work-Related Stress: a Guide for Employers HS(G)128, HSE Management Standards for Stress*)

Civil liability

In the last decade the number of civil claims for stress-induced injury has increased dramatically. To this extent the Court of Appeal has produced guidelines with respect to an employer's obligations when faced with a reasonably foreseeable risk of such injury.

Court of appeal guidelines: employers' obligations

1. The employer should pay regard to the size of the enterprise and its administrative resources, as there are limits as to what can be reasonably expected of an employee.

2. Before considering what action should be taken, an employer must pay regard to:

a) the magnitude of the risk of psychiatric injury occurring;

b) the seriousness of the potential injury;

c) the cost and practicability of taking action to prevent such injury; and

d) whether these steps would actually prevent the injury from occurring.

3. Whilst it may be reasonable to consider granting an employee:

a) a sabbatical;

b) transferring him to another department;

c) redistributing work; or

d) granting assistance,

an employer would not be obliged to dismiss or demote an employee in order to remove him from a stressful situation.

Moreover, an employer who provides a confidential support and advice service is unlikely to be found in breach of duty unless he has placed unreasonable demands upon an individual when the risk of psychiatric injury to that individual was obvious.

Court of appeal general guidelines

As a result of a series of cases involving injury arising from work-related stress, the Court of Appeal issued the following general guidelines.

- The ordinary principles of employer's liability apply to claims for psychiatric illness arising from stress at work.

- Employers are generally entitled to accept at face value what employees tell them, unless there is good reason not to do so.

- No occupation should be regarded as intrinsically dangerous to mental health.

- An employer is entitled to assume that an employee is able to withstand the normal pressures of the job unless they have some particular problem or vulnerability.

- For an employer to have a duty to take action, indications of impending harm to health must be apparent enough to show that the action should be taken.

- An employer is only in breach of duty if he has failed to take steps that are reasonable in all the circumstances.

- An employer who makes available a confidential counselling service with access to treatment is unlikely to be found in breach of duty.

Proving liability for psychiatric illness

Proving an employer's liability for psychiatric injury may be difficult in some cases. A claimant employee must demonstrate the following:

- that the employer had breached the duty of care owed to the employee to provide a safe place of work and to keep him safe from harm;

- that the employee is suffering from recognizable psychiatric illness, that is, not simply stress but clinical depression or post-traumatic stress disorder;

- that the recognizable psychiatric injury was caused by the employer's negligence and not by any other factors; and

- that the stress to which the employee was exposed was sufficient to create a *reasonably foreseeable risk of injury.*

The two main issues

In the leading judgement, the Court of Appeal held that liability depends primarily on two main issues.

1. Was it reasonably foreseeable that the employee would suffer psychiatric injury as a result of the working conditions?

2. If so, did the employer do all he reasonably could to address the problem?

These two main issues should feature strongly in any stress risk assessment undertaken by an employer.

> **See:**
>
> - *Common law liability*
> - *Homeworking*
> - *Human factors and safety*
> - *Negligence*
> - *Risk assessment*
> - *Safety culture*
> - *Violence at work*

Structural safety

Accidents associated with structural features of workplaces are common. These may include slips, trips and falls on the same level, falls down staircases, contact with fixed structural features and vehicles using traffic routes, falls through teagle openings and from elevated work/storage platforms.

Floors and traffic routes

Specific provisions relating to the safety of floors and traffic routes in work places are dealt with in Regulation 12 of the WHSWR.

- Floors and the surfaces of traffic routes must be of suitable construction, free from dangerous holes, slopes and uneven and slippery surfaces, and provided with effective means of drainage where necessary. So far as is reasonably practicable, they must be kept free from obstruction and from articles and substances which could cause slips, trips or falls.

- Floors should be of sound construction, free from obstruction and sudden changes in level, and of non-slip finish. Where safety levels, production or the storage of goods are materially assisted, storage areas should be clearly marked by the use of yellow or white lines. 'No Go' areas should be cross-hatched with yellow lines. All openings in floors or significant differences in floor level should be fenced. Attention should also be paid to ensuring that floor loading does not produce structural instability.

- Where a wet process is carried out, or where frequent floor washing is necessary, the floor should be laid to a fall to a drainage system. Floor channels, incorporating metal gratings or covers, can sometimes be used as an alternative.

Stairs, ladders and catwalks

- Suitable and sufficient handrails and, if appropriate, guards must be provided on all traffic routes which are staircases except in circumstances in which a handrail cannot be provided without obstructing the traffic route. In the case of very wide staircases, further handrails may be necessary in addition to those at the sides. If necessary, the space between the handrail and the treads should be filled in, or an intermediate rail fitted.

- Fixed vertical ladders and catwalks, including bridges to them, should be securely fixed. Where practicable, back rings should be fitted to vertical ladders from a height of 2m upwards and spaced at 1m intervals. Catwalks and bridges should be adequately fenced by means of m high guard rails, 500mm high intermediate rails and toe boards.

External areas, traffic routes and approach roads

- Every workplace shall be organized in such a way that pedestrians and vehicles can circulate in a safe manner. A 'traffic route' is defined as meaning a route for pedestrian traffic, vehicles or both and includes any stairs, staircase, fixed ladder, doorway, gateway, loading bay or ramp.

- Traffic routes must be suitable for the persons or vehicles using same, sufficient in number, in suitable positions and of sufficient size. Particular precautions must be taken to prevent pedestrians or vehicles causing danger to persons near that route, ensure there is sufficient separation of traffic routes for vehicles from doors, gates and pedestrian routes, and where pedestrians and vehicles use the same traffic routes, ensure there is sufficient separation between them. Traffic routes must be suitably indicated where necessary for reasons of health and safety.

- To facilitate access to, and egress from, the workplace by people and vehicles, external areas should have impervious and even surfaces and be adequately drained to a drainage system. The provision of water supply points and hoses for washing down yards and approaches is recommended.

Windows, doors, gates and walls, etc.

Specific provisions relating to structural items such as windows, doors, gates, walls, skylights and ventilators are incorporated in the WHSWR thus:

- Every window or other transparent or translucent surface in a wall or partition and every transparent or translucent surface in a door, gate or wall shall, where necessary for reasons of health and safety:

  a) be of safety material or be protected against breakage; and

  b) be appropriately marked or incorporate features so as, in either case, to make it apparent.

- No window, skylight or ventilator which is capable of being opened shall be likely to be opened, closed or adjusted in a manner which exposes any person performing such operations to a risk to his health or safety. No window, skylight or ventilator shall be in a position to expose any person in the workplace to a risk to his health or safety.

- All windows and skylights in a workplace shall be of a design or so constructed that they may be cleaned safely. In considering whether a window or skylight is safe, account may be taken of any equipment used in conjunction with the window or skylight or of devices fitted to the building.

- Doors and gates shall be suitably constructed (including fitted with any necessary safety devices). Specific safety provisions apply to sliding doors/gates, powered doors and doors/gates which are capable of being opened by being pushed from either side. Thus:

a) any sliding door or gate must be fitted with a device to prevent it coming off its track during use;

b) any upward opening door or gate must be fitted with a device to prevent it falling back;

c) any powered door or gate must incorporate suitable and effective features to prevent it causing injury by trapping any person;

d) where necessary for reasons of health or safety, any powered door or gate must be capable of being operated manually unless it opens automatically if the power fails; and

e) any door or gate which is capable of opening by being pushed from either side must be of such a construction as to provide, when closed, a clear view of the space close to both sides.

- Interior walls have a contribution to make to illuminance levels, colour schemes, the maintenance of physical cleanliness, sound insulation and the prevention of fire spread. They should be substantial, durable, smooth, easily cleaned and reflect light.

- Ceilings and inner roof surfaces of workrooms should also assist in the maintenance of appropriate illuminance levels, heat insulation, sound insulation and physical cleanliness. Ceiling heights should be a minimum of 2.4m.

Escalators and moving walkways

Special provisions apply in the case of escalators and moving walkways.

- In both cases, they shall:
  a) function safely;
  b) be equipped with any necessary safety devices; and
  c) be fitted with one or more emergency stop controls which are easily identifiable and readily accessible.

In all the above cases, further detail is provided in the ACOP accompanying the Regulations.

> **See:**
>
> - *Confined spaces*
> - *Health and Safety at Work etc Act 1974*

T

Temperature control in the workplace

Legal requirements

The WHSWR require that during working hours, the temperature in all workplaces inside buildings shall be reasonable.

The ACOP qualifies the requirement thus:

- The temperature in workrooms should provide reasonable comfort without the need for special clothing. Where such a temperature is impractical because of hot or cold processes, all reasonable steps should be taken to achieve a temperature which is as close as possible to comfortable.

- The temperature in workrooms should normally be at least $16^{o}C$ unless much of the work involves severe physical effort in which case the temperature should be at least $13^{o}C$. These temperatures may not, however, ensure reasonable comfort, depending upon other factors such as air movement and relative humidity.

Comfort conditions

A temperature of 16oC, however, does not provide reasonable comfort conditions in, for instance, an office, and the following temperatures are recommended (*see overleaf*):

Offices	18-21°C	(65-70°F)
Production areas (sedentary work)	18°C	(65°F)
Production areas (active work)	16°C	(60.8°F)
Amenity areas	18-21°C	(65-70°F)

Table 15: Recommended temperatures

In certain workplaces, e.g. depots, stores, which are sparsely or spasmodically occupied, localized space heating points should be provided for use during excessively cold periods of weather.

Central heating should operate independently of the hot water or steam installation so that central heating can be turned off in summer months. Individual control of radiators and heaters should be provided, together with the installation of thermostat control switches where central heating is by electrical means.

Where excessive heat is produced by processes, the adequacy of control and removal of this heat must be considered. Local exhaust ventilation (LEV) will, in many cases, solve this problem.

Safety requirements

Heating units with exposed electrical elements should not be used, nor heating appliances producing gases as a result of combustion, unless efficient flues are installed. The use of privately-owned heating appliances, particularly those of the open radiant type, should be prohibited in view of the fire risk associated with such appliances.

See:

- *Electrical installations*
- *Health surveillance and health protection*
- *Occupational diseases and conditions*

Temporary workers

A temporary worker is defined in the MHSWR as a person:

a) employed under a fixed term contract of employment; or

b) employed in an employment business, but working for a user organization.

Under the regulations, employers must provide temporary workers working under a fixed term contract of employment with comprehensible information on:

a) any special occupational qualifications or skills required to be held by that employee if he is to carry out his work safely; and

b) any health surveillance required to be provided to that employee by or under any of the relevant statutory provisions,

and shall provide that information before the employee concerned commences his duties.

In the case of persons employed in an employment business, employers must provide the operator of the employment business with the above information who must, in turn, ensure that the information is provided to employees.

Temporary employment

Where an employee has been hired out to another employer, but control over the work he is carrying out remains with his permanent employer, the permanent employer may be liable for any injuries sustained. In *Mersey Docks and Harbour Board v Coggins and Griffiths (Liverpool) Ltd (1947) AC1* this Board hired out the services of a skilled crane driver to a firm of stevedores. The Board was held liable for injuries caused by the crane driver whilst working for the stevedores.

The test of whether an employee has been 'temporarily employed' by another employer is one of control. If the temporary employer, either personally or through his employees, can direct that employee not only on what to do but how to do his work, control has passed to that temporary employer.

See:

- *Risk assessment*
- *Work away from base*

Toxicology

Toxicology is the study of the body's responses to toxic substances. On the other hand, the toxicity of a substance is related to the ability of a chemical molecule to produce injury once it reaches a susceptible site in or on the body.

Effects of exposure to toxic substances

Exposure to toxic substances may produce a number of effects on the body.

Acute effect

A rapidly produced effect following a single exposure to an offending agent.

Chronic effect

An effect produced as a result of prolonged exposure or repeated exposures of long duration. Concentrations of the offending agent may be low in both cases.

Sub-acute effect

A reduced form of acute effect.

Progressive chronic effect

An effect which continues to develop after exposure ceases.

Local effect

An effect usually confined to the initial point of contact. The site may be the skin, mucous membranes of the eyes, nose or throat, liver, bladder, etc.

Systemic effects

Such effects occur in parts of the body other than at the initial point of contact, and are associated with a particular body system e.g. respiratory system, central nervous system.

Routes of entry of toxic substances to the body

Toxic substances may enter the body in a number of ways.

Inhalation

Inhalation of toxic substances, in the form of a dust, gas, mist, fog, fume or vapour accounts for approximately 90% of all ill health associated with toxic substances. The results may be acute (immediate) as in the case of gassing accidents e.g. chlorine, carbon monoxide, or chronic (prolonged, cumulative) as in the case of exposure to chlorinated hydrocarbons, lead compounds, benzene, numerous dusts, which produce pneumoconiosis, mists and fogs, such as that from paint spray, oil mist, and fume, such as that from welding operations.

Pervasion

The skin, if intact, is proof against most, but not all, inputs. There are certain substances and micro-organisms which are capable of passing straight through the intact skin into underlying tissue, or even into the bloodstream, without apparently causing any changes in the skin, however.

The resistance of the skin to external irritants varies with age, sex, race, colour and, to a certain extent, diet. Pervasion, as a route of entry, is normally associated with occupational dermatitis, the causes of which may be broadly divided into two groups:

a) **primary irritants** are substances which will cause dermatitis at the site of contact if permitted to act for a sufficient length of time and in sufficient concentrations e.g. strong alkalis, acids and solvents;

b) **secondary cutaneous sensitisers** are substances which do not necessarily cause skin changes on first contact, but produce a specific sensitization of the skin. If further contact occurs after an interval of, say, seven days or more, dermatitis will develop at the site of the second contact. Typical skin sensitisers are plants, rubber, nickel and many chemicals.

It should be noted that, for certain people, dermatitis may be a manifestation of psychological stress, having no relationship with exposure to toxic substances (an endogenous response).

Ingestion

Certain substances are carried into the gut from which some will pass into the body by absorption. Like the lung, the gut behaves as a selective filter which keeps out many but not all harmful agents presented to it.

Injection and implantation

A forceful breach of the skin, frequently as a cause of injury, can carry substances through the skin barrier.

Chemical poisoning at work

Toxic substances are widely used in industry. Some indication of the most common substances and the occupations associated with them are listed in the Social Security (Industrial Injuries) (Prescribed Diseases) Regulations 1985.

The responses of the body to toxic substances

Dose-response relationship

A basic principle of occupational disease prevention rests upon the reality of threshold levels of exposure for the various hazardous agents below which Man can cope successfully without significant threat to his health. This concept derives from the quantitative characteristic of the dose-response relationship, according to which there is a systematic down change in the magnitude of Man's response as the dose of the offending agent is reduced.

$$\text{Dose} = \text{Level of environmental contamination} \quad \times \quad \text{Duration of exposure}$$

With many dusts, for instance, the body's response is directly proportional to the dose received over a period of time, the greater the dose, the more serious the condition, and vice versa.

However, in the case of airborne contaminants, such as gases or mists, there is a concentration in air or dose below which most people can cope reasonably well. Once this concentration in air is reached (threshold dose), some form of body response will result. This concept is most important in the correct use and interpretation of Occupational Exposure Limits (formerly known as 'Threshold Limit Values').

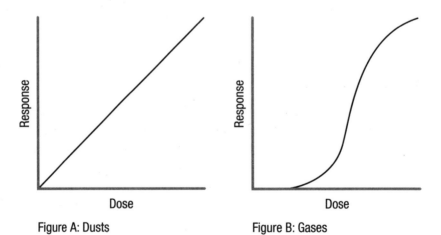

Figure A: Dusts   Figure B: Gases

Figure A shows a typical direct dose-response relationship, whereas in Figure B the dose-response curve reaches a level of 'no response' at a point greater than zero on the dose axis. This point of cut-off identifies the threshold dose which was the original basis for the setting of Threshold Limit Values (Occupational Exposure Limits).

Target organs and systems

It is a well-established fact that certain substances have a direct or indirect effect on certain body organs (target organs) and certain body systems (target systems).

Target organs include the lungs, liver, brain, skin and bladder.

Target systems, on the other hand, include the central nervous system, circulatory system and reproductive system

Protective mechanisms

The protective mechanisms within the body respond largely according to the shape and size of particulate matter which may be inhaled. Such mechanisms are as follows:

Nose

The coarse hairs in the nose, assisted by mucus from the nasal lining, act as a filter, trapping the larger particles of dust.

Ciliary escalator

The respiratory tract consists of the trachea (wind pipe) and bronchi which branch to the lungs. The lining of the trachea consists of quite tall cells, each of which has a cilium growing from its head (ciliated epithelium). These cilia exhibit a wave-like motion so that a particle falling onto the cilia is returned back to the throat. Mucus assists these particles to stick.

Macrophages

These are wandering scavenger cells. They have an irregular outline and large nucleus, and can move freely through body tissue, engulfing bacteria and dust particles. They secrete hydrolytic enzymes which attack the foreign body.

Lymphatic system

This is a drainage system which acts as a clearance channel for the removal of foreign bodies, many of which are retained in the lymph nodes throughout the body. In certain cases, a localized inflammation will be set up in the lymph node.

Tissue response

A typical example of tissue response is in byssinosis, (the 'Monday fever' or 'Monday feeling'), a chest condition of cotton workers, where the lung becomes sensitised to cotton dust through continuing exposure.

Safe handling of toxic substances

Assuming that substitution as a control strategy has been considered and found impracticable, then in order of merit:

- substances should be used in diluted form wherever possible;
- only limited quantities should be used or stored at any one time; large quantities should be stored in a purpose-built bulk chemical store;
- containment of the specific area may be necessary, together with safe venting and drainage requirements;
- handling and dispensing from bulk should be eliminated by the use of automatic systems;
- adequate exhaust ventilation should be provided;
- adequate separation of substances e.g. acids from alkalis; with
- personal protective equipment as an extra means, not the sole means, of protection.

Personal protective equipment and associated facilities

Protective clothing

This should take the form of one-piece overalls, aprons, gloves for specific duties; the frequency of laundering and replacement of body protection is important.

Footwear

Employees should wear wellington boots with steel toe-caps and insoles or safety boots and gaiters.

Eye protection

The use of spectacles, goggles or visors will depend on the extent of handling and degree of risk. Specific recommendations for various jobs may be necessary.

Respiratory protection

This should incorporate a full face mask of the ori-nasal air-fed types. This aspect should feature in health risk assessments.

Emergency arrangements

These include first aid, emergency showers and eye wash bottles, together with decontamination chemicals and procedures.

Welfare amenity provisions

There should be adequate provision for sanitation, hand washing, showers and clothing storage, together with the provision and use of barrier creams and skin cleansers.

See:

- *Biological agents*
- *Hazardous substances*
- *Health risk assessment*
- *Health surveillance and health protection*
- *Information, instruction and training*
- *Occupational diseases and conditions*
- *Occupational exposure limits*
- *Ventilation in the workplace*
- *Welfare amenity provisions*

Traffic management on site

An effective system of traffic management on site is essential in order to prevent accidents involving people and vehicles of all types. Legal requirements relating to internal transport arrangements are covered by the WHSWR thus:

- Every workplace shall be organized in such a way that pedestrians and vehicles can circulate in a safe manner.

- Traffic routes in a workplace shall be suitable for the persons or vehicles using them, sufficient in number, in suitable positions and of sufficient size.

- Without prejudice to the generality of paragraph (2), traffic routes shall not satisfy the requirement of that paragraph unless suitable measures are taken to ensure that:

  a) pedestrians, or as the case may be, vehicles may use a traffic route without causing danger to the health or safety of persons at work near it; and

  b) there is sufficient separation of any traffic route for vehicles from doors or gates or from traffic routes for pedestrians which lead onto it;

  c) where vehicles and pedestrians use the same traffic route, there is sufficient separation between them.

All traffic routes shall be suitably indicated where necessary for reasons of health or safety.

General considerations

Particular attention must be given to providing and maintaining a safe system for the loading and unloading of vehicles and for regulating the activities of drivers in terms of internal routes taken, parking locations used, speed and the potential for coming into contact with pedestrians, cyclists and other vehicles.

Specific considerations

In any consideration of the movement of people and vehicles, the following points are important:

Road system

- number of vehicles using the internal road system
- travelling distances
- relative safety of entrances and exits
- widths of roads
- obstructions – overhead, parked vehicles, plant, spillages
- bends, corners and junctions
- the use of speed limiters/retarders
- signage
- construction of roads – suitable materials, drainage, gradients
- maintenance – state of repair, freedom from spillages
- external road lighting
- escape points

Pedestrians and cyclists

- specific routes – separate from vehicles
- footpaths, crossings, barriers, bridges, subways

- separate entrances and exits

- separate personnel entrance doors to vehicle workshops and internal parking areas

- specific provisions at start and termination of work/shifts

Gangways

- 1m minimum width and as straight as possible

- emergency exits clearly indicated

- delineation by use of painted lines or marking tape

- gangways maintained clear and unobstructed

- maximum travel distance to reach marked gangway 6m, 12m or 25m depending upon fire risk

- effective natural and/or artificial lighting

- securely fixed barriers to prevent stack displacement

- all doors to open outwards readily from the inside

Workplace risk assessment

The hazards arising from the interface between pedestrians and vehicles should be taken into account in a workplace risk assessment.

> **See:**
>
> - *Contractors and visitors on site*
> - *Damage control*
> - *Machinery and work equipment*
> - *Mechanical handling*
> - *Safety signs*

V

Ventilation in the workplace

'Ventilation' is defined as the process of simultaneously removing used or vitiated air from a building and replacing it with fresh air. The objectives of a ventilation system are:

- to maintain healthy and comfortable conditions for employees (comfort ventilation);

- to ensure the removal of airborne contamination from a building (exhaust or extract ventilation).

Ventilation may be provided:

- by natural means, that is, through the use of windows which open, airbricks, and other openings in the fabric of a building;

- by mechanical means such as by the use of fans pushing air into, or extracting air from, a building; and

- by the use of air conditioning systems.

In many cases a combination of these processes may be used.

Comfort ventilation

Comfort is essentially a subjective feeling or assessment of the conditions in which a person works, sleeps, travels, etc and the sensation of comfort is commonly associated with age, state of health and vitality. Comfort is associated with the ambient air temperature, relative humidity and the rate of air movement in a building. Comfort ventilation, therefore, may be related to the rate of air movement, the number of air changes per hour and the external ambient temperature. When external temperatures are low, the rate of air movement should be reduced to maintain comfort whereas, in hot summer months, the opposite must take place.

Ventilation systems, whether natural or artificial, are commonly designed assuming a maximum air temperature of 32°C and a minimum air temperature of 0°C and should operate within these extremes. Much will depend upon the nature of the work undertaken as to the appropriate comfortable ambient workplace temperature.

A commonly used standard for recommended air changes per hour is shown at Table 16.

	SUMMER	WINTER
Offices	6	4
Corridors	4	2
Amenity areas	6	4
Storage areas	2	2
Production areas with heat producing plant	20	20
Production area – assembly, finishing	6	6
Workshops	6	4

Table 16: Recommended air change rates

Comfort ventilation criteria

In assessing design features for comfort ventilation systems, the following criteria should be considered:

- incoming air should be drawn from a clean external source or subjected to a filtration process;

- an atmosphere which is cool rather that hot, dry rather than damp, and with a variable rate of air movement according to season, must be produced;

- relative humidity should vary between 40% and 70%;

- every occupied part of a workplace should be separately ventilated;

- input units should be located so as to give a flow of air from operating positions towards sources of heat and finally to extract units;

- total extract volume should be around 80% of the input volume to allow for a positive plenum or pressure within the building;

- fresh air intakes at roof level should stand at least 0.66m above the roof surface to avoid collecting heated, and sometimes contaminated, air and from extracts.

Legal requirements

Section 2(2)(e) of the HSWA requires the provision and maintenance by an employer of a working environment for his employees that is, so far as is reasonably practicable, safe, without risks to health and adequate as regards arrangements for their welfare at work.

More specifically, the WHSWR place an absolute duty on an employer to ensure that effective and suitable provision is made to ensure that every enclosed workplace (as defined), for example, a factory, office, shop, workshop, is ventilated by a sufficient quantity of fresh or purified air.

The ACOP accompanying the Regulations makes the following points:

- Enclosed workplaces should be sufficiently well-ventilated so that stale air, and air which is hot or humid because of the processes or equipment in the workplace, is replaced at a reasonable rate.

- The air which is introduced should, as far as possible, be free of any impurity which is likely to be offensive or cause ill health. Air which is taken from the outside can normally be considered to be 'fresh', but air inlets for ventilation systems should not be sited where they may draw in excessively contaminated air (for example close to a flue, an exhaust ventilation system outlet, or an area in which vehicles manoeuvre). Where necessary the air inlet should be filtered to remove particulates.

- In many cases, windows or other openings will provide sufficient ventilation in some or all parts of the workplace. Where necessary, mechanical ventilation systems should be provided for parts or all of the workplace, as appropriate.

- Workers should not be subject to uncomfortable draughts. In the case of mechanical ventilation systems it may be necessary to control the direction or velocity of air flow. Workstations should be re-sited or screened if necessary.

- In the case of mechanical ventilation systems which recirculate air, including air conditioning systems, recirculated air should be adequately filtered to remove impurities. To avoid air becoming unhealthy, purified air should have some fresh air added to it before being recirculated. Systems should therefore be designed with fresh air inlets which should be kept open.

- Mechanical ventilation systems (including air conditioning systems) should be regularly and properly cleaned, tested and maintained to ensure that they are kept clean and free from anything which may contaminate the air.

Further information is provided in the HSE Guidance to this Regulation.

Maintenance of ventilation systems

Regulation 5 of the WHSWR is of an all-embracing nature. This states:

1. The workplace, equipment, systems and devices to which this regulation applies shall be maintained (including cleaned as appropriate) in an efficient state, in efficient working order and in good repair.

2. Where appropriate, the equipment, devices and systems to which this Regulation applies shall be subject to a suitable system of maintenance.

3. The equipment, devices and systems to which this Regulation applies are:

   a) equipment and devices a fault in which is liable to result in a failure to comply with any of these Regulations; and

   b) mechanical ventilation systems provided pursuant to Regulation 6 (whether or not they include equipment or devices within sub-paragraph (a) of this paragraph).

Local exhaust ventilation (LEV) systems

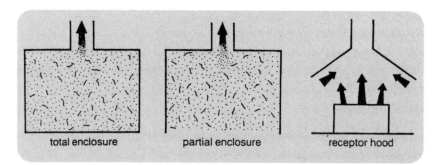

Fig 17: Local exhaust ventilation (LEV) systems – Receptor systems

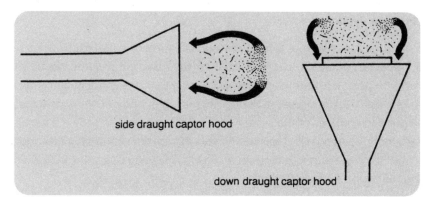

Fig 17: Local exhaust ventilation (LEV) systems – Captor systems

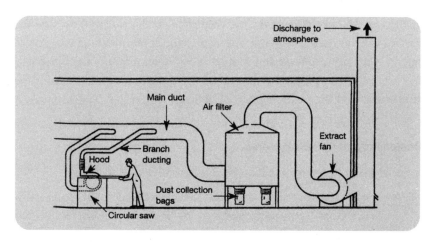

Fig 17: Local exhaust ventilation (LEV) systems – Typical LEV system

A local exhaust ventilation system should remove the airborne contaminant at the point of, or close to, the site of production and before the contaminant can be inhaled. LEV systems may be fixed, as with, for instance, a laboratory fume cupboard, or portable, as in the case of a welding fume extraction unit.

Current HSE Guidance is provided in booklet HS(G)37 *An Introduction to Local Exhaust Ventilation* which draws the distinction between receptor systems and captor systems.

Receptor systems

With this type of system, which may take the form of a total enclosure, e.g. a laboratory fume cupboard, partial enclosure e.g. a welding booth, or receptor hood e.g. the canopy above a plating tank, the contaminant enters the system with inducement. Fundamentally, the contaminant is produced within the confines of the system and a fan is used to provide the necessary air flow, along with thermal currents, taking the contaminant through a system of ducting to a collection system. In many cases, the collection unit incorporates a filtration device.

Captor systems

In the case of captor systems, the contaminant is produced outside the confines of the system. Moving air entrains the contaminant at some point outside the capture hood and induces flow into the hood. On this basis, the rate of air flow into the hood must be great enough to capture the contaminant at the furthest point of origin.

Design factors for LEV systems

In most cases LEV systems incorporate the following features:

- a hood, enclosure or other inlet to collect and contain the contaminant close to the source of its generation or point of emission;

- ductwork to convey the contaminant away from the source;

- a filter or other cleaning device to remove the contaminant from the extracted airstream; (Note: the filter should normally be located between the hood and the fan);

- a fan or other air-moving device to provide the necessary airflow; and

- further ductwork to discharge the cleaned air to the outside atmosphere at a suitable point.

In particular, the design capture velocity should be appropriate to the aerosol contaminant in terms of particle size and weight (see Figure 17: *Local exhaust ventilation systems*).

Examination and testing

Regulation 9 of the COSHH Regulations stipulates that employers must ensure that all physical control measures provided to prevent or control exposure to substances hazardous to health are maintained in an efficient state, in efficient working order and in good repair. This implies the operation of a system of visual checks, inspection, testing and servicing of LEV systems. Manufacturers and suppliers of LEV systems must specify the means of testing and examination.

Where engineering controls are provided, the employer must ensure that through examination and tests of those engineering controls are carried out:

a) in the case of LEV plant, at least once every 14 months; and

b) in any other case, at suitable intervals.

In addition to the general duty to ensure effective preventive maintenance, there are specific requirements on employers to undertake formal examination and testing of LEV systems in certain industries e.g. ceramics.

For effective examination and testing, it is helpful to have available comprehensive information on the system and the design specification. This information should have been provided at the commissioning stage of the

LEV system. Employers must keep records of examination and test of LEV systems, which must be kept available for inspection by employees, Employment Medical Advisers and inspectors of the relevant enforcing authority.

Maintenance requirements

Apart from the absolute duty on employers under the COSHH Regulations to maintain engineering controls, there is a similar duty on employers under the PUWER to maintain any item of work equipment (including an LEV system) in an efficient state, in efficient working order and in good repair. By implication, all such systems should be incorporated in a formal planned preventive maintenance system.

Management procedures

To ensure effective ventilation systems, a number of procedures are necessary, including:

- ensuring the competence of maintenance and monitoring personnel;
- arranging for the training of such persons if necessary;
- introduction of procedures for employees to formally report defects in LEV systems;
- establishment of priorities for maintenance of control measures (these priorities should feature in the planned preventive maintenance system);
- implementation of a programme of six monthly tests and weekly visual examinations;
- record keeping procedures.

See:

- *Hazardous substances*
- *Risk assessment*
- *Smoking at work*

Vibration

Many people are exposed to the risk of vibration-induced injury whilst at work. Vibration can be transmitted to the body (whole-body vibration) during the driving of heavy vehicles on uneven ground, such as in construction activities, or in the long-distance driving of heavy goods vehicles. Alternatively, people using hand-held vibratory power tools, such as pneumatic drills, chain saws and grinders may be exposed to vibration transmitted from work processes into the hand and arms (hand-arm vibration).

Hand-arm vibration syndrome (HAVS)

HAVS arises through regular exposure to vibration from the use of vibratory hand tools. This exposure can cause damage to the circulatory system, as in the case of vibration white finger (VWF), sensory nerves, bones, joints and muscular tissue. Symptoms of HAVS include parasthesia ('pins and needles') in the fingers, a loss of the sense of touch and grip strength, severe pain and numbness in the hand and arm and pain in the wrist, in some cases leading to the development of carpal tunnel syndrome.

The various forms of HAVS are outlined below.

Vibration-induced white finger (VWF)

The first signs of VWF are mild tingling and numbness in the fingers. As exposure continues, the tips of the fingers take on a white appearance, particularly early in the morning and during cold weather. This blanching of the fingers increases to the full extent of the fingers and eventually they take on a blue-black appearance. Unless the condition is treated, it can progress to gangrene and necrosis (death of tissue) resulting in the need for surgical amputation of parts of fingers or whole fingers.

Osteoarthritis

Osteoarthritis is encountered most commonly in the elbow joint, but also in the wrist and shoulder joints.

Dupuytren's contracture

This very painful condition is associated with injury to the soft tissues of the hand, principally the palm, resulting in atrophy (shrinkage) of the palmar muscles, together with, in limited cases, injury to the ulnar nerve. The condition results in an inability to straighten the fingers.

Whole-body vibration (WBV)

WBV is caused by vibration transmitted through the vehicle's seat and to the feet of the driver. Drivers of many mobile machines in construction projects, such as earth moving machines, industrial tractors and excavators, may be exposed to WBV. In most cases this causes shocks to the back with the resulting back pain. Other symptoms of WBV include blurred vision, loss of balance and loss of concentration, the latter being a contributory factor in accidents involving vehicles.

Control of Vibration at Work Regulations 2005

The Regulations impose duties on employers to protect employees who may be exposed to risk from exposure to vibration at work, and other persons who might be affected by the work, whether they are at work or not.

The Regulations lay down exposure limit values and action values for both hand-arm vibration and whole body vibration thus:

For HAV:

a) the daily exposure limit value normalized to an eight hour reference period is 5 m/s^2;

b) the daily exposure action value normalized to an eight hour reference period is 2.5 m/s^2;

c) daily exposure shall be ascertained on the basis set out in Schedule 1 Part 1.

For WBV:

a) the daily exposure limit value normalized to an eight hour reference period is 1.5 m/s^2;

b) the daily exposure action value normalized to an eight hour reference period is 0.5 m/s^2;

c) daily exposure shall be ascertained on the basis set out in Schedule 2 Part 1.

Principal requirements of the regulations

- Risk from exposure of employees to vibration should be eliminated at source or reduced as low as is reasonably practicable.

- When an employee is exposed to risk from vibration, an assessment shall be made of that risk by observation, reference to relevant information and, if necessary, by measurement.

- Action values and limit values are established for HAV and WBV assessed on an eight hour reference period.

- If the risk assessment indicates that an action value is exceeded the employer shall implement a programme of measures to reduce exposure to vibration as low as reasonably practicable.

- A limit value shall not be exceeded, or alternatively if it is exceeded immediate action shall be taken by the employer to identify the reason, to remedy the situation and to amend the programme of measures taken in accordance with the above paragraph to prevent a recurrence.

An alternative assessment of exposure on a one week reference period may allow the limit value to be exceeded in specified circumstances.

The employer shall provide suitable health surveillance when the risk assessment indicates a risk to health of employees or an action value is exceeded, where such health surveillance is appropriate, and shall take specified steps if the health surveillance indicates that an employee has a disease or adverse health effect as a result of exposure to vibration.

The employer shall provide suitable and sufficient information, instruction and training to the employees if there is a risk to their health from vibration or if they are exposed to vibration in excess of an exposure action value, and to any person who carries out work in connection with the employer's duties under the Regulations.

> **See:**
>
> - *Health surveillance and health protection*
> - *Information, instruction and training*
> - *Occupational diseases and conditions*

Vicarious liability

The doctrine of vicarious liability is based on the fact that if an employee, while acting in the course of his employment, negligently injures another employee or the employee of a contractor working on the premises, or even a member of the public, the employer, rather than the employee, will be liable for that injury. As most accidents at work are caused in this way, rather than as a result of personal negligence on the part of the employer, vicarious liability is the ground on which many civil claims for injury-type accidents are won.

Vicarious liability rests on the employer, simply as a result of the fact that he is the employer and is deemed to have ultimate control over the employee in what is known as 'a master and servant relationship'.

This liability must be insured against under the Employers' Liability (Compulsory Insurance) Act 1969. Employers cannot contract out of this liability as such practices are prohibited by the Law Reform (Personal Injuries) Act 1948 and the Unfair Contract Terms Act 1977.

The key to liability is that the accident causing the injury, disease or death arises, firstly, out of, and secondly, in the course of employment. This does not, however, normally include the time travelling to and from work, though it would if the mode of transport for such travelling was within the employer's control or was provided by them or in arrangement with them.

Notwithstanding vicarious liability, an employee can be sued instead of, or as well as, an employer where the employee has been negligent. *Lister v Romford Ice & Cold Storage Co.Ltd (1957) 1 AER 125*

See:

- *Common law liability*
- *Negligence*

Violence at work

The question of people suffering various forms of violence at work has received considerable attention in recent years. In particular, employees who deal directly with the public, such as security staff, police officers, people working behind bars or serving customers in licensed premises, and public officials, commonly face aggressive or violent behaviour.

In certain cases, this behaviour may arise through the effects of drugs and drug abuse. They may further come into contact with people who have behavioural disorders associated with their attitudes, personalities and perceptions. As a result, they may be verbally abused, threatened or even physically assaulted. Apart from physical injuries sustained, this can be a common cause of stress for the people concerned.

Work-related violence

The HSE define this aspect of 'violence' as 'any incident in which a person is abused, threatened or assaulted in circumstances relating to their work'. Verbal abuse and threats are the most common type of incident, whereas physical attacks are comparatively rare.

Who is at risk?

Any person whose job entails dealing with members of the public can be at risk. According to the HSE, those most at risk are people engaged in:

- giving a service, e.g. supermarket check-out operators, bar staff, petrol station staff;

- caring, e.g. nurses, midwives, care assistants;

- education e.g. teachers;

- cash transactions, eg bank employees, those collecting cash from banks or, for instance, gaming machines in public houses;

- delivery/collection e.g. postal service employees, deliverymen, bailiffs;

- controlling e.g. car park attendants;

- representing authority e.g. enforcement officers, police officers, security staff.

The legal situation

The general duties on employers to take measures to protect employees at work, which may include the risk of exposure to violence, are incorporated in:

- Health and Safety at Work etc Act 1974 – general duties on employers

- Management of Health and Safety at Work Regulations 1999 – risk assessment, management systems, emergency procedures

- Reporting of Injuries, Diseases and Dangerous Occurrences Regulations 1995 – notification and reporting of death, major injury, etc

- Safety Representatives and Safety Committees Regulations 1977 and Health and Safety (Consultation with Employees) Regulations 1996 – procedures for joint consultation on health and safety at work.

Effective management of violence

The HSE recommend employers follow the four stage management process set out below.

1. Find out if you have a problem

Employers must undertake a risk assessment to identify the hazards and evaluate the risks arising from these hazards.

This assessment should be assisted by:

- consultation with employees;
- keeping detailed records of previous incidents;
- classifying all incidents.

Fundamentally, a risk assessment should endeavour to predict what might happen in certain situations, such as a bank raid, aggressive drunken behaviour or regular harassment of staff by certain customers, and the measures necessary to protect staff.

2. Decide what action to take

The risk assessment should take account of who might be harmed and how this harm could arise. In certain cases, potentially violent people may be known to the organization and measures must be taken immediately that those people are identified, including disciplinary action in the case of employees and reporting aggressive customers and clients to the police.

Evaluation of the risk entails checking existing arrangements, including any precautions already being taken. There is also a need to consider:

- the level of training and information provided e.g. spotting early signs of aggression, clients with a history of aggression;
- the environment e.g. video cameras and alarm systems, coded security locks on doors;
- the design of the job e.g. checking the credentials of clients prior to entry, regular radio communication with base, avoiding lone worker situations;
- ensuring staff get home safely.

The significant findings of the assessment should be recorded, including the preventive and protective measures necessary to comply with legal requirements.

The risk assessment should be reviewed and revised on a regular basis.

3. Take action

Procedures for dealing with violence should be produced and staff informed, instructed and trained in these procedures. Reference to these procedures should be incorporated in the organization's Statement of Health and Safety Policy

4. Check what you have done

Regular checks and reviews of the procedures should be made, accompanied by consultation with staff on the success or otherwise of these procedures. Records of incidents should be maintained.

What about the victims?

Where there has been a violent incident involving employees, employers must act quickly to avoid any long-term distress. Employees must be provided with support, which may include:

- debriefing – they will need to talk through their experience as soon as possible after the event;
- time off work – different people need differing amounts of time off to recover; some may need specific counseling;
- legal help – this may need to be offered;
- other employees – they may need guidance and/or training to help them react appropriately.

Implications for employers

Employers have a duty of care with respect to their employees. Recent civil cases have indicated that employers must recognize this problem and provide confidential support and counselling services for employees, particularly in the case of bullying and harassment by other employees and members of the public.

An employer who has provided these support services is less likely to be found in breach of his duty of care unless he has placed unreasonable demands on an individual when the risk of psychiatric injury to that individual was obvious.

See:

- Common law liability

- Health and Safety at Work etc Act 1974

- Stress at work

W

Welding and similar operations ('Hot work')

Hot work involving welding and flame cutting operations involve the application of intense heat, either from an electrical source (electric arc welding) or by the use of a compressed gas, such as acetylene or propane, with a view to joining two metals together, or for cutting sheet metal to a specific shape or for a specific purpose, e.g. metal fabrication operations.

The principal hazards likely to be encountered during hot work operations are outlined below.

Fire and explosion

Arcs, flames, sparks and metal spatter (the ejection of small particles of molten metal in all directions) are sources of ignition which will readily ignite flammable materials and waste in the immediate vicinity of the welding operation. Welding on systems or vessels under pressure can result in explosion.

In the case of gas welding, gases commonly used are acetylene and propane, both of which are flammable and form mixtures with air or oxygen. Any leakage of fuel gas is potentially hazardous, as ignition may lead to rapid or explosive combustion, particularly in confined spaces or poorly ventilated areas. Propane is heavier than air, can accumulate at floor level and will readily ignite. Acetylene, an unstable gas, can decompose explosively when subjected to heat or shock. This can occur in the absence of oxygen and under pressure.

One of the classic causes of explosion is associated with welding operations carried out on a vehicle chassis in close proximity to the vehicle's petrol tank. The welding of tanks, drums and vessels which have not been completely freed of their flammable contents and/or purged with an inert gas can frequently result in explosions, in many cases having fatal results.

Electric arc welding hazards can arise through poor maintenance and/or repair of equipment, improper use, and the use of unsuitable materials, e.g. insulation tape, to effect repairs to equipment and connections.

With portable welding sets the use of an inadequate power supply circuit, the need to remake earth connections for each job, and strain or damage to terminals and connections to the welding set can result in danger to operators and others in the immediate vicinity.

Burns

Welders are commonly exposed to hot surfaces and may suffer burns, in particular, to the hands and arms. Flying metal spatter may also burn other parts of the body, such as the face and neck.

Exposure to toxic fumes and gases

The inhalation of welding and cutting fumes can lead to the condition known as 'welder's lung' or siderosis. Metallic fumes in the form of oxides can be evolved according to the nature of the base metals and electrodes in use. This is also the case with flux coatings. The action of heat and ultra violet leads to the evolution of ozone, carbon monoxide and oxides of nitrogen. Heavy particulate matters in the form of respirable dusts can be created as smoke and metal spatter. Many of the gases, vapours, fumes and dusts evolved are invisible, colourless and odourless, so considerable care must be taken when welding in confined spaces or unventilated areas.

Oxygen enrichment

Most welding and cutting operations use oxygen to support combustion of the fuel gas. Accidental leakage of oxygen has, therefore, considerable hazard potential. Oxygen enrichment will cause a change in the ignition characteristics of all combustible materials, including those considered to be non-combustible. Any oxygen leakage in confined or unventilated areas is a matter for immediate concern.

Activities which can cause oxygen enrichment include flame cutting, which can discharge up to 30% unconsumed oxygen into the atmosphere. On this basis, flame cutting should not be carried out in a confined space or area until special arrangements to control ventilation have been made.

Exposure to infra-red and ultra-violet radiation

Welding and flame cutting operations can expose both operators and other persons in the immediate vicinity to electric arcs radiating both infra-red (radiant heat) and ultra-violet (UV) radiation. UV radiation can be hazardous in that it affects the skin and eyes in a similar way to the sun.

Exposure to UV radiation can also result in the condition known as 'arc eye', a painful but temporary form of conjunctivitis. This can have an acute effect on the eye with extensive irritation and the painful sensation of 'grittiness' of the surface of the eyeball. Chronic effects can include permanent visual damage and, in extreme cases, blindness following prolonged exposure.

Shock and electrocution

Electric welding sets operate on a circuit incorporating:

a) the welding lead, which carries the current from the welding set to the electrode and to the workpiece;

b) the welding return lead, which returns the current from the workpiece to the welding set; and

c) the welding earth, which must be connected to the workpiece.

The welding return lead is essential to prevent current taking random paths, for instance, via structural steelwork, metal pipes, etc. A particular danger is that if a random path includes a loosely bolted connection, a high resistance is set up which will cause heat to generate as the current flows through it, possibly resulting in fire. The welding return lead should be firmly clamped to the workpiece.

The welding earth is necessary to maintain the workpiece at earth potential and thus prevent electric shock by safeguarding against the possibility of the workpiece becoming energized at mains voltage, or energized because of the lack of continuity in the welding return.

employees, including those of contractors, and members of the public in the vicinity.

Risk assessment

A suitable and sufficient risk assessment must be undertaken taking into account the requirements and prohibitions imposed by or under the relevant statutory provisions.

Each of the hazards identified should be considered, as well as any hazards specific to a particular workplace, e.g. a construction site, engineering workshop or transport maintenance workshop, perhaps incorporating an inspection pit which could be used for welding activities.

More specific risk assessments, such as those required under the COSHHR, Noise at Work Regulations, Control of Lead at Work Regulations and the PUWER, may be required prior to work commencing.

Factors for consideration

Layout

The layout of the working area should be such that there is sufficient space for welding operations to be undertaken safely. Safe access to, and egress from, the work area should be provided. There should be no obstructions or physical barriers which prevent rapid egress from the work area.

The work area should be segregated by the use of fire resistant screens or covers to prevent persons other than the welder being exposed to intense light.

Storage of hazardous substances

Storage areas should be of fire resistant construction and designed in such a way that, in the event of a fire, cylinders can be removed quickly.

Hazardous compressed gas cylinders, such as those containing acetylene, should be stored in an upright position and used in conjunction with a trolley or cradle. Full and empty cylinders should be kept apart and notices displayed indicating their specific storage positions.

All LPG cylinders should be stored either in the open air or in a purpose-built store room or storage area. Small quantities can be stored in a purpose-made cupboard or bin. LPG storage tanks, cylinders and store rooms should be marked:

HIGHLY FLAMMABLE – LPG

Stored cylinders should be suitably restrained and their valves protected from impact damage.

Where acetylene or other combustible gas cylinders are kept in a store, the lighting should be of the approved flameproof type. Switches must also be flameproof and located outside the store.

Fuel gas and oxygen cylinders should be stored separately, at least 6m apart in the open, or in a store of fire-resistant construction, with permanent high and low-level ventilation to allow any leaking gases to disperse.

Containers which have held a flammable liquid should be made safe by cleaning and/or inerting, and then purging with air. The container should be certified as free of flammable vapour and posing no harmful inhalation risk.

Cylinders should be stored well away from any heat source and combustible material.

'Flashback' is a hazard commonly associated with the use of oxygen and fuel gas cylinders. Flashback arrestors and hose check valves must be installed to fuel gas and oxygen regulators and manifolds. Similarly acetylene manifolds must be fitted with a flashback arrestor. (The purpose of a flashback arrestor is to stop and extinguish a flashback, to prevent a reverse flow of gases and to close off the supply of gas in the event of a flashback.)

Particular care must be taken in the handling of cylinders with a view to preventing damage to valves and regulators, sudden impact with other cylinders and mechanical damage which could result in leakage from, or explosion of, the cylinder.

Information, instruction, training and supervision

Welders should be appropriately trained and supervised and be provided with any information and instructions necessary prior to commencing work.

Welders must use the equipment in accordance with training and instructions received and report to their supervisor situations of serious danger and any shortcomings in the protection arrangements.

Emergency equipment

Emergency situations can arise as a result of fire stemming from welding and flame cutting operations. Portable fire appliances should always be readily available, particularly where operations are undertaken in areas other than welding workshops, e.g. production and storage areas.

Emergency procedures

There should be a fully established emergency procedure to cover situations of serious or imminent danger, such as explosion or fire.

Extensive fire and explosions may require evacuation of surrounding industrial and residential premises.

Competent persons should be trained and appointed to deal with the established emergency procedure.

Personal protective equipment

Those involved in welding and flame cutting operations must be provided with appropriate PPE, namely goggles, welding masks or face shields, gloves, aprons, overalls and safety footwear. This may entail undertaking some form of risk assessment of the PPE prior to the task commencing.

Under the Personal Protective Equipment at Work Regulations 1992, a PPE risk assessment must ensure that PPE is 'suitable' (see *Personal protective equipment*).

In the selection of PPE for use in welding and flame cutting operations, the following points should be noted:

a) face masks and goggles should be fitted with dark glass to BS 679 standard in order to protect eyes from ultra violet radiation and intense light;

b) overalls should be flame retardant and specially designed with flaps on pockets to prevent sparks being trapped, and zip or Velcro fastenings;

c) the use of a safety helmet incorporating a welding mask is common practice for many welding and flame cutting operations; in certain cases, where welding fume may not disperse quickly, for instance, in confined spaces, 'Airstream' helmets and face masks, using an independent fresh air supply, may be necessary;

d) welders should wear safety boots with gaiters where there may be a risk of spatter; and

e) ear protection, e.g. ear muffs, may be necessary where sound pressure levels exceed 85 dB(A) over a normal eight hour working period.

Manual handling

The manual handling of cylinders, in particular, may expose personnel to the risk of back injury, such as a hernia, prolapsed intervertebral disc or ligamental strain. Such activities should be subject to a manual handling risk assessment.

Fumes and other airborne contaminants

The risk of inhalation of toxic gases, fumes and other airborne contaminants arising from welding and flame cutting operations must be considered. A complex combination of airborne gases and particulates can be produced according to the type of equipment used, the metals being worked on, the fluxes used and the secondary effects of metallic coatings and paints when exposed to intense heat.

A number of management systems must be operated to prevent the risk of inhalation of airborne contaminants by operators. These include:

a) health risk assessment;

b) monitoring of the effectiveness of local exhaust ventilation systems;

c) supervision of the wearing and use of PPE; and

d) health surveillance.

Ventilation

Wherever practicable, welding and flame cutting should take place in a controlled environment, such as a welding workshop. Such workshops should be provided with mechanical ventilation capable of achieving six to ten air changes per hour. Local exhaust ventilation (LEV) should be provided at the point of fume emission. In the case of specific welding booths and work benches, an LEV system of the receptor type, capable of achieving a face velocity of 0.5m/sec generally and at least 1m/sec at the weld, should be installed. Where welding is undertaken in situ on machinery, plant or structures, portable extraction and filtration units should be used.

The LEV systems should be subject to regular maintenance, examination and testing.

Welding in confined spaces

Dangerous levels of fumes and gases, oxygen enrichment or a lack of oxygen can arise during welding in confined spaces, such as tanks or unventilated spaces.

In accordance with the Confined Spaces Regulations 1997, a work activity risk assessment must take these specific factors into account. Immediate action arising from a risk assessment should include the need to operate a Permit to Work system and the preparation of an emergency procedure which will also safeguard rescuers, together with the training of designated competent persons to implement the emergency procedure when necessary. Continuous air monitoring is also necessary in these cases.

Lead fume

Wherever welding may expose operators to risk of exposure to lead fume, the requirements of the Control of Lead at Work Regulations must be taken into account in the health risk assessment undertaken prior to commencing work.

Factors to be considered include:

a)   control and maintenance of protective measures, e.g. LEV systems;

b)   provision of the appropriate respiratory protective equipment and protective clothing where necessary;

c)   continuous air monitoring;

d)   the provision of medical surveillance;

e)   the provision and maintenance of appropriate welfare amenities, including separate storage arrangements for protective clothing, and clothing not worn during working hours; and

f)   a total ban on eating, drinking and smoking in places liable to become contaminated by lead fume.

Information, instruction and training

It is essential that everyone i.e. operators, supervisors and other persons exposed to welding hazards, understands the hazards and risks arising from welding and flame cutting operations.

Welfare amenity provisions

A high standard of washing and showering facilities should be provided for all those involved in hot work.

See:

- *Contractors and visitors on site*
- *Damage control*
- *Electrical installations*
- *Hazardous substances*
- *Health risk assessment*
- *Lead at work*
- *Occupational diseases and conditions*
- *Permit to Work systems*
- *Risk assessment*
- *Welfare amenity provisions*

Welfare amenity provisions

General requirements for welfare amenities (sanitary accommodation, washing facilities, clothing storage, etc) are laid down in the WHSWR, with specific guidance incorporated in the accompanying ACOP and Guidance. It should be appreciated that the majority of the requirements relating to the provision and maintenance of welfare amenity provisions under the Regulations are of an absolute nature. These Regulations apply to all types of workplace.

Sanitary accommodation

Suitable and sufficient sanitary conveniences shall be provided at readily accessible places. Conveniences shall not be suitable unless:

a) the rooms containing them are adequately ventilated and lit;

b) they and the rooms containing them are kept in a clean and orderly condition; and

c) separate rooms containing conveniences are provided for men and women, except where and so far each convenience is in a separate room the door of which can be secured from inside.

In existing workplaces, compliance with Part II of Schedule 1 to the Regulations shall be sufficient compliance with the requirement in paragraph 1.

Schedule 1 – Provisions applicable to factories which are not new workplaces, extensions or conversions

Part II – Number of sanitary conveniences

4. In workplaces where females work, there shall be at least one suitable water closet for use by females only for every 25 females.

5. In workplaces where males work, there shall be at least one suitable water closet for use by males only for every 25 males.

6. In calculating the number of males or females who work in any workplace for the purposes of this Part of this Schedule, any number not itself divisible by 25 without fraction or remainder shall be treated as the next number higher than it which is so divisible.

Washing facilities

Suitable and sufficient washing facilities, including showers if required by the nature of the work or for health reasons, shall be provided at readily accessible places. Washing facilities shall not be suitable unless:

a) they are provided in the immediate vicinity of every sanitary convenience, whether or not provided elsewhere as well;

b) they are provided in the vicinity of any changing rooms required by the regulations, whether or not provided elsewhere as well;

c) they include a supply of clean hot and cold, or warm water (which shall be running water so far as is practicable);

d) they include soap or other suitable means of drying;

e) they include towels or other suitable means of drying;

f) the rooms containing them are sufficiently ventilated and lit;

g) they and the rooms containing them are kept in a clean and orderly condition and are properly maintained; and

(h) separate facilities are provided for men and women, except where and so far as they are provided in a room the door of which is capable of being secured from inside and the facilities in each room are intended to be used by only one person at a time.

Paragraph (h) above shall not apply to facilities which are used for washing the hands, forearms and face only.

Minimum numbers of facilities

Table 17 shows the minimum number of sanitary conveniences and washing stations which should be provided. The number of people at work shown in column 1 refers to the maximum number likely to be in the workplace at any one time. Where separate sanitary accommodation is provided for a group of workers, for example, men, women, office workers or manual workers, a separate calculation should be made for each group.

1	2	3
Number of people at work	Number of water closets	Number of wash stations
1-5	1	1
6-25	2	2
26-50	3	3
51-75	4	4
76-100	5	5

Table 17: Sanitary accommodation

In the case of sanitary accommodation used only by men, Table 18 may be followed if desired, as an alternative to column 2 of Table 17. A urinal may be either an individual urinal or a section of urinal space which is at least 600mm long.

1	2	3
Number of men at work	Number of water closets	Number of urinals
1-15	1	1
16-30	2	1
31-45	2	2
46-60	3	2
61-75	3	3
76-90	4	3
91-100	4	4

Table 18: Sanitary accommodation for men

The ACOP further recommends that an additional water closet, and one additional washing station, should be provided for every 25 people above 100 (or fraction of 25). In the case of water closets used only by men, an additional water closet for every 50 men (or fraction of 50) above 100 is sufficient provided at least an equal number of additional urinals are provided.

Where work activities result in heavy soiling of face, hands and forearms, the number of washing stations should be increased to one for every ten people at work (or fraction of ten) up to 50 people; and one extra for every additional 20 people (or fraction of 20).

Where facilities provided for workers are also used by members of the public the number of conveniences and washing stations specified above should be increased as necessary to ensure that workers can use the facilities without undue delay.

The ACOP also makes specific recommendations covering remote workplaces and temporary work sites.

Ventilation, cleanliness and lighting (ACOP)

Any room containing a sanitary convenience shall be well ventilated, so that offensive odours do not linger. Measures should also be taken to prevent odours entering other rooms. This may best be achieved by, for example, providing a ventilated area between the room containing the convenience and the other room. Alternatively it may be possible to achieve it by mechanical ventilation or, if the room containing the convenience is well sealed from the workroom and has a door with an automatic closer, by good natural ventilation.

However, no room containing a sanitary convenience should communicate directly with a room where food is processed, prepared or eaten.

Arrangements should be made to ensure that rooms containing sanitary conveniences or washing facilities are kept clean. The frequency and thoroughness of cleaning should be adequate for this purpose. The surfaces of the internal walls and floors of the facilities should normally have a surface which permits wet cleaning, for example, ceramic tiling or a plastic coated surface. The rooms should be well lit; this will also facilitate cleaning to the necessary standard and give workers confidence in the cleanliness of the facilities. Responsibility for cleaning should be clearly established, particularly where facilities are shared by more than one workplace.

Drinking water

An adequate supply of wholesome drinking water shall be provided for all persons at work in the workplace. Every supply of drinking water required by paragraph (1) above shall be:

a)   readily accessible at suitable places; and

b)   conspicuously marked by an appropriate sign where necessary for reasons of health or safety.

Where a supply of drinking water is required, there shall also be provided a sufficient number of suitable cups or other drinking vessels unless the supply of drinking water is in a jet from which persons can drink easily.

The ACOP makes specific recommendations relating to adequacy of water supplies, the prevention of contamination of taps, the provision of disposal or non-disposable cups, with facilities for washing the latter and marking of supplies where there is a risk of people drinking from non-drinkable water supplies. The Guidance accompanying the ACOP recommends marking of supplies which could become grossly contaminated.

Any such supply of water shall be:

a) clean and wholesome;

b) constant, if the provision of a constant supply is reasonably practicable and is in accordance with good practice at premises used for business of a similar class.

Accommodation for clothing

Suitable and sufficient accommodation shall be provided:

a) for any person at work's own clothing which is not worn during working hours; and

b) for special clothing which is worn by any person at work but which is not taken home.

Without prejudice to the generality of paragraph (1) the accommodation mentioned in that paragraph shall not be suitable unless:

a) where facilities to change clothing are required, it provides suitable security for clothes not so worn;

b) where necessary to avoid risks to health or damage to the clothing, it includes separate accommodation for clothing worn at work and for other clothing;

c) so far as is reasonably practicable, it allows or includes facilities for drying clothing; and

d) it is in a suitable location.

The ACOP recommends that accommodation for work clothing and workers' own personal clothing should enable it to hang in a clean, warm, dry, well-ventilated place where it can dry out during the course of a working day if necessary. If the workroom is unsuitable for this purpose, then accommodation should be provided in another convenient place. The accommodation should consist of, as a minimum, a separate hook or peg for each worker.

Where facilities to change clothing are required, effective measures should be taken to ensure the security of clothing. This may be achieved, for example, by providing a lockable locker for each worker.

Where work clothing (including personal protective equipment) which is not taken home becomes dirty, damp or contaminated due to the work it should be accommodated separately from the worker's own clothing. Where work clothing becomes wet, the facilities should enable it to be dried by the beginning of the following work period unless other dry clothing is provided.

It should be noted that civil action lies against a factory occupier in the event of personal clothing being stolen. (McCarthy v. Daily Mirror Newspapers Ltd. [1949] 1 AER 801.

Facilities for changing clothing

Suitable and sufficient facilities shall be provided for any person at work in the workplace to change clothing in all cases where:

a) the person has to wear special clothing for the purpose of work; and

b) the person cannot, for reasons of health or propriety, change in another room.

Without prejudice to the generality of paragraph (1), the facilities mentioned in that paragraph shall not be suitable unless they include separate facilities for, or separate use of, facilities by men and women where necessary for reasons of propriety.

The ACOP recommends that a changing room should be provided for workers who change into special work clothing and where they remove more than outer clothing. Changing rooms should also be provided where necessary to prevent workers' own clothing being contaminated by a harmful substance. Changing facilities should be readily accessible from workrooms and eating facilities, if provided. They should be provided with adequate seating and should contain, or communicate directly with, clothing accommodation and showers or baths if provided. They should be constructed and arranged to ensure privacy of the user. Furthermore, the facilities should be large enough to enable the maximum number of persons at work expected to use them at any one time, to do so without over-crowding or unreasonable delay. Account should be taken of starting and finishing times and the time available to use the facilities.

Facilities for rest and to eat meals

Suitable and sufficient rest facilities shall be provided at readily accessible places. Rest facilities provided shall:

a) where necessary, for reasons of health or safety include, in the case of a new workplace, extension or conversion, rest facilities provided in one or more rest rooms, or, in other cases, in rest rooms or rest areas;

b) include suitable facilities to eat meals where food eaten in the workplace would otherwise be likely to become contaminated.

Rest rooms and rest areas shall include suitable arrangements to protect non-smokers from discomfort caused by tobacco smoke.

Suitable facilities shall be provided for any person at work who is a pregnant woman or nursing mother to rest.

Suitable and sufficient facilities shall be provided for persons at work to eat meals where meals are regularly eaten in the workplace.

The ACOP makes extensive recommendations on the question of rest facilities and facilities for taking meals in the workplace. These include:

a)   where workers have to stand to carry out their work, suitable seats should be provided for their use if the type of work gives them an opportunity to sit from time to time;

b)   suitable seats should be provided for workers for use during breaks;

c)   rest areas or rooms should be large enough, and have sufficient seats with backrests and tables, for the number of workers likely to use them at any one time;

d)   where workers frequently have to leave their work area, and wait until they can return, there should be a suitable rest area where they can wait;

e)   where workers regularly eat meals at work suitable and sufficient facilities should be provided for the purpose;

f)   seats in working areas can be counted as eating facilities provided they are in a sufficiently clean place and there is a suitable surface on which to place food;

g)   eating facilities should include a facility for preparing or obtaining a hot drink, such as an electric kettle, vending machine or a canteen;

h)   workers who work during hours or at places where hot food cannot be obtained in, or reasonably near to, the workplace should be provided with the means for heating their own food;

j)   eating facilities should be kept clean to a suitable hygiene standard;

k)   canteens or restaurants may be used as rest facilities, provided there is no obligation to purchase food in order to use them; and

l)   good hygiene standards should be maintained in those parts of rest facilities used for eating or preparing food and drinks.

See:

- *Lighting in the workplace*
- *Ventilation in the workplace*

Work at height

Falls of people from heights is one of the principal causes of fatal accidents at work. Whilst this type of accident is commonly associated with workers carrying out a wide range of tasks in the construction industry, such people working on roofs, scaffolds and from ladders, other workers, such as window cleaners, painters and decorators, dockers and maintenance staff are exposed to this risk.

Work at Height Regulations 2005

These extensive Regulations apply both to employers and self-employed persons. 'Work at height' is defined as meaning:

a)   work in any place, including a place at or below ground level;

b)   obtaining access to or egress from such place while at work, except by a staircase in a permanent workplace.

The Regulations:

- impose duties on employers relating to the organizing and planning of work at height;

- require that persons at work be competent, or supervised by competent persons;

- prescribe steps to be taken to avoid risk from work at height;

- impose duties relating to the selection of work equipment;

- impose duties in relation to particular work equipment, such as guard rails, toe boards, barriers, working platforms, nets, airbags, personal fall protection systems and ladders;

- impose duties for the avoidance of risks from fragile surfaces, falling objects and danger areas;

- require the inspection of certain work equipment and of places of work at height;

- impose duties on persons at work.

Much of the detailed requirements is to be found in the Schedules to the Regulations:

Schedules

1. Requirements for existing places of work and means of access or egress at height.

2. Requirements for guard rails, toe boards, barriers and similar collective means of protection.

3. Requirements for working platforms:
   a) Requirements for all working platforms;
   b) Additional requirements for scaffolding.

4. Requirements for collective safeguards for arresting falls.

5. Requirements for personal fall protection systems:
   a) requirements for all personal fall protection systems;
   b) additional requirements for work positioning systems;
   c) additional requirements for rope access and positioning techniques;
   d) additional requirements for fall arrest systems;
   e) additional requirements for work restraint systems.

6. Requirements for ladders.

7. Particulars to be incorporated in a report of inspection.

See:

- *Competent persons*
- *Construction safety*
- *Contractors and visitors on site*
- *Method statements*
- *Permit to work systems*
- *Risk assessment*

Work away from base

Many people work away from their normal base of operation, such as employees of building contractors, those involved in the installation and servicing of machinery, plant and equipment, sales representatives and drivers of delivery vehicles. As such, they can be exposed to a wide range of hazards through, in many cases, their unfamiliarity with premises, processes and individual working practices. In some organizations, 20-25% of accidents to employees take place on other people's premises.

Employers need to be aware of the legal requirements relating to this form of work.

Occupiers' Liability Act 1975

Occupiers of premises owe a common duty of care to all lawful visitors in respect of dangers due to the state of the premises or things done or omitted to be done on them (see *Occupiers' liability*).

Health and Safety at Work etc Act 1974

An employer must conduct his undertaking in such a way as to ensure, so far as is reasonably practicable, that persons not in his employment who may be affected thereby are not thereby exposed to risks to their health or safety (Section 3).

Every person who has, to any extent, control of premises must ensure, so far as is reasonably practicable, that the premises, all means of access thereto and egress there from, and any plant or substances in the premises or provided for use there, is or are safe and without risks to health (Section 4).

Management of Health and Safety at Work Regulations 1999

Regulation 12 covers persons working in 'host employers" or self-employed persons' undertakings.

Every employer and every self-employed person shall ensure that the employer of any employees from an outside undertaking who are working in his undertaking is provided with comprehensible information on:

a) the risks to those employees' health and safety arising out of or in connection with the conduct by that first-mentioned employer or by that self-employed person of his undertaking; and

b) the measures taken by that first-mentioned employer or by that self-employed person in compliance with the requirements and prohibitions imposed upon him by or under the relevant statutory provisions and by Part II of the Fire Precautions (Workplace) Regulations 1997 in so far as the said requirements and prohibitions relate to those employees.

Every employer shall ensure that any person working in his undertaking who is not his employee and every self-employed person (not being an employer) shall ensure that any person working in his undertaking is provided with appropriate instructions and comprehensible information regarding any risks to that person's health and safety which arise out of the conduct by that employer or self-employed person of his undertaking.

The ACOP to the Regulations explains these requirements thus:

The risk assessment carried out under Regulation 3 will identify risks to people other than the host employers' employees. This will include other employers' employees and self-employed people working in that business.

Employers and self-employed people need to ensure that comprehensible information on those risks, and the measures taken to control them is given to other employers and self-employed people.

Host employers and self-employed people must ensure that people carrying out work on their premises receive relevant information. This may be done by either providing them with information directly or by ensuring that their employers provide them with the relevant information. If you rely on their employers to provide information to the visiting employees, then adequate checks should be carried out to ensure that the information is passed on. The information should be sufficient to allow the employer of the visiting employees to comply with their statutory duties, and should include the identity of the people nominated by the host employer to help with an emergency evacuation.

In the light of these requirements, it is essential that organizations have a formal procedure for regulating the activities of visitors, including the employees of contractors, and for the provision of information to such persons. This may include the running of formal health and safety briefing sessions for these persons before commencing work in the host employer's undertaking.

Practical procedures

1. Provision of written instructions to non-employees with regard to safe working practices generally.

2. Provision of comprehensible written information to non-employees on the hazards that may arise and the precautions necessary.

3. Formal health and safety training sessions for all non-employees prior to commencing work on the host employer's premises.

4. Specification of the health and safety competence necessary for non-employees at the tender stage of contracts.

5. Operation of a formal hazard reporting system by non-employees.

6   Disciplinary procedures against non-employees for failure to comply with written instructions and safety signs, including dismissal from the site or premises in serious case of non-compliance.

7. General supervision of non-employees and regular meetings to reinforce the safety requirements for such persons.

8. Liaison with external employers, and certification where necessary, to ensure employees concerned have received the appropriate information, instruction and training necessary prior to commencing work in the host employer's undertaking.

9. Pre-tender and on-going site inspections by the external employer to ensure his employees are following the host employer's safety instructions and are not exposed to risks to their health or safety.

See:

- *Common law liability*

- *Hazard reporting*

- *Health and Safety at Work etc Act 1974*

- *Negligence*

- *Occupiers' liability*

- *Risk assessment*

- *Shared workplaces*

Work in compressed air

People engaged in tunnelling and similar construction work in compressed air can be exposed to the risk of contracting a number of health conditions, namely:

- decompression illness (sickness), a condition associated with joint pains or as a more serious condition which may affect the heart, central nervous system or the lungs;

- barotraumas, where a change in the surrounding pressure causes direct damage to those air-containing cavities in the body which are directly concerned with the surrounding atmosphere, principally, the ears, sinuses and lungs; and

- dysbaric osteonecrosis, a long-term condition, causing damage to the long bones, hip and shoulder joints.

Work in Compressed are Regulations 1996

These regulations impose requirements and prohibitions with respect to the safety, health and welfare of persons working in compressed air. They apply to construction work (as defined) but not to diving operations within the meaning of the Diving Operations at Work Regulations 1981.

The Regulations:

- provide for the appointment of a competent contractor ('the compressed air contractor') to execute or supervise the work in compressed air included in any project;

- require specified information to be notified in writing to the HSE and to specified hospitals and other bodies before work in compressed air is commenced and for further notification of the termination or suspension of such work;

- require work in compressed air to be carried out only in accordance with a safe system of work and under adequate supervision;

- impose requirements with regard to the provision, use and maintenance of adequate and suitable plant and equipment;

- provide that a contract medical adviser be appointed to advise the compressed air contractor on matters relating to the health of persons who work in compressed air;

- impose a requirement on employers for adequate medical surveillance to be carried out in respect of such of their employees who work in compressed air;

- require compression and decompression to be carried out safely and in accordance with any procedures approved by the HSE and impose requirements for the making and maintenance of records;

- require adequate medical facilities to be provided and maintained for those who work in compressed air;

- impose requirements with regard to the preparation of adequate emergency arrangements;

- impose requirements with regard to the provision of suitable fire precautions and prohibit the possession of smoking materials in compressed air;

- require adequate instruction, information and training to be given to persons who work in compressed air;

- impose requirements on:
  - the compressed air contractor to ensure, so far as is reasonably practicable, that persons who are to work in compressed air are fit to do so; and
  - persons who work in compressed air to inform the compressed air contractor if they are unfit for such work;

- prohibit persons working in compressed air if impaired by drink or drugs and prohibit the consumption of alcohol in compressed air;

- impose requirements for the provision and maintenance of suitable welfare facilities for persons who work in compressed air;

- impose a requirement that, in specified circumstances, badges are to be supplied to persons who have worked in compressed air; and

- provide a defence in proceedings in respect of specified duties of the compressed air contractor.

See:

- *Health surveillance and health protection*

- *Permit to work systems*

- *Risk assessment*

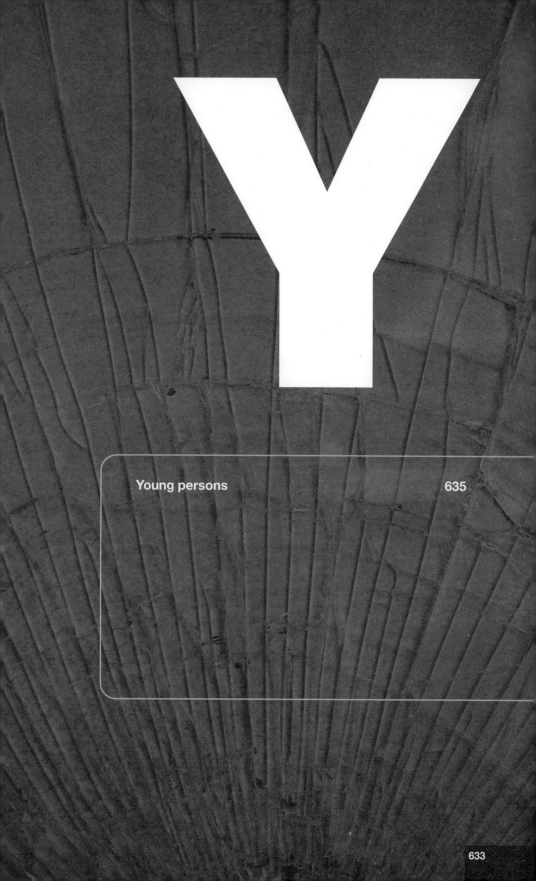

Y

Young persons

Under the MHSWR a 'young person' means any person who has not attained the age of eighteen. Regulation 19 places an absolute duty on every employer to ensure that young persons are protected at work from any risks to their health or safety which are a consequence of their lack of experience, or absence of awareness of existing or potential risks or the fact that young persons have not yet fully matured.

More specifically, no employer shall employ a young person for work:

- which is beyond his physical or psychological capacity;

- involving harmful exposure to agents which are toxic or carcinogenic, cause heritable genetic damage or harm to the unborn child or which in any other way chronically affects human health;

- involving harmful exposure to radiation;

- involving the risk of accidents which it may reasonably be assumed cannot be recognized or avoided by young persons owing to their insufficient attention to safety or lack of experience or training; or

- in which there is a risk to health from extreme cold or heat, noise or vibration;

- and in determining whether work will involve harm or risks for the purposes of this paragraph, regard shall be had to the results of the (risk) assessment.

Nothing in the above paragraph shall prevent the employment of a young person who is no longer a child for work:

- where it is necessary for his training;

- where the young person will be supervised by a competent person; and

- where any risk will be reduced to the lowest level that is reasonably practicable.

Risk assessment

In making or reviewing a risk assessment an employer who employs, or is about to employ, a young person must take particular account of:

- the inexperience, lack of awareness of risks and immaturity of young persons;

- the fitting out and layout of the workplace and workstation;

- the nature, degree and duration of exposure to physical, biological and chemical agents;

- the form, range and use of work equipment and the way in which it is handled;

- the organization of processes and activities;

- the extent of the health and safety training provided or to be provided;

- risks from agents, processes and work listed in the Annex to Council Directive 94/33/EC on the protection of young people at work.

The ACOP to the Regulations stresses the need for employers to undertake risk assessment before young workers start work and to see where risk remains, taking account of control measures in place, as described in Regulation 3.

When control measures have been taken against these risks and if a significant risk still remains, no child (a young worker under the compulsory school age) can be employed to do this work.

Further guidance on young workers is contained in *Young People at Work: A Guide for Employers HS(G)165:1997 (HSE Books).*

See:

- *Information, instruction and training*

- *Risk assessment*

Other titles from Thorogood

COMPANY DIRECTOR'S DESKTOP GUIDE

David Martin
£16.99 paperback • Published June 2004

The role of the company director is fundamental to the success of any business, yet the tasks, responsibilities and liabilities that directors' face become more demanding with every change to the law.

Written in a clear, jargon-free style, this is a comprehensive guide to the complex legislation and procedures governing all aspects of the company director's role. The author's wide experience as a Director and Secretary of a plc and consultant and author provides a manual that is expert, practical and easy to access.

THE COMPANY SECRETARY'S DESKTOP GUIDE

Roger Mason
£16.99 paperback • Published April 2004

Written in a clear, jargon-free style, this is a comprehensive guide to the complex legislation and procedures governing all aspects of the company secretary's work. The Company Secretary's role becomes more demanding with every change to the law and practice. The author's considerable experience as both Company Secretary and lecturer and author has ensured a manual that is expert, practical and easy to access.

DEVELOPING AND MANAGING TALENT

How to match talent to the role and convert it to a strength

Sultan Kermally
£12.99 paperback, £24.99 hardback
Published May 2004

Effective talent management is crucial to business development and profitability. Talent management is no soft option; on the contrary, it is critical to long-term survival.

This book offers strategies and practical guidance for finding, developing and above all keeping talented individuals. After explaining what developing talent actually means to the organization, he explores the e-dimension and the global dimension. He summarizes what the 'gurus' have to say on the development of leadership talent. Included are valuable case studies drawn from Hilton, Volkswagen, Unilever, Microsoft and others.

GURUS ON BUSINESS STRATEGY

Tony Grundy
£14.99 paperback, £24.99 hardback
Published May 2003

This book is a one-stop guide to the world's most important writers on business strategy. It expertly summarizes all the key strategic concepts and describes the work and contribution of each of the leading thinkers in the field.

It goes further: it analyses the pro's and con's of many of the key theories in practice and offers two enlightening case-studies. The third section of the book provides a series of detailed checklists to aid you in the development of your own strategies for different aspects of the business.

More than just a summary of the key concepts, this book offers valuable insights into their application in practice.

SUCCESSFUL BUSINESS PLANNING

Norton Paley
£14.99 paperback, £29.99 hardback
Published June 2004

"Growth firms with a written business plan have increased their revenues 69 per cent faster over the past five years than those without a written plan."

FROM A SURVEY BY PRICEWATERHOUSECOOPERS

We know the value of planning – in theory. But either we fail to spend the time required to go through the thinking process properly, or we fail to use the plan effectively. Paley uses examples from real companies to turn theory into practice.

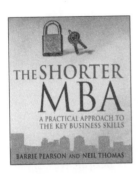

THE SHORTER MBA

A practical approach to the key business skills

Barrie Pearson and Neil Thomas
£35.00 Hardback • Published July 2004

A succinct distillation of the skills that you need to be successful in business. Most people can't afford to give up two years to study for an MBA. This pithy, practical book presents all the essential theory, practiced and techniques taught to MBA students – ideal for the busy practising executive. It is divided into three parts:

- Personal development
- Management skills
- Business development

Thorogood also has an extensive range of reports and special briefings which are written specifically for professionals wanting expert information.

For a full listing of all Thorogood publications, or to order any title, please call Thorogood Customer Services on 020 7749 4748 or fax on 020 7729 6110. Alternatively view our website at **www.thorogood.ws**.

Focused on developing your potential

Falconbury, the sister company to Thorogood publishing, brings together the leading experts from all areas of management and strategic development to provide you with a comprehensive portfolio of action-centred training and learning.

We understand everything managers and leaders need to be, know and do to succeed in today's commercial environment. Each product addresses a different technical or personal development need that will encourage growth and increase your potential for success.

- Practical public training programmes
- Tailored in-company training
- Coaching
- Mentoring
- Topical business seminars
- Trainer bureau/bank
- Adair Leadership Foundation

The most valuable resource in any organization is its people; it is essential that you invest in the development of your management and leadership skills to ensure your team fulfil their potential. Investment into both personal and professional development has been proven to provide an outstanding ROI through increased productivity in both you and your team. Ultimately leading to a dramatic impact on the bottom line.

With this in mind Falconbury have developed a comprehensive portfolio of training programmes to enable managers of all levels to develop their skills in leadership, communications, finance, people management, change management and all areas vital to achieving success in today's commercial environment.

What Falconbury can offer you?

- Practical applied methodology with a proven results
- Extensive bank of experienced trainers
- Limited attendees to ensure one-to-one guidance
- Up to the minute thinking on management and leadership techniques
- Interactive training
- Balanced mix of theoretical and practical learning
- Learner-centred training
- Excellent cost/quality ratio

Falconbury In-Company Training

Falconbury are aware that a public programme may not be the solution to leadership and management issues arising in your firm. Involving only attendees from your organization and tailoring the programme to focus on the current challenges you face individually and as a business may be more appropriate. With this in mind we have brought together our most motivated and forward thinking trainers to deliver tailored in-company programmes developed specifically around the needs within your organization.

All our trainers have a practical commercial background and highly refined people skills. During the course of the programme they act as facilitator, trainer and mentor, adapting their style to ensure that each individual benefits equally from their knowledge to develop new skills.

Falconbury works with each organization to develop a programme of training that fits your needs.

Mentoring and coaching

Developing and achieving your personal objectives in the workplace is becoming increasingly difficult in today's constantly changing environment. Additionally, as a manager or leader, you are responsible for guiding colleagues towards the realization of their goals. Sometimes it is easy to lose focus on your short and long-term aims.

Falconbury's one-to-one coaching draws out individual potential by raising self-awareness and understanding, facilitating the learning and performance development that creates excellent managers and leaders. It builds renewed self-confidence and a strong sense of 'can-do' competence, contributing significant benefit to the organization. Enabling you to focus your energy on developing your potential and that of your colleagues.

Mentoring involves formulating winning strategies, setting goals, monitoring achievements and motivating the whole team whilst achieving a much improved work life balance.

Falconbury – Business Legal Seminars

Falconbury Business Legal Seminars specializes in the provision of high quality training for legal professionals from both in-house and private practice internationally.

The focus of these events is to provide comprehensive and practical training on current international legal thinking and practice in a clear and informative format.

Event subjects include, drafting commercial agreements, employment law, competition law, intellectual property, managing an in-house legal department and international acquisitions.

For more information on all our services please contact Falconbury on +44 (0) 20 7729 6677 or visit the website at: www.falconbury.co.uk.